THE SETTLEMENT OF THE ISRAELITE T
IN PAL

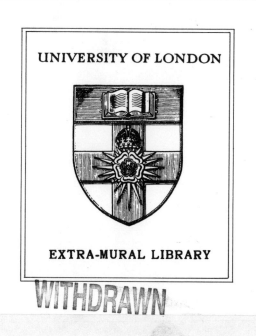

STUDIES IN BIBLICAL THEOLOGY

A series of monographs designed to provide clergy and laymen with the best work in biblical scholarship both in this country and abroad

STUDIES IN BIBLICAL THEOLOGY

Second Series · 21

THE SETTLEMENT OF THE ISRAELITE TRIBES IN PALESTINE

A Critical Survey of Recent Scholarly Debate

MANFRED WEIPPERT

SCM PRESS LTD
BLOOMSBURY STREET LONDON

Translated from the German
Die Landnahme der israelitischen Stämme in der neueren wissenschaftlichen Diskussion
(Forschungen zur Religion und Literatur des Alten und Neuen Testaments 92,
Vandenhoeck und Ruprecht, Göttingen 1967)
by James D. Martin

334 01567 7
FIRST PUBLISHED IN ENGLISH 1971

PRINTED IN GREAT BRITAIN BY
W & J MACKAY & CO LTD, CHATHAM

CONTENTS

PREFACE

THE AIM OF the present book is, as expressed in the phraseology of its title, strictly limited, namely the critical presentation, in their various forms, of the hypotheses concerning the Israelite settlement which may nowadays be regarded as 'classical' and whose main lines may be denoted in summary fashion by the names of Alt and Albright. It is, therefore, of the nature of a survey in which the relationship of the individual authors and 'schools' to each other and to the available material is presented from a primarily methodological and systematic point of view, in which, also, the attempt is made, with the aid of means which are now at our disposal, to place on a firmer footing individual aspects of theories which are now thirty or forty years old. In this respect, individual problems of the literary tradition may, for the most part, be left out of consideration. The time has not yet come to deal with these within a survey monograph; they should, rather, in the first place, be the subject, individually, of thorough examination. The connection established with the so-called 'deuteronomistic history' has convinced me that in this sphere there are still innumerable questions waiting to be answered or even still to be asked.

A work such as the present one, which concentrates on the broad lines, must, in a certain sense, take as its maxim the sentence of Lytton Strachey, 'Ignorance is the first requisite of the historian – ignorance which simplifies and clarifies, which selects and omits'.[1] I have, therefore, not regarded it as a duty to refer, even approximately completely, to what is by now a vast literature on the subject of the Israelite settlement. I have even mentioned only marginally such important contributions as those of Y. Kaufmann because they promised too slight an advantage in the clear formulation of the questions. For the same reason, hardly any reference is made to the most recent and very divergent discussions in numerous articles in periodicals. However, in the

[1] Preface to *Eminent Victorians*, quoted from the reprint in L. Strachey, *Five Victorians* (London 1942), p. 221.

citing of literature I believe that I have sometimes been overgenerous.

The German edition of the book (Göttingen 1967) goes back to my Master's thesis which was accepted in July 1965 by the Theological Faculty of the Georg-August University in Göttingen. I have made no fundamental alterations in the text of the English edition, but some oversights have been corrected and, in a few places, references to further evidence and additional literature have been added. In this connection I should like to draw attention only to the amplification of the remarks concerning the rite of the 'slaying of the ass' (below pp. 113f. n. 52) and to my altered conception of the text *ARM* II 102.9–16 (below p. 115). I should also like to draw attention to the fact that in quoting the earliest information about the Aramaeans (below p. 103 and n. 67) I was no longer able to refer to the evidence from the funeral temple of Amenophis III which E. Edel has published and interpreted ('Die Ortsnamenlisten aus dem Totentempel Amenophis III', *BBB* 25, 1966, pp. 28f.) and which takes us back a good two hundred and fifty years before the time of Tiglath-pileser I. In spite of this, I am still of the opinion that the Aramaean colouring of the patriarchal narratives is anachronistic. In the nomadic question in future, more notice will have to be taken than here of the *š3s.w* mentioned in the Egyptian texts once the book by R. Giveon on this subject has appeared with its convenient presentation of the material. Finally, mention should be made of the important article by P. W. Lapp, 'The Conquest of Palestine in the Light of Archaeology', *Concordia Theological Monthly* 38 (1967), pp. 283–300, which provides a welcome complement to the section 'The Archaeological Solution'.

I must thank the translator, the Rev. James D. Martin, M.A., B.D., Ph.D. for his work, the SCM Press for being willing to publish this English edition and also the early reviewers of the German edition, of whose criticisms and suggestions I have taken account as far as possible and in so far as I have been convinced by them.

Tübingen, 30 March 1969 MANFRED WEIPPERT

TRANSLATOR'S PREFACE

THE READER will notice that Dr Weippert's Preface to this English edition of his book is dated March 1969, while this one is dated March 1971. I must apologize both to him and to the reader for the delay in the appearance of this translation, a delay occasioned partly by other commitments on my part and partly by the complex nature of the book itself.

In the German edition of the book the reader was referred for an explanation of the abbreviations used to *RGG*³ and *AHw*, which were supplemented by a short list of additional abbreviations provided by Dr Weippert. I thought it more convenient for English readers to provide a complete list of abbreviations, and I trust that this does not contain too many lacunae.

Where English translations of German works exist, I have given references to these, retaining at the same time the reference to the original German work for the sake of bibliographical completeness. On the few occasions, however, on which Dr Weippert refers to a German translation of an English work I have given the reference to the English version only.

I should like to thank my colleague Mr Peter Coxon for help with the proofs, and Miss Jean Cunningham of the SCM Press for doing much more than ought reasonably to have been expected of her in preparing this translation for publication.

St Mary's College
University of St Andrews
March 1971

JAMES D. MARTIN

ABBREVIATIONS

A	A-stem (Aram. Aphel, Arab. IV stem)
AAA	*Annals of Archaeology and Anthropology* (Liverpool)
AAB	Abhandlungen der Deutschen (bis 1944: Preussischen) Akademie der Wissenschaften zu Berlin
AASOR	*The Annual of the American Schools of Oriental Research* (New Haven)
ABSA	*Annual of the British School at Athens* (London)
ADAJ	*Annual of the Department of Antiquities of Jordan* (Amman)
AfO	*Archiv für Orientforschung* (Graz)
ÄgA	Ägyptologische Abhandlungen (Wiesbaden)
ÄgF	Ägyptologische Forschungen (Glückstadt)
AGI	*Archivio glottologico italiano* (Rome)
AHw	W. v. Soden, *Akkadisches Handwörterbuch* (Wiesbaden 1965ff.)
AJA	*American Journal of Archaeology* (Norwood, Mass.)
AJSL	*American Journal of Semitic Languages and Literatures* (Chicago)
AKA	L. W. King, *The Annals of the Kings of Assyria* I (London 1902)
Akk.	Akkadian
AKM	Abhandlungen für die Kunde des Morgenlandes (Leipzig)
AnBibl	Analecta Biblica (Rome)
AnOr	Analecta Orientalia (Rome)
AnSt	*Anatolian Studies* (London)
Ant.	Josephus, *Antiquitates*
AO	Catalogue number of tablets in the Louvre Museum, Paris
AO Leipzig	Der Alte Orient (Leipzig)
AOS	American Oriental Series (New Haven)
Arab.	Arabic

Aram.	Aramaic
ARM(T)	*Archives Royales de Mari* (Paris 1950ff.). See ch. III 2, n. 15.
ArOr	*Archiv Orientální* (Prague)
AS	*Antiquity and Survival* (The Hague)
ASAE	*Annales du Service des Antiquités de l'Égypte* (Cairo)
AssSt	Assyriological Studies (Chicago)
ATD	Das Alte Testament Deutsch (Göttingen)
ATh	Arbeiten zur Theologie (Stuttgart)
B	Book of the Covenant
BA	*The Biblical Archaeologist* (New Haven)
Bab.	Babylonian
BAH	Institut Français d'Archéologie à Beyrouth, Bibliothèque Archéologique et Historique (Paris)
BAL	R. Borger, *Babylonisch-assyrische Lesestücke* (Rome 1963)
BASOR	*Bulletin of the American Schools of Oriental Research* (New Haven)
BAss	Beiträge zur Assyriologie (Leipzig)
BBB	*Bonner Biblische Beiträge* (Bonn)
BE	1. The Babylonian Expedition of the University of Pennsylvania (Philadelphia)
BE	2. (without volume number) Catalogue number of unpublished Babylonian tablets
Bell.	Josephus, *Bellum Judaicum*
Bh.	Beiheft
BHK^3	*Biblia Hebraica* edidit R. Kittel (3rd and following editions)
BHTh	Beiträge zur historischen Theologie (Tübingen)
Bibl	*Biblica* (Rome)
Bibl.Aram.	Biblical Aramaic
BIES	*The Bulletin of the Israel Exploration Society* (Jerusalem)
BIFAO	*Bulletin de l'Institut Français d'Archéologie Orientale* (Cairo)
BIN	Babylonian Inscriptions in the Collection of J. B. Nies (New Haven)
BJ	Bonner Jahrbücher (Cologne)

BJRL	*The Bulletin of the John Rylands Library* (Manchester)
BKAT	Biblischer Kommentar-Altes Testament (Neukirchen)
Bo.	Catalogue number of unpublished Boğazköy tablets
BO	*Bibliotheca Orientalis* (Leiden)
Bott.	See ch. III 1, n. 1
BRL	K. Galling, *Biblisches Reallexikon* (HAT I, 1, Tübingen 1937)
BSA	Berichte über die Verhandlungen der Sächsischen Akademie der Wissenschaften zu Leipzig, phil.-hist. Kl. (Leipzig till 1949, then Berlin)
BWANT	Beiträge zur Wissenschaft vom Alten und Neuen Testament (Stuttgart)
BZ	*Biblische Zeitschrift* (Freiburg i. B.)
BZAW	Beihefte zur *Zeitschrift für die Alttestamentliche Wissenschaft* (Giessen till 1934, then Berlin)
CAD	*The Assyrian Dictionary of the University of Chicago* (Chicago-Glückstadt 1956ff.)
Can.	Canaanite
CBQ	*The Catholic Biblical Quarterly* (Washington)
CGC	Catalogue Général des Antiquités égyptiennes du Musée du Caire (Cairo)
Chr.Pal.	Christian Palestinian
CILUP	*Conférences de l'Institut de Linguistique de l'Université de Paris*
CT	*Cuneiform Texts from Babylonian Tablets in the British Museum,* ed. E. A. W. Budge, London (London 1896ff.)
CTA	A. Herdner, *Corpus des tablettes en cunéiformes alphabétiques découvertes à Ras Shamra-Ugarit de 1929 à 1939* (Mission de Ras Shamra 10, Paris 1963)
D	1. Doubled stem (Hebr. Piel etc.)
	2. The 'Deuteronomic' source according to the classical theory of the 'Pentateuchal' sources
DISO	(Ch.-F. Jean and) J. Hoftijzer, *Dictionnaire des inscriptions sémitiques de l'ouest* (Leiden 1965)

DMOA	Documenta et Monumenta Orientis Antiqui (Leiden)
DP	Mémoires de la Délégation en Perse/Mission Archéologique de Perse (Paris)
Dt	The D-stem of an Akkadian verb with infixed *-ta-*, generally the passive of D. See *GAG* § 93.
Eg.	Egyptian
EI	*Eretz-Israel* (Jerusalem)
EKI	F. W. König, *Die elamischen Königsinschriften* (*AfO* Bh. 16, 1965)
EM	*'enṣiqlōpēdiyā miqrā'īt* (Jerusalem 1950ff.)
Era	F. Gössmann, *Das Era-Epos* (Würzburg 1957), cited by tablet nos.
ET	English Translation
ExpT	*Expository Times* (Edinburgh)
Eth.	Ethiopic
EvTh	*Evangelische Theologie* (Munich)
FRLANT	Forschungen zur Religion und Literatur des Alten und Neuen Testaments (Göttingen)
G	1. Septuagint 2. Ground-stem (Hebr. Qal etc.)
GAG	W. von Soden, *Grundriss der akkadischen Grammatik* (AnOr 33, 1952)
gen.	Genitive
$GesB^{17}$	*Wilhelm Gesenius' Hebräisches und Aramäisches Handwörterbuch über das Alte Testament* . . . bearbeitet von F. Buhl. Unveränderter Nachdruck der 1915 erschienenen 17. Auflage (Berlin, Göttingen, Heidelberg 1954 *et al.*)
GGA	*Göttingische Gelehrte Anzeigen* (Göttingen)
GLECS	*Groupe Linguistique d'Études Chamito-Sémitiques, comptes rendus* (Bordeaux)
GN	Name of a god
GOST	*Transactions of the Glasgow University Oriental Society* (Glasgow)
H	H-stem (Hebr. Hiphil etc.)

HAT	Handbuch zum Alten Testament, ed. O. Eissfeldt (Tübingen)
Hebr.	Hebrew
Ḫḫ	The lexical list ḪAR-ra = *ḫubullu*, ranged in subjects
Hitt.	Hittite
HSAT	*Die Heilige Schrift des Alten Testaments . . . übers. v. E. Kautzsch*, 4th edition ed. by A. Bertholet (Tübingen 1922f.)
HSS	Harvard Semitic Series (Cambridge, Mass.)
HT	L. King, *Hittite Texts in the Cuneiform Character from Tablets in the British Museum* (London 1920)
HThR	*The Harvard Theological Review* (Cambridge, Mass.)
HUCA	*Hebrew Union College Annual* (Cincinnati)
Hurr.	Hurrian
IEJ	*Israel Exploration Journal* (Jerusalem)
JA	*Journal Asiatique* (Paris)
JAOS	*Journal of the American Oriental Society* (New Haven)
JBL	*Journal of Biblical Literature* (Philadelphia)
JBR	*Journal of Bible and Religion* (Wolcott., N.Y.)
JCS	*Journal of Cuneiform Studies* (New Haven)
JEA	*The Journal of Egyptian Archaeology* (London)
JEN	Joint Expedition with the Iraq Museum at Nuzi (= American Schools of Oriental Research. Publications of the Baghdad School. Texts: Vol. 1ff., Paris 1927ff.)
JEOL	*Jaarbericht . . . Ex Oriente Lux* (Leiden)
JESHO	*Journal of the Economic and Social History of the Orient* (Leiden)
JNES	*Journal of Near Eastern Studies* (Chicago)
JPOS	*The Journal of the Palestine Oriental Society* (Jerusalem)
JRAS	*Journal of the Royal Asiatic Society* (London)
JSOR	*Journal of the Society of Oriental Research* (Chicago)
JSS	*Journal of Semitic Studies* (Manchester)
JTVI	*Journal of the Transactions of the Victoria Institute* (London)

KAH	*Keilschrifttexte aus Assur historischen Inhalts* (= WVDOG 16 and 31, 1911 and 1922)
KAV	*Keilschrifttexte aus Assur verschiedenen Inhalts* (= WVDOG 35, 1920)
KBo	*Keilsschrifttexte aus Boghazköi* (= WVDOG, various volumes, 1916ff.)
KBw	H. Guthe (ed.), *Kurzes Bibelwörterbuch* (Tübingen 1903)
KlF	*Kleinasiatische Forschungen* I (Weimar 1930)
Kl.Schr.	A. Alt, *Kleine Schriften zur Geschichte des Volkes Israel*, I^2, II^2, III (Munich 1959)
KUB	*Keilschrifturkunden aus Boghazköi* (Berlin 1926ff.)
LRS	Leipziger rechtswissenschaftliche Studien (Leipzig)
M	Massoretic Text
MAD	Materials for the Assyrian Dictionary (Chicago 1952–7; I by no., III by page)
Mand.	Mandaean
MAOG	*Mitteilungen der Altorientalischen Gesellschaft*
MDOG	*Mitteilungen der Deutschen Orient-Gesellschaft* (Leipzig, then Berlin)
Mél.Duss.	*Mélanges Syriens offerts à Monsieur René Dussaud* (Paris 1939), see ch. III 2 n. 45
MGWJ	*Monatschrift für Geschichte und Wissenschaft des Judentums* (Breslau)
MIO	*Mitteilungen des Instituts für Orientforschung* (Berlin)
Moab.	Moabite
MSL	B. Landsberger and others, *Materialen zum sumerischen Lexikon* (Rome 1937ff.)
MSS	Münchner Studien zur Sprachwissenschaft (Munich)
MVAeG	Mitteilungen der Vorderasiatisch-Ägyptischen Gesellschaft (Berlin/Leipzig)
N	1) Name 2) N-stem (Hebr. Niphal etc.)
NAG	Nachrichten der Akademie der Wissenschaften in Göttingen

n.d.	No date
NF	Neue Folge
NRTh	*Nouvelle Revue Théologique* (Paris)
NS	Nova series, nouvelle série, new series
NThT	*Nieuw Theologisch Tijdschrift* (Haarlem)
OA	*Oriens Antiquus* (Rome)
OIP	Oriental Institute Publications (Chicago)
OLZ	*Orientalistische Literaturzeitung* (Leipzig)
On.	Eusebius, *Onomastikon*, cited from E. Klostermann (ed.), *Die griechischen christlichen Schriftsteller der ersten drei Jahrhunderte* II.1 (Leipzig 1904, reprint Hildesheim 1966)
Or	*Orientalia* (Rome)
OSArab.	Old South Arabian
OTS	*Oudtestamentische Studiën* (Leiden)
Pap.	Papyrus
PBH	Post-biblical Hebrew
PEFA	*Palestine Exploration Fund Annual* (London)
PEFQS	*Palestine Exploration Fund Quarterly Statement* (London)
PEQ	*Palestine Exploration Quarterly* (London)
Pers.	Persian
Phoen.	Phoenician
PJ	*Palästinajahrbuch* (Berlin)
PN	Proper name
PP	*La Parola del Passato* (Naples)
PPS	The Museum of the University of Pennsylvania, Publications of the Palestine Section (Philadelphia)
PRU	J. Nougayrol and others, *Le Palais Royal d'Ugarit* (Paris 1955ff.)
PSBA	*Proceedings of the Society of Biblical Archaeology* (London)
QDAP	*The Quarterly of the Department of Antiquities in Palestine* (London)
RA	*Revue d'Assyriologie et d'Archéologie Orientale* (Paris)

RB	*Revue Biblique* (Paris)
RDE	*Rowohlts Deutsche Enzyklopädie* (Hamburg)
RecTrav	*Recueil de travaux relatifs à la philologie et à l'archéologie égyptiennes et assyriennes* (Paris and Leipzig)
RevHist	*Revue Historique* (Paris)
*RGG*³	K. Galling and others (ed.), *Die Religion in Geschichte und Gegenwart: Handwörterbuch für Theologie und Religionswissenschaft* (Tübingen ³1957–65)
RHA	*Revue Hittite et Asianique* (Paris)
*RHPh*R	*Revue d'Histoire et de Philosophie Religieuses* (Strasbourg and Paris)
RHR	*Revue de l'Histoire des Religions* (Paris)
RivBibl	*Rivista biblica* (Rome)
RLV	*Reallexikon der Vorgeschichte,* ed. M. Ebert (Berlin 1924–32)
RS	Catalogue number of the discoveries from *rās eš-šamrā* (Ugarit)
RSO	*Rivista degli Studi Orientali* (Rome)
S	Syriac Peshitta
SAB	*Sitzungsberichte der Deutschen* (bis 1944: *Preussischen*) *Akademie der Wissenschaften zu Berlin* (Berlin)
SAT	Die Schriften des Alten Testaments in Auswahl übers u. erkl. v. H. Gunkel u.a., 2nd edition (Göttingen, 1920–5)
SBT	Studies in Biblical Theology (London)
SEM	E. Chiera, *Sumerian Epics and Myths* (= OIP XV, 1934)
ŠL	A. Deimel, *Šumerisches Lexikon* (Rome 1925–50)
SPIB	Scripta Pontificii Instituti Biblici (Rome)
StANT	Studien zum Alten und Neuen Testament (Munich)
StC	Studia Catholica (Roermond)
Sum.	Sumerian
SVT	Supplements to *Vetus Testamentum* (Leiden)
Syr.	Syriac (language)
T	Targum

TCL	*Textes Cunéiformes*. Musée du Louvre (Paris 1910ff.)
ThB	Theologische Bücherei (Munich)
ThLZ	*Theologische Literaturzeitung* (Leipzig)
ThR	*Theologische Rundschau* (Tübingen)
ThSt	Theologische Studien (Zürich)
ThZ	*Theologische Zeitschrift* (Basle)
TR	The numbered list of finds made at *tell er-rīma* by the British expedition
TU	F. Thureau-Dangin, *Tablettes d'Uruk à l'usage des prêtres du temple d'Anu au temps des Seleucides* (TCL VI, 1922)
TuU	Texte und Untersuchungen zur Geschichte der Altchristlichen Literatur (Leipzig)
UB	Urban-Bücher (Stuttgart)
UCP	University of California. Publications in Semitic Philology (Berkeley–Los Angeles)
UET	*Ur Excavations, Texts* (London 1928ff.)
Ug.	Ugaritic
Urk.	*Urkunden des ägyptischen Altertums* (Leipzig 1903ff.)
V	Vulgate
VAB I	F. Thureau-Dangin, *Die sumerischen und akkadischen Königsinschriften* (Vorderasiatische Bibliothek I, Leipzig 1907)
VAB II and VII	J. A. Knudzton, *Die El-Amarna Tafeln* (VAB II and VII, 1907 and 1915)
VAB III	E. H. Weissbach, *Die Keilinschriften der Achämeniden* (VAB III, 1911)
VAB VI	A. Ungnad, *Babylonische Briefe aus der Zeit der Hammurapi-Dynastie* (VAB VI, 1914)
VAS	Vorderasiatische Schriftdenkmäler (Leipzig)
VAT	Catalogue number of unpublished tablets in the Near Eastern section of the Berlin Museum
VD	*Verbum Domini* (Rome)
VIO	Deutsche Akademie der Wissenschaften zu Berlin, Veröffentlichungen des Instituts für Orientforschung (Berlin)
VT	*Vetus Testamentum* (Leiden)

WMANT	Wissenschaftliche Monographien zum Alten und Neuen Testament (Neukirchen-Vluyn)
WO	*Die Welt des Orients* (Göttingen)
WUS	J. Aistleitner, *Wörterbuch der ugaritischen Sprache*, ed. by O. Eissfeldt (BSA 106.3, Berlin 1963)
WVDOG	Wissenschaftliche Veröffentlichungen der Deutschen Orient-Gesellschaft (Leipzig till 1941, then Berlin)
WZ Berlin	*Wissenschaftliche Zeitung* (of the University of) Berlin
WZKM	*Wiener Zeitschrift für die Kunde des Morgenlandes* (Vienna)
YOS	Yale Oriental Series (New Haven)
ZA	*Zeitschrift für Assyriologie und verwandte Gebiete* (Leipzig, Berlin)
ZÄS	*Zeitschrift für Ägyptische Sprache und Altertumskunde* (Leipzig)
ZAW	*Zeitschrift für die alttestamentliche Wissenschaft* (Giessen, then Berlin)
ZDMG	*Zeitschrift der Deutschen Morgenländischen Gesellschaft* (Leipzig)
ZDPV	*Zeitschrift des Deutschen Palästinavereins* (Wiesbaden)
ZThK	*Zeitschrift für Theologie und Kirche* (Tübingen)

I

THE PROBLEM

1. The further back one goes, from the point of view of scientific investigation, into the pre-history and early history of Israel, the more difficult does it become to handle the relevant source material and the more uncertain, too, are the results of the inquiry. To anyone familiar with the work of the last two hundred years on the 'historical books' of the Old Testament, this is not particularly surprising. However, work on the books of Genesis to Kings by the methods of literary criticism, form analysis and traditio-analysis, has shown just how heterogeneous is the material of which these books are composed and that it is only the editorial framework which holds them together and the occasional fusion of disparate elements which give the impression that these books are self-contained units and provide a historical progression. With the destruction of this framework, a destruction which was necessary in the interests of exact analysis, there disappeared, of course, that lead through the maze of individual narratives which had guided earlier generations in their reception of 'salvation history', and we moderns, in our quest for the actual course of the pre-history and early history of Israel, are directed to a much smaller number of obvious indications within the Old Testament itself, to conclusions from analogy and to 'external evidence' which is basically scanty. In these circumstances, the place of the picture of 'what actually happened', a picture which it is possible to read directly, if naïvely, from the texts, must necessarily be taken by the reconstruction of history, by the 'ideal pattern', by what – on grounds of historical analogy – can or must have happened. Into this the historical information which can be gathered from the sources must then be meaningfully inserted. The fragmentary character of this information and a certain liberty in the choice of a pattern admit, however, of different

possibilities of reconstruction. It follows, therefore, that different points of view, hypotheses and theories about the pre-history and early history of Israel have been proposed with greater or less conviction, and it is necessary from time to time, by means of systematization and criticism, to shed light on the probability and the dubiety of what has been produced. This is what is attempted in the present work with regard to the problem of the Israelite settlement. For methodical and technical reasons this review is directed at 'recent scholarly debate', and before entering upon the exposition of it we must inquire about its limitations with regard to time and especially about its ἐποχή.

2. Even a superficial review of the extensive literature[1] on our subject soon reveals that at the beginning of the twenties of this century the possibilities of the older methods were, on the whole, virtually exhausted, and any really new results, able to face penetrating criticism, could no longer be obtained unless they were based on newly discovered material. The method of regarding the problem from the point of view of tribal history,[2] especially linked, as this method was, with the traditional methods of intensive literary criticism, had led to the distinguishing of several waves of 'Israelite' penetration into Palestine which were usually, and certainly not incorrectly, recognized as being the 'Leah' and 'Rachel' tribes, and many attempts were made to link these waves with the results of research in Egyptology and Assyriology and with the fruits of the flourishing ('biblical') archaeology of Syria–Palestine.

[1] Of important older works, besides the 'Histories of Israel', we might mention the following: E. Meyer, 'Kritik der Berichte über die Eroberung Palaestinas (Num. 20, 12 bis Jud. 2, 5)', *ZAW* 1, 1881, 117–46; 'Nachtrag', *ibid.* 3, 1883, 306–9; C. Steuernagel, *Die Einwanderung der israelitischen Stämme in Kanaan. Historisch-kritische Untersuchungen*, Berlin, 1901; E. Meyer, *Die Israeliten und ihre Nachbarstämme. Mit Beiträgen von B. Luther*, Halle/S. 1906; E. Sellin, *Gilgal. Ein Beitrag zur Geschichte der Einwanderung Israels in Palästina*, Leipzig 1917; C. F. Burney, *Israel's Settlement in Canaan* (Schweich Lectures 1917), London 1918. A detailed report of scholarly debate until about 1948 may be found in H. H. Rowley, *From Joseph to Joshua. Biblical Traditions in the Light of Archaeology* (Schweich Lectures 1948), London [4]1958, with detailed bibliography (pp. 165–88). Cf. also the book by J. Bright which is primarily concerned with a criticism of method, *Early Israel in Recent History Writing. A Study in Method* (SBT, First Series, 19), 1956. A review of the more recent literature on the books of Joshua and Judges is found in E. Jenni, 'Zwei Jahrzehnte Forschung an den Büchern Josua bis Könige', *ThR*, NF 27, 1961, 1–32, 97–146.

[2] Cf. W. Duffy, *The Tribal-Historical Theory on the Origin of the Hebrew People*, Washington, D.C., 1944 (unavailable to me).

So, again and again in the discussion we find the Hyksos,[3] the *ʿapiru*[4] of the cuneiform archives from *el-ʿamārna*,[5] the so-called 'Israel stele' from the fifth year of the Egyptian king Merenptah,[6] the supposed mention of Jacob,[7] Joseph[8] or the tribe of Asher[9] in the city lists of the Pharaohs, or the attempt to determine somehow from the conflagration levels of *tell es-sulṭān* (the site of pre-Roman Jericho) a point of reference for the dating of Josh. 2 and 6[10] and thus for the campaigns of Joshua or else, from the discoveries in the 'cultic' sphere, to find evidence for a change in the religious situation of the country beginning with the penetration of the Israelites[11] – all this without such undertakings having, in

[3] The 'anti-Semitic' ancient world had already connected the expulsion of the Hyksos from Egypt with the Israelite exodus and settlement; cf. J. Schwartz, 'Le "Cycle de Petoubastis" et les commentaires égyptiens de l'Exode', *BIFAO* 49, 1950, 75–83.

[4] Since 1939 (Ch. Virolleaud; cf. *AfO* 13, 1939–41, 88; *Syria* 21, 1940, 143; A. Goetze, *BASOR* 77, 1940, 32–4) it has been known definitively that the correct form of the word which appears in cuneiform as *ḫa*-BI-*ru*/*rù*/*ri* is *ʿpr* (i.e. **ʿapiru*) (cf. already W. F. Albright, *The Vocalization of the Egyptian Syllabic Orthography* [AOS 5, 1934], 42 No. VII B 4). In view of the Ugaritic (Pl.) *ʿprm* and the Egyptian (Pl.) *ʿpr.w*, the Akkadian should therefore be transcribed as *ḫa-pí-ru* or *'a4-pí-ru* (for *'a4* instead of ḪA cf. W. v. Soden, *Das akkadische Syllabar,* AnOr 27, 1948, 7f., 88 No. 317). The material on the *ʿapiru* can be found collected in J. Bottéro (ed.), *Le problème des Ḫabiru à la 4e Rencontre Assyriologique Internationale* (Cahiers de la Société Asiatique 12, Paris, 1954); M. Greenberg, *The Ḫab/piru* (AOS 39, 1955).

[5] See p. 10 n. 18 below.

[6] Cairo 34025 v°.: W. Spiegelberg, 'Die Inschrift des Merneptah', *ZÄS* 34, 1896, 1–25; W. M. F. Petrie, *Six Temples at Thebes,* London 1897, plates XIII and XIV; P. Lacau, *Stèles du Nouvel Empire* (CGC 45) I, 1909, 52–9 and plates XVII–XIX. A duplicate from *karnak*: Ch. Kuentz, 'Le double de la Stèle d'Israël à Karnak', *BIFAO* 21, 1923, 113–17 and plates.

[7] *ya-ʿ-q-b-'i-r* (= **yʿqb'l*), place name, no. 102 in the city list of Tuthmosis III. See below pp. 9f. n. 17.

[8] *ya-š()-p-'()-r()*, *ibid.* No. 78, but on phonological grounds on no account to be traced back to **ysp'l.*

[9] On this cf., with examples, W. Helck, *Die Beziehungen Ägyptens zu Vorderasien im 3. und 2. Jahrtausend v. Chr.* (ÄgA 5, 1962), 297 n. 24. The real equivalent of the proper name Asher is found (in the feminine form) in W. F. Albright, *JAOS* 74, 1954, 229f., line 23.

[10] The discussion of this was naturally based on the results of Sellin's excavations of 1907–09 (E. Sellin and C. Watzinger, *Jericho*, WVDOG 22, 1912) with their inaccurate dating of strata (corrections in W. F. Albright, *AASOR* 4, 1922/23, 11, 14f.; C. Watzinger, *Svenska Orientsällskapets Årsbok* 1, 1923, 104f. with nn. 2 and 3; *ZDMG* 80, 1926, 131–6). On the more recent excavations by J. Garstang and K. M. Kenyon see generally, J. and J. B. E. Garstang, *The Story of Jericho*, London and Edinburgh ²1948; K. M. Kenyon, *Digging up Jericho*, London 1957 and below p. 50 n. 24.

[11] Cf., e.g., L. H. Vincent, *Canaan d'après l'exploration récente*, Paris 1907, 204.

the last resort, achieved the expected result. Too many elements in the total picture were being achieved only by the ingenious filling in of enormous gaps.

3. Then in 1925 there appeared Albrecht Alt's essay, 'The Settlement of the Israelites in Palestine',[12] which claimed to be able to carry further a discussion which had come to a standstill and to lead it to more accurately based results with the help of a new method, logically carried through, that of the history of the country's territorial divisions.[13] Whether the claim of this first work of Alt's and of later work of his own and of his followers could be fulfilled either approximately or entirely is discussed in the course of the present work. Since, however, it is clear in restrospect to what extent Alt has stimulated the debate, it appears justified to begin our review with him, the more so since all other scholars after 1925 were obliged to discuss Alt's methods, results, theories or hypotheses if their own work was not to appear out of date in advance.[14]

[12] *Kl.Schr.* I, 89–125, ET *Essays on Old Testament History and Religion*, Oxford 1966, 133–69.

[13] On this method cf. in general F. Curschmann, 'Historisch-geographische Probleme und die neuen deutschen historischen Atlanten', *1er Congrès International de Géographie Historique, II Mémoires*, Brussels 1931, 33–61. For what is dealt with in what follows I indicate only two separate investigations into German conditions, but they represent a great number of others with similar results: E. Rubow, 'Die Beständigkeit der Gemarkungsgrenzen und die Bedingungen für ihre Veränderung', *Pommersche Jahrbücher* 25, 1929, 3–27; W. Koch, *Die deutschen Gemeindegrenzen und ihr historischer Wert: Untersuchungen zur Frage der Beständigkeit der Gemeindegrenzen und ihrer Verwendbarkeit als Grundlage für historische Atlanten* (Diss. phil. Greifswald 1932), Quakenbrück, 1935.

[14] The work of Y. Kaufmann stands in an isolated position within the whole of the scholarly debate concerning the Israelite settlement and will not be dealt with in this book in order not to obscure the clear confrontation of views (cf. above p. ix). Reference might be made especially to the following works: Y. Kaufmann, *Tōlᵉdōt hā'ᵉmūnā hayyiśrā'ēlīt, mīmē qedem ʿad sōp bayit šēnī*, I–VIII, Tel-Aviv 1937–56 (abridged English translation by M. Greenberg with the title *The Religion of Israel, from its Beginnings to the Babylonian Exile*, Chicago 1960); *The Biblical Account of the Conquest of Palestine*, Jerusalem 1953; *Sēfer yᵉhōšūaʿ ʿim mābō' lihōšūaʿ wᵉšōpᵉṭīm*, 1–3, Jerusalem 1959. For a discussion of him cf. O. Eissfeldt, 'Die Eroberung Palästinas durch Altisrael', *WO* 2.2, 1955, 158–71; A. Alt, 'Utopien', *ThLZ* 81, 1956, 521–8; J. Bright, *Early Israel in Recent History Writing*, 56–78.

II

ATTEMPTS SINCE 1925 TO SOLVE THE SETTLEMENT PROBLEM

1. THE SOLUTION BY MEANS OF THE HISTORY OF TERRITORIAL DIVISIONS AND THE HISTORY OF TRADITIONS

1. According to Albrecht Alt,[1] the picture which the deuteronomistic school has presented – above all in the book of Joshua – of the Israelite settlement and which has long served as the basis of all research in this sphere, is not wholly inaccurate, but it has to be corrected at certain important points. It is not the case, as might appear from the narrative of the book of Joshua, that the Israelite confederacy of twelve tribes under the leadership of the Ephraimite Joshua ben Nun[2] gained victory over the Canaanite kings in a series of consecutive campaigns in central Palestine, southern Palestine and Galilee, conquering and burning their cities and slaughtering the inhabitants, thus taking possession of the whole land. On the contrary, this tribal confederacy did not exist at the time when those who later became the Israelites entered Palestine. It is extremely doubtful whether in that period one can speak at all of 'Israelite' tribes in the later sense.[3] According to Alt, one must suppose, rather, that it was a question of individual clans or confederacies of clans of nomads with small cattle who, during the winter rainy season and the spring, lived with their herds in the border territory between the desert and the cultivated land and

[1] A. Alt, 'Die Landnahme der Israeliten in Palästina' (1925), *Kl.Schr.* I, 89–125 (ET 'The Settlement of the Israelites in Palestine' in *Essays in Old Testament History and Religion*, 133–69); 'Erwägungen über die Landnahme der Israeliten in Palästina' (1939), *ibid.*, 126–75. In what follows, only direct quotations are provided with precise references.

[2] See below p. 37 n. 110.

[3] M. Noth, *Geschichte Israels* (Göttingen [5]1963), 71 (ET *The History of Israel*, 2nd revised edition, 1960, 72f.).

who were forced, when the vegetation in that area ceased in summer, to penetrate further into the cultivated land and to come to an understanding with the owners of the land about summer pasturage in the harvested fields and in the woods. In Alt's opinion the clans who entered the country in this way in the course of a regular change of pasture[4] then gradually settled in the relatively thinly populated, wooded areas of the uplands, areas which were not directly exposed to the reach either of the Canaanite city-states or of Egyptian sovereignty, and began to practise agriculture once they had turned these wooded areas into arable land. This peaceful process of transition on the part of nomads to a sedentary life was, according to Alt, the real process of settlement and it was, in the nature of things, a peaceful development since the interests of any landowners there might be would not be harmed by it. Only gradually, at a second stage, did the 'Israelites' expand also into the fruitful plains and valleys which had long been occupied by closely packed groups of Canaanite cities. In this way there occurred isolated military encounters in which the 'Israelites' were not always the victors (a fact which is not exactly surprising in view of the superior military technique of the Canaanites, especially in the use of the chariot)[5] but in which they nevertheless succeeded from time to time in taking a fortified city, massacring or driving away its inhabitants and themselves taking over the cultivation of its arable land. Alt called this second stage of 'Israelite' settlement in Palestine 'territorial expansion'.

2. The basis of this presentation which, in the face of the different tenor of the biblical narratives, runs the risk of being called arbitrary and contradictory to the sources,[6] was formed by

[4] On the question of the change of pasture (transhumance) cf. for the western Mediterranean R. Leonhard, 'Die Transhumanz im Mittelmeergebiet. Eine wirtschafts-geographische Studie über den Seminomadismus', *Festschrift für Lujo Brentano zum siebzigsten Geburtstag* (Munich and Leipzig 1916), 327–49. On the phenomenon in the 'present-day' Middle East cf. the numerous scattered references in the literature on the Arabian bedouin which does not need to be detailed here. The application to the 'Israelites' in M. Weber, *Gesammelte Aufsätze zur Religionssoziologie*: III. Das antike Judentum (Tübingen [3]1963), 11, 44–46; L. Rost, 'Weidewechsel und altisraelitischer Festkalender' (1943), *Das kleine Credo und andere Studien zum Alten Testament* (Heidelberg 1965), 101–12; and in the works of Alt cited in n. 1 above.

[5] The 'iron chariots' of the Canaanites are often mentioned as weapons which could not be defeated and which therefore were sources of fear and terror; cf. Deut. 20.1; Josh. 17.16; Judg. 1.19; 4.3; *et al.*

[6] Thus, e.g., most of those to be discussed in ch. II 2.

research into extra-biblical and, as far as possible, contemporary records with the aid of the so-called method of the 'history of territorial divisions' which was introduced into the debate consciously for the first time by Alt in his essay of 1925. This method takes as its starting point the view that the territorial divisions in a country are always, and therefore in Palestine too, conservative, so that a change in the political and economic relationships, even a change in the population, can at the most modify only details but not fundamentally alter the larger or smaller units or their delimitations. Applied to the problem that is of immediate interest to us, this means that a comparison of the territorial relationships in Palestine *before* and *after* the 'Israelite' settlement (in so far as these relationships can be discerned in the sources) must provide the possibility of drawing conclusions, based on whether these relationships remain the same or are changed, about the effect of the process on 'the history of territorial divisions' and, on this basis, about the nature and manner of the process itself. Unlike his predecessors, who had usually begun with an analysis of the biblical narrative of the settlement and of the Israelite tribal system[7] and had tried to find the connection between these and the 'external evidence',[8] i.e. Egyptian and cuneiform texts and the results of archaeology – unlike them, Alt first of all examined only those records which could definitely be called original (above all those of Egyptian provenance) and which referred to Palestine and the territorial relationships of the country which were reflected in them, and endeavoured to determine from this starting point the place and the purpose of the Old Testament accounts of the settlement.

Since the views of Alt which were presented dogmatically at the beginning of this chapter cannot stand without fairly detailed proof, we shall proceed in the first place along the lines which he laid down in his fundamental essays and then follow the threads which lead from him to his followers, above all to Martin Noth.

3. According to Alt, and according to the view generally held both before him and still today, the political organization of Palestine in the pre-Israelite period was characterized by the well-

[7] Cf. e.g., C. Steuernagel, *Die Einwanderung der israelitischen Stämme in Kanaan* (Berlin 1901), 1–55.

[8] This is a basic term frequently used by Albright (see below p.47), but I use it here in a non-technical sense.

known system of city-states for which there is evidence in written sources[9] from as far back as the twelfth dynasty of Egypt, i.e. since the beginning of the second millennium BC and which, on archaeological evidence, is certainly much older still and is surely already prefigured in the great fortified cities of the late Chalcolithic and Early Bronze Ages.[10] 'System of city-states' means that the country was divided up into a fairly large number of small regions each centred round a fortified city which was usually the seat of a ruler with the title 'king' (Canaanite **milku/malku*, Hebrew *melek*).[11] In his essay of 1925, Alt had deduced this from the feudalism of the Hyksos empire;[12] however, under the influence of the Egyptian 'execration texts' of the twelfth dynasty published soon after – 1926 – by Sethe and later by Posener,[13] he revised his opinion. The result is that in a detailed discussion of his hypothesis of the broader pattern of systems of government in nineteenth-century Palestine we can no longer include in particular the 'kingdom of Lydda' or *rṯnw*[14] or the 'foreign country (*ḫ3ś.t*;

[9] The evidence is in the so-called 'execration texts' (see below n. 13).

[10] The neolithic predecessor of later Jericho (*tell es-sulṭān*) already had strongly fortified walls and can be described as a 'city' (cf. K. M. Kenyon, *Digging up Jericho* [London 1957], 65–69; E. Anati, 'Prehistoric Trade and the Puzzle of Jericho,' *BASOR* 167, 1962, 25–31). 'Ai' (*et-tell* between *bētīn* and *dēr dubwān*) is an Early Bronze walled city (on the excavations cf. below n. 53), so too 'Arad' (*tell ʿarād/tell ʿarād*; cf. Y. Aharoni, '*ʿOnat ha-ḥapīrōt ha-šenīyā be-tel ʿarād*', *BIES* 28, 1964, 154–63; Y. Aharoni and R. Amiran, 'Arad – A Biblical City in Southern Palestine', *Archaeology* 17, 1964, 46–48; M. Weippert, 'Archäologischer Jahresbericht', *ZDPV* 80, 1964, 180).

[11] The Canaanite term **milku/malku* (on the noun form see below p. 82 n. 110) is inferred from the Akk. *šarru* (occasionally in the Amarna letters; cf. Alt, 'Settlement', 145 and n. 36; J. de Koning, *Studiën over de El-Amarnabrieven en het Oude-Testament inzonderheid uit historische oogpunt* [Diss. theol. Amsterdam 1940], 162) and Hebr. *melek* (OT). The Egyptians themselves write *wr* 'great one' with the name of the city in the 'indirect' genitive (e.g. *p3wr n rḥb* on the great stele of Sethos I from Beth-shan, lines 17f.; A. Rowe, *The Topography and History of Beth-Shan* [PPS 1, 1930], 27 fig. 5 and plate 41). In the Amarna letters, as elsewhere (Mari, Alalaḫ), we frequently find (Sum. LÚ) Akk. *awīlu* with the name of the city in the genitive.

[12] A discussion of the so-called 'Second Intermediate Period' in Egypt as well as of the special views of Alt on the 'Hyksos' lies outside the scope of this work.

[13] K. Sethe, *Die Ächtung feindlicher Fürsten, Völker und Dinge auf altägyptischen Tongefässscherben des Mittleren Reiches* (AAB 1926.5); G. Posener, *Princes et pays d'Asie et de Nubie. Textes hiératiques sur des figurines d'envoûtement du Moyen Empire* (Brussels 1940). The extensive secondary literature cannot be cited here.

[14] Alt referred in particular to the occurrence of *rṯnw* on the stele of *Ḫw-śbk* from Abydos (K. Sethe, *Ägyptische Lesestücke zum Gebrauch im aka-*

according to Alt 'region') called *śkmm* (Shechem)'.[15] The city-state system can be clearly seen in the relatively rich source-material on the Asiatic campaigns of Tuthmosis[16] III, i.e. in his 'Annals', in the poetically stylized stele of *jebel barkal* and in his city lists.[17] The most important sources of information, however,

---

demischen Unterricht [Leipzig ^{2}1928; reprint Darmstadt 1959], 83:10). His identification of *rṯnw* with Lod (Lydda) (A. Alt, 'Ein Reich von Lydda. Thesen zur ältesten Geschichte Palästinas', *ZDPV* 47, 1924, 169–185; 'Die älteste Schilderung Palästinas im Lichte neuer Funde', *PJ* 37, 1941, 19–49, esp. 26ff.) cannot, however, bear examination. The equation of *rṯnw* with the place name *rú-ṯ-n* (city list of Tuthmosis III, no. 64), which A. Mariette, *Les listes géographiques des pylônes de Karnak comprenant la Palestine, l'Éthiopie, le pays de Somâl* (Leipzig, Cairo, Paris 1885), 32 (cf. also G. Maspero, *JTVI* 22, 1888/9, 53 and note ‡; G. Daressy, *RecTrav* 21, 1899, 33) had first connected with Lydda, cannot be proved (nor is *rw-ṯ-n* to be understood with Daressy, *op. cit.*, as an error of writing for *rṯnw*) even if *rú-ṯ-n* is really supposed to correspond to Can. **lud(d)ōn-*, a correspondence which cannot be excluded on the basis of the orthography of the period of Tuthmosis III. On the other hand, the name *rṯnw* cannot be identified with the supposed **lud(d)ōn-* since *rṯnw* is already attested at a period when the Eg. *ṯ* is regularly used to reproduce Can. *s* (which at least until the Amarna period was pronounced as a fricative */ts/* or */č/*). Moreover, it follows from the use of the name already for the Middle Kingdom that it cannot be a question of a strictly delimited political power; here, and later until the Ptolemaic period, *rṯnw* is a fairly general name for Palestine-Syria whose origin (which must, in any case, be Egyptian, not Syrian!) and original meaning we do not know. If it had really been the place name 'Lod', then in the nineteenth century (cf. the orthography of the 'execration texts') one would have expected something like **ꜣr/d/t(j)* for **ludd-* and **ꜣr/d/tn* for **luddōn-*. Finally, Lod is first attested in literature in the Chronistic history (I Chron. 8.12; Ezra 2.33; Neh. 7.37; 11.35); it seems to be a settlement which was first established in the Iron Age.

On *rṯnw* see also A. H. Gardiner, *Ancient Egyptian Onomastica* (*Text*) *I* (London 1947), 142*–149*; G. Posener, 'Le Pays de Retenou au Moyen Empire', *Actes du XXIe Congrès International des Orientalistes, Paris, 23–31 Juillet 1948* (Paris 1949), 72f.

15 *ḫꜣś.t śkmm rn-ś*, stele of *Ḫw-śbk*, Sethe, *op. cit.*, 83:9. The identification of *śkmm* as Shechem which was doubted at first is now correctly regarded as certain; it is phonetically exact (Hebr. *š^{e}kem* < **ṯakm-*, cf. **Šakmu* in KUR *šakmi* [gen.] 'the land of Shechem' VAB II 289, 23 and Ug. *ṯkm* 'back') and historically probable.

16 Thus the correct Greek form for *ḏḥwty-mś* in Manetho (*Τουθμωσις, Τεθμωσις*), which should be used in place of the incorrect forms 'Thutmosis/Thutmose' (German) and 'Thothmes' (English).

17 'Annals': *Urk.* IV, 465ff.; Stele of *jebel barkal*: G. A. and M. B. Reisner, 'Inscribed Monuments from Gebel Barkal: II The granite Stele of Thutmosis III', *ZÄS* 69, 1933, 24–39; *Urk.* IV, 1227–43. City list: *Urk.* IV, 779–94; J. Simons, *Handbook for the Study of Egyptian Topographical Lists Relating to Western Asia* (Leiden 1937), 109–22; A. Jirku, *Die ägyptischen Listen*

are the letters, written in Akkadian, from the city princes of Syria-Palestine in the archives of the kings Amenophis III and IV (Akh-en-Aton) which were discovered in the ruins of Akh-en-Aton's residence in the region of *el-ʿamārna* ('*tell el-ʿamārna*').[18] From the evidence of these texts the conclusion may be drawn that the city-state system was, on the whole, not affected by the changing balance of power, that, therefore, the Pharaohs of the eighteenth and nineteenth dynasties, like the Hyksos rulers in earlier times, were dependent for their continuing authority as well as for substantial parts of their administration[19] on the faithful homage of the city princes who were responsible for military security along with contingents of Egyptian troops and for the collection of taxes. In view of the clash of interests and other sources of conflict on the part of the participants, this practice may well, even in times of peace, have produced considerable difficulties for

---

palästinensischer und syrischer Ortsnamen in Umschrift und mit historisch-archäologischem Kommentar (*Klio* Bh. 38 1937; reprint Aalen 1962), 5–23. Fragments of other city lists in Simons, *op. cit.*, 123–6.

[18] The basic treatment, though now out of date in many places: J. A. Knudtzon, *Die El-Amarna-Tafeln mit Einleitung und Erläuterungen. Anmerkungen and Register bearbeitet von O. Weber und E. Ebeling* (VAB II) (1915; reprint Aalen 1964). Later publications of additional texts from *el-ʿamārna*: O. Schroeder, *Die Tontafeln von el-Amarna* (VAS 11/12, 1915), nos. 179 and 193; O. Schroeder, 'Zu Berliner Amarnatexten', *OLZ* 20, 1917, 105f. (VAT 3780); F. Thureau-Dangin, 'Nouvelles Lettres d'El-Amarna', *RA* 19, 1922, 91–108; S. Smith and C. G. Gadd, 'A Cuneiform Vocabulary of Egyptian Words', *JEA* 11, 1925, 230–40; G. Dossin, 'Une nouvelle lettre d'El Amarna', *RA* 31, 1934, 125–36; C. H. Gordon, 'The New Amarna Tablets', *Or*, NS 16, 1947, 1–21; A. R. Millard, 'A Letter from the Ruler of Gezer', *PEQ* 97, 1965, 140–43. An English adaptation of Knudtzon's book (though in parts by no means an improvement on it) was made by S. A. B. Mercer, *The Tell el-Amarna Tablets* (Toronto 1939), including new texts published to date.

[19] A detailed exposition of Egyptian rule in the Asiatic provinces which, in view of the state of the sources, would have to be largely hypothetical, is outside the scope of this work. On the subject cf. A. Alt, 'Ägyptische Tempel in Palästina und die Landnahme der Philister' (1944), *Kl.Schr.* I, 216–30; 'Hettitische und ägyptische Herrschaftsordnung in unterworfenen Gebieten' (1949), *Kl.Schr.* III, 99–106; 'Das Stützpunktsystem der Pharaonen an der phönikischen Küste und im syrischen Binnenland' (1950), *ibid.*, 107–40; M. A.-K. Mohammad, 'The Administration of Syro-Palestine during the New Kingdom', *ASAE* 56, 1959, 105–37; W. Helck, 'Die ägyptische Verwaltung in den syrischen Besitzungen', *MDOG* 92, 1960, 1–13; *Die Beziehungen Ägyptens zu Vorderasien im 3. und 2. Jahrtausend v. Chr.* (ÄgA 5, 1962), 256–67; C. Kühne, 'Zum Status der syro-palästinensischen Vasallen des Neuen Reiches', *Andrews University Seminary Studies* 1, 1963, 71–3.

the central government; the result must have been chaos, however, when the central government was no longer strong enough to control the conflicting forces in the country, to settle the conflicts and, if necessary, to intervene with a show of strength. The Amarna letters[20] just mentioned reveal just such a state of anarchy. The fact that the Egyptians, in spite of the imperfections of the system and of continual difficulties, were unable to achieve a unified administration for their Asiatic possessions, is a striking illustration of how much respect for the autochthonous system had to be shown even by the great powers.[21]

4. By analysing the Egyptian sources such as the letters from Palestine found in the Amarna archives, Alt established that there existed remarkable differences in political structure between the plain and the hill country. While the former contained the majority of the known city-states and of settlements in general, there was in the hill country only a small and diminishing number of royal cities. Thus the 'Annals' and city lists of Tuthmosis III mention hardly any cities in the hill country.[22] From the Amarna archives there is no evidence of a single city-state for the whole area between the plain of Jezreel and Jerusalem with the exception of Shechem, in the case of which special circumstances are operative. In the hill country south of Jerusalem the situation is less well known; yet here, too, there seem to have been scarcely

[20] I use the simplified form 'Amarna' when 'Amarna texts/tablets/letters' and the so-called 'Amarna period' are meant. The place itself will continue to be written *el-ʿamārna*.

[21] The Assyrians acted ruthlessly when transforming into a province a territory which had hitherto been independent or had been in one of the various stages of vassalage; on their methods see now H. Donner, 'Neue Quellen zur Geschichte des Staates Moab in der zweiten Hälfte des 8. Jahrhunderts v. Chr.', *MIO* 5, 1957, 163–5; *Israel unter den Völkern* (SVT 11, 1964), 2f. Under the subsequent foreign dominations older structures reappeared, in part, alongside those created by the Assyrians.

[22] To begin with, Alt had considered all the place names mentioned in the great lists of Tuthmosis III to be names of city-states ('Settlement', 146ff.) but then accepted (*ibid.*, 146 n. 43) the view of Noth and Grapow that they were simply the names of places referred to in and taken over from war diaries (whether they were autonomous or not); cf. M. Noth, 'Die Wege der Pharaonenheere in Palästina und Syrien. Untersuchungen zu den hieroglyphischen Listen palästinischer und syrischer Städte: III. Der Aufbau der Palästinaliste Thutmoses III' *ZDPV* 61, 1938, 52ff.; 'Die Annalen Thutmoses III als Geschichtsquelle', *ZDPV* 66, 1943, 159–74; H. Grapow, *Studien zu den Annalen Thutmosis des Dritten* (AAB 1947: 2, 1949), 45–54. This correction does not affect Alt's argument in any essential.

any city-states. There is controversy about the actual location of the 'cities of the land of Garu' (URU.DIDLI.ḪÁ^{KUR}*ga-ri*, VAB II 256.22–28). According to Alt,[23] who cites Steuernagel,[24] Dhorme[25] and Sellin[26] as his predecessors, they are in the Negeb, to be precise in the neighbourhood of the city of Gerar which is identified with *tell eš-šerīʿa*; according to Noth[27] they are in the region which he claims to be the land of Goshen mentioned in Josh. 10.41; 11.16 and are perhaps identical with the land of Goshen; finally, according to Clauss, Albright and Mazar,[28] they are, rather, in Transjordan in the province of Golan (Gaulanitis,

[23] 'Beiträge zur historischen Geographie und Topographie des Negeb: II. Das Land Gari' (1932), *Kl.Schr.* III, 396–409. Identifications: ^{URU}*ú-du-mu* = Dumah (Josh. 15.52), *k̲h̲irbet ed-dōme*; ^{URU}*a-du-ri* = Adoraim (II Chron. 11.9), *dūrā*; ^{URU}*a-ra-ru* = *Ararah (**ʿrʿrh* Josh. 15.22) or Aroer (I Sam. 30.28), *k̲h̲irbet ʿarʿara*; ^{URU}*ʿme-iš-tú'* = *mmšt* (*lmlk*-jar seal), *kurnub*?; ^{URU}*ma-ag-da-lì* = Migdal-gad (Josh. 15.37), *tell-el-mejādil*; ^{URU}*ḫi-ni-a-na-bi* = Anab (Josh. 15.50), *k̲h̲irbet ʿanāb*; ^{URU}*ḫa-wi*(PI)*-ni* = Anim (Josh. 15.50)), *k̲h̲irbet ġuwēn et-taḥtā* (*op. cit.*, 402). K. Elliger, *PJ* 31, 1935, 55f., regards ^{URU}*a-ra-ru* as a place **hrr* which he derives from the gentilic *hārārī* II Sam. 23.11, 33; I Chron. 11.34f. and identifies with *k̲h̲irbet eṭ-ṭarrāme* (which Noth, on the other hand, thinks is Debir: *JPOS* 15, 1935, 45–49; see below n. 84).

[24] *Die Einwanderung der israelitischen Stämme in Kanaan* (Berlin 1901), 122.

[25] 'Les pays bibliques au temps d'el-Amarna d'après la nouvelle publication des lettres', *RB* NS 5, 1908, 514f.

[26] *Geschichte des israelitisch-jüdischen Volkes* I (Leipzig 1924), 21.

[27] 'Zur historischen Geographie Südjudäas', *JPOS* 15, 1935, 42–44. Identifications of ^{URU}*ḫi-ni-a-na-bi*, ^{URU}*ḫa-wi-ni*, ^{URU}*a-ra-ru*, ^{URU}*ú-du-mu*, ^{URU}*a-du-ri* as Alt, the remainder 'uncertain'. Noth's proposal (*loc. cit.*, 44) to read *ga-ša*$_7$ (improbably equated with *gošen*) instead of *ga-ri* founders on the fact that the value '*ša*$_7$' for RI is only Sumerian (cf. R. Labat, *Manuel d'épigraphie akkadienne,* Paris ^{3}1959, 269^b) and what is, apparently, the only occurrence *CT* XIX 18 III 24 (cf. *ŠL* II No. 86.49) is in any case obscure (R. Borger states in a letter: the glossing of RI by NINDA [*ša*] need not necessarily indicate the reading *ša*$_7$; *gar* would also be possible).

[28] H. Clauss, 'Die Städte der El-Amarnabriefe und die Bibel', *ZDPV* 30, 1907, 5, 9f., 27, 30f., 32, 41, 43, 51, 64. W. F. Albright: cf. 'The Jordan Valley in the Bronze Age', *AASOR* 6, 1924/25 (1926), 41, and more recently 'Two Little Understood Amarna Letters from the Middle Jordan Valley', *BASOR* 89, 1943, 14f. Identifications: ^{URU}*a-du-ri* = *dūrā* in northern *jōlān*; ^{URU}*ma-ag-da-lì* = *mgdl ṣbʿyy'* near *el-ḥamme*? (also *mgdl gdr*; on this cf. H. Graetz, *MGWJ* 29, 1880, 487–95; E. L. Sukenik, *JPOS* 15, 1935, 109, 114); ^{URU}*ḫe-ni-a-na-bi* = *ʿēn nāb* (haplology for **ʿēn 'enāb*) in central *jōlān*; ^{URU}*ḫa-ya*$_8$/*yú*(PI)*-ni* = *ʿayyūn* 3 km. (2 miles) north-west of *el-ḥamme*; ^{URU}*ya*$_8$*-bi-lì*$^!$*-ma*$^!$ (so instead of *ya*$_8$*-bi-ši-ba*) = *ābil*?; ^{URU}*me-iš-tú* to be read as URU *me-iš-qí*$^!$ (without identification; on the etymology cf. now W. F. Albright, *BASOR* 163, 1961, 46f., n. 53. B. Mazar, 'Geshur and Maaca', *JBL* 80, 1961, 18–21. Mazar, *loc. cit.*, 20, wishes to emend KUR *ga-ri* to KUR *ga*(*-šu*)*-ri* and to connect it with the land of *g^{e}šūr* Josh. 13.13 *et al.*

modern *jōlān*).[29] The only hill cities which appear are Jerusalem and Shechem, to which may be added at the most the tetrapolis, known from Josh. 9.17: Gibeon, Chephirah (*khirbet kefīre*), Beeroth and Kiriath-jearim (*dēr el-azhar* near *el-qerye*).[30] In the

[29] In the nature of things the question must remain open. If Albright, whose readings undoubtedly mark an advance on the attempts of his predecessors, interprets VAB II 256, 19ff. correctly, his siting of the towns of the land of *Garu* in *jōlān* near Pella (*Piḫilu, khirbet faḥil*) has probability on its side even if many of his identifications must remain dubious.

[30] While the identification of Chephirah and Kiriath-jearim is certain, that of Beeroth and Gibeon is still strongly contested. Earlier, in the case of Gibeon, a fairly general claim was put forward for *el-jīb* (cf., e.g., E. Robinson, *Palästina und die südlich angrenzenden Länder II* [Halle/S. 1841], 353; *KBw* 215, *s.v.* Gibeon) and even today, mostly on the basis of the excavations of J. B. Pritchard on this site, this identification is made by an ever increasing group of writers. Cf. J. B. Pritchard, 'The Water System at Gibeon', *BA* 19, 1956, 70; *Hebrew Inscriptions and Stamps from Gibeon* (Philadelphia 1959), 17; 'Gibeon's History in the Light of Excavation', *SVT* 7, 1960, 1–3; 'A Bronze Age Necropolis at Gibeon', *BA* 24, 1961, 23; *Gibeon Where the Sun Stood Still—The Discovery of the Biblical City* (Princeton 1962), 5, 27–29, 45–52, 136f.; W. F. Albright, *BASOR* 159, 1960, 37 ('there can no longer be any doubt that the site has been correctly identified'); E. F. Campbell Jr., *BA* 26, 1963, 30; J. Liver, 'The Literary History of Joshua IX', *JSS* 8, 1963, 237. n.1; K.-D. Schunck, *Benjamin: Untersuchungen zur Entstehung und Geschichte eines israelitischen Stammes* (BZAW 86, 1963), 22f.; cf. also A. Jirku, 'Wo lag Gibeon?', *JPOS* 8, 1928, 187–90; Y. Aharoni, *'Ereṣ yiśrā'ēl bi-tqūfat ha-miqrā'. Gē'ōgrafyā hisṭōrīt* (Jerusalem 1962), 347; M. Avi-Yonah, *The Madaba Mosaic Map with Introduction and Commentary* (Jerusalem 1954), 49 No. 48. Now Gibeon is certainly to be located in the region circumscribed by the places *en-nebī samwīl, er-rām, el-bīre, rāmallāh* and *el-jīb*, and *el-jīb* also suits very well the position of Gibeon that is to be presupposed for the campaign of Cestius (*Γαβαω* Josephus, *Bell.* II 19.1, 7–9, §§516, 540–55) and the (uncertain) information about distance given by Josephus, i.e. 40 stadia (= 7.7 km. or 4¾ miles) or 50 stadia (= 9.6 km. or nearly 6 miles) from Jerusalem (*Ant.* VII 11.7, §283; or *Bell.* II 19.1, §516) but not the information (equally uncertain and certainly not entirely correct) given by Eusebius (*On.* 66.11–16, Klostermann). The name *el-jīb* cannot, as G. Kampffmeyer, *Alte Namen im heutigen Palästina und Syrien: I. Namen des Alten Testaments* (Leipzig 1892), 112–14, has already convincingly shown, be understood as a variant of the old name *gibʿōn*. But even the results of Pritchard's excavations – unfortunately extremely inadequate (cf. on this generally K. Galling, 'Kritische Bemerkungen zur Ausgrabung von eğ-ğib', *BO* 22, 1965, 242–5) – do not agree with the history of the town of Gibeon as this can be deduced from the written sources. For Pritchard has found in *el-jīb* neither a settlement stratum of the Late Bronze Age nor a wall of the same period; only seven graves in the cemetery show that after an interment of the Middle Bronze Age there was a second interment of the Late Bronze Age in the fourteenth century (J. B. Pritchard, *The Bronze Age Cemetery at Gibeon* [Philadelphia 1963], 17, 18, 21, 22, 36, 37, 72). Pritchard assumes that the scant remains of Late Bronze pottery are indicative of the existence of a Late Bronze Age town and thinks that this lies in a part of the *tell* which has not yet been excavated; but against this suggestion one must

Shephelah the Amarna texts mention, in addition, the cities of Gezer (*tell jezer*), Rubute, Zorah (*ṣarʿā*), Aijalon (*yālō*), Lachish (*tell ed-duwēr*) and Keilah (*k͟hirbet qīlā*).[31] In the mountainous parts

---

hold the fact that the few Late Bronze Age burials in the cemetery do not necessarily presuppose a fortified town of that period at *el-jīb* and that, in the relatively thorough excavations around the town spring and the installations for securing the water supply, a Late Bronze Age wall would, in all probability, have been found if there had really been a fortified town of that period on the site. From similar considerations, therefore, E. F. Campbell Jr. (*loc. cit.*) has dated the events of Josh. 9, which lead to the supposition of a pre-Israelite, i.e. Late Bronze Age city state of Gibeon, forward into Iron I, a very dubious *ad hoc* procedure which, on methodological grounds, cannot be permitted without further examination. Thus, in view of the discrepancy between the literary and the archaeological data, the equation Gibeon = *el-jīb* would be very uncertain if Pritchard, in the course of his excavations, had not discovered a large number of inscribed jar handles of the sixth century (so F. M. Cross Jr., 'Epigraphical Notes on Hebrew Documents of the Eighth-Sixth Centuries B.C.: III. The Inscribed Jar Handles from Gibeon', *BASOR* 168, 1962, 18–23; J. B. Pritchard, *Hebrew Inscriptions and Stamps from Gibeon* [Philadelphia 1959]; 'More Inscribed Jar Handles from el-Jîb', *BASOR* 160, 1960, 1–6) which also mention the place name *gbʿn* = Gibeon and are generally regarded as positive corroboration of the identification. In this case, too, one must beware of interpreting difficult facts too quickly and uncritically. The jar handle inscriptions have, over a long period, not been interpreted with any certainty; the result is that we can say nothing about the function of Gibeon in connection with the unknown event of which we are informed in the handle inscriptions. One must grant to Pritchard without qualification that discoveries of inscriptions which mention the old name of the place where they are discovered can provide confirmation of the identification; this is, of course, true of the boundary stones of Gezer which he cites and perhaps also of the stele of Sethos I from Bethshan (better examples would have been Ugarit/*rās eš-šamrā*, Mari/*tell ḥarīrī*, Guzana/*tell ḥalāf*), but it is problematical even in the case of the Lachish letters (where the equation Lachish = *tell ed-duwēr* is established on other grounds). Meanwhile, therefore, the *gbʿn* jar handles contribute nothing to the identification of *el-jīb* (cf. also K. Galling, *op. cit.*, 245). Against the equation cf. A. Alt, 'Neue Erwägungen über die Lage von Mizpa, Ataroth, Beeroth und Gibeon', *ZDPV* 69, 1953, 1–27; K. Elliger, 'Beeroth und Gibeon', *ZDPV* 73, 1957, 125–32; M. Weippert, 'Archäologischer Jahresbericht', *ZDPV* 79, 1963, 172 n.63.

Beeroth, on the basis of the doubtful assonance of the names, is usually equated with *el-bīre*, although this common place name most probably goes back not to Hebr. *beʾēr* and its derivatives but to Aram. *bīrā* 'fortress'. On Beeroth cf. A. Alt, *op. cit.*; Z. Kallai-Kleinmann, '*Beʾērōt-le-ʾōr ha-gevūl bēn binyāmīn le-ʾefrayim*', *EI* 3, 1954, 111–15 (*nebī samwīl*); K. Elliger, *op. cit.*; K. Elliger, 'Noch einmal Beeroth' in *Mélanges bibliques rédigés en l'honneur de André Robert* (Travaux de l'Institut Catholique de Paris 4, n.d.; 1957), 82–94; R. T. O'Callaghan, 'Is Beeroth on the Madaba Map?', *Bibl* 32, 1951, 57–64; H. Donner, *ZDPV* 81, 1965, 44–46. On this whole question one might compare with advantage *BRL*, 193–7.

[31] Cf. the summary in Aharoni, *op. cit.*, 152.

I have scruples about the identification of the place which is written

of the country, there may be observed, rather, according to Alt, a tendency towards the formation of larger territorial units. This tendency first comes to light perhaps already in the above-mentioned 'foreign country called Shechem' in the period of Sesostris III, if one accepts the sense which Alt gives to the somewhat vague term *ḫ3s.t*. It is clear in the Amarna letters. Thus a large territory in central Palestine, with its centre probably precisely at Shechem (**šakmu*, *tell balāṭa*), is ruled by a dynasty called Lab'ayu which extends its power and spreads into the adjacent plains to the west and north.[32] A similar process may be supposed in the case of Tagu which, certainly also from central-Palestinian bases, spreads into the territory of Bethshan (*tell el-ḥuṣn* near *bēsān*).[33] According to Alt, the king of Hazor (*tell el-qedaḥ*) was a kind of Galilean 'Lab'ayu'.[34]

From this Alt produces the following schema of the territorial division of Palestine in the Amarna period:

(*a*) *Galilean Hill Country*: Fairly large territorial units, especially the kingdom of Hazor.
(*b*) *Chain of City States* from Acco (*'akkā*) to Bethshan in the plains of Megiddo, Jezreel and Bethshan.
(*c*) *Central Palestinian Hill Country* (Mountains of Ephraim): Fairly large territorial units, including the kingdom of Shechem under Lab'ayu and his sons and the domain of Tagu.
(*d*) *Chain of City States* from the coastal plain up towards Jerusalem with Zorah and Aijalon; Gibeonite tetrapolis.
(*e*) *Judean Hill Country*: No information, perhaps fairly large territorial units (the land of Garu??).

URUÉ.DNIN.URAŠ, VAB II 290.16, according to line 15 a 'town of the country of Jerusalem' (URU KUR *ú-ru-ša-lim*KI) with Bethlehem (so O. Schroeder, 'Zu Berliner Amarnatexten: 2. Die jerusalemische Stadt *alubît-ilu*NIN.IB = Bethlehem', *OLZ* 18, 1915, 294f.: the reading **Bīt-*D*Laḫama* by using *CT* XXIV 1.4f., 15 in a somewhat too 'mathematical' way). But the question can be left open here since we are not dealing with an independent city-state. W. F. Albright identifies the place, probably correctly, with Lower Beth-horon: *AJSL* 53, 1936/37, 7 n. 20; *Yahweh and the Gods of Canaan* (London 1968), 120; so now also, with detailed proof, Z. Kallai and H. Tadmor, *EI* 9, 1969, 138–47.

32 VAB II 244 (Megiddo); 250.11–14 (*Gittipadalla*), 42–50 (Shunem, *Burkūna*, *Ḫarabu*, *Gittirimmūnīma*); 253.18–22; 254.20–22 (Gezer).

33 VAB II 289.19f.; cf. also 289.13 (*Rubūte*), 18f. (*Gittikirmil*).

34 VAB II 148.41–43; AO 7094.17–20 (*RA* 19, 1922, 96, 104).

(*f*) *Shephelah*: City states of Lachish, Gezer and Keilah.
(*g*) *Coastal Plain*: City states.

5. After the collapse of Egyptian domination in the Ramessid period, Palestine offers quite another picture. The territory west and east of the Jordan is now divided up among several larger states, distinguished from the earlier system that had been characterized by city governments in that they bear tribal or ethnic names, names which had hitherto apparently played no role in the history of the country: Edom, Moab, Ammon, Judah, Israel, Peleseth. The old city-state system has not yet disappeared, but on the fringes of the new states (at any rate west of the Jordan) it is in the process of breaking up (even among the Philistines, whose particular type of settlement most demanded a link with the older system, it is admitted only with modifications).[35] We have evidence for this state of affairs in the case of Israel in the so-called 'negative account of the conquest' which is contained primarily in Judg. 1.[36] This deals with a list of Canaanite cities claimed by the tribes of Benjamin,[37] Manasseh, Ephraim, Zebulun, Asher and Naphtali, but which could become subjugated only 'when Israel grew strong',[38] that is with the setting up of a central monarchy in the process of the formation of the state, at

[35] The Philistines certainly settled in a region where Gaza (*ġazze*) at least was no longer a royal town but was a possession of the Egyptian crown. But, perhaps in a second stage of their settlement, they took over the Palestinian city state system, and the so-called 'Philistine pentapolis' was organized politically under their own princes (Hebr. *s^e^rānīm*) in the five cities of Ashdod (*esdūd*), Ashkelon (*ʿasqelān*), Ekron (*k̲h̲irbet el-muqannaʿ*; cf. J. Naveh, 'Khirbat al-Muqannaʿ – Ekron: An Archaeological Survey', *IEJ* 8, 1958, 87–100, 165–70), Gath (*tell eṣ-ṣāfī*; see below n. 81) and Gaza. Cf. A. Alt, 'Ägyptische Tempel in Palästina und die Landnahme der Philister' (1944), *Kl.Schr.* I, ^{2}1959, 216–30; H. Donner, *RGG*^{3} V (1961), 339 *s.v.* Philister; M. Weippert, *Lexikon der alten Welt* (Zürich 1965), 2296f. *s.v.* Philister.

[36] The list includes Judg. 1.21 (Benjamin; variant Judah in Josh. 15.63; see below n. 37), 27f. (Manasseh; variant Josh. 17.11–13), 29 (Ephraim; variant Josh. 16.10), 30 (Zebulun), 31f. (Asher), 33 (Naphtali), 34f. (Dan). Against E. Täubler, *Biblische Studien: Die Epoche der Richter* (Tübingen 1958), 70f.; Schunck, *Benjamin*, 77, the section on Dan is to be retained. Josh. 13.13 is not original.

[37] Against Schunck, *op. cit.* 76, 78f., who, on the basis of the linguistic usage (*b^e^nē binyāmīn*) in Judg. 1.21, considers the reference to Benjamin to be secondary and suggests the insertion of Judah as in Josh. 15.63, I adhere to the reading 'Benjamin', so that Judah does not occur and could not occur in the list as it has been preserved (in its entirety?).

[38] Josh. 17.13 = Judg. 1.28; Judg. 1.35.

the earliest under David, not under Saul.[39] What is important here is that the cities mentioned in this list form the same chains of city states which Alt established on the basis of the Amarna texts: in the north, the line Acco (*ʿakkā*), Nahalol (*maʿlūl*?), Megiddo (*tell el-mutesellim*), Taanach (*tell taʿannek*), Ibleam (*k̲h̲irbet belʿame*), Bethshan (*tell el-ḥuṣn* near *bēsān*), in the south Gezer (*tell jezer*), Aijalon (*yālō*), Shaalbim (in the region of *selbīṭ*),[40] Jerusalem. The regions where the Israelite tribes settled must then, as is shown by the geographical distribution of these cities, be sought in the hill country between the Canaanite 'diagonals', and the Old Testament data concerning their settlements, especially the lists in Josh. 13–19,[41] leave no doubt that this was indeed the case. We can see here, then, at close quarters, the end of the old city-state system as far as one part of the country is concerned and may conclude that a similar process took place in other

39 As Alt concluded from II Sam. 2.8f. ('Settlement', 160f.) the Canaanite cities were not part of Saul's kingdom.

40 The old identification of Shaalbim with *selbīṭ* itself (cf. GesB[17], 853[b], *s.v. šaʿalebīm*) has not been confirmed by archaeology and cannot be supported by the alleged similarity of names. Cf. K. Elliger, 'Die dreissig Helden Davids', *PJ* 31, 1935, 52f.; Y. Aharoni, *'Ereṣ-yiśrā'ēl bi-tqūfat ha-miqrā'. Gē'ōgrafyā hisṭōrīt* (Jerusalem 1962), 100, 102, 261, 354 and against this M. Noth, *Das Buch Josua* (HAT I 7, [1]1938, 93; [2]1953, 121) on Josh. 19.42. If Aharoni's spelling of the Arabic name as *selbīt* is correct, then a connection with *šaʿalebīm* (via an Aramaic-Greek form of the name) could not be excluded.

41 In the first place, reference need be made only to the old 'system of tribal frontiers' in the book of Joshua, in second place also to the later complex of city lists which Alt has connected with the division of the kingdom of Judah into administrative districts under Josiah (this, in my opinion, is true of the final form of the lists, but their point of origin must be earlier). Cf. on this, amongst others, A. Alt, 'Judas Gaue unter Josia' (1925), *Kl.Schr.* II, [2]1959, 276–88; 'Das System der Stammesgrenzen im Buche Josua' (1927), *Kl.Schr.* I, [2]1959, 193–202; M. Noth, 'Studien zu den historisch-geographischen Dokumenten des Josuabuches', *ZDPV* 58, 1935, 185–255; *Josua*[1], IXf., 47ff.; *Josua*[2], 13–15, 73ff.; S. Mowinckel, 'Zur Frage nach dokumentarischen Quellen in Josua 13–19' (Avhandlinger utgitt av det Norske Videnskaps-Akademi i Oslo, hist.-filos. Kl. 1946:1); A. Alt, 'Bemerkungen zu einigen judäischen Ortslisten des Alten Testaments' (1950), *Kl.Schr.* II, [2]1959, 289–305; F. M. Cross Jr. and G. E. Wright, 'The Boundary and Province Lists of the Kingdom of Judah', *JBL* 75, 1956, 202–26; Z. Kallai-Kleinmann, 'The Town Lists of Judah, Simeon, Benjamin and Dan', *VT* 8, 1958, 134–60; Y. Aharoni, 'The Northern Boundary of Judah', *PEQ* 90, 1958, 27–31; 'The Province List of Judah', *VT* 9, 1959, 225–46; Z. Kallai-Kleinmann, *Gevūlōtehā ha-ṣefōnīyīm šel yehūdā le-min teqūfat ha-hitnaḥalūt we-ʿad rēšīt yemē ha-ḥašmōnā'īm* (Jerusalem 1960), 9–19, 21–34, 45; 'Note on the Town Lists of Judah, Simeon, Benjamin and Dan', *VT* 11, 1961, 223–7; Schunck, *Benjamin*, 156–67.

parts of the country such as Galilee or the hill country of Judah.

6. In these circumstances it is very probable that the settlement of the Israelite tribes in the gaps in the city-state system took place peacefully and that, therefore, in these extremely thinly populated regions no resistance worthy of mention was to be expected from an old-established population, with the exception of a few isolated cities such as Luz-Bethel (cf. Judg. 1.22–26) and perhaps Laish-Dan (cf. Judg. 18). The hypothesis of a settlement growing out of the regular change of pasture on the part of nomads with small cattle fits very well into the picture which can be derived from the sources of the territorial divisions in Palestine and the changes in them.

7. There are also references in the Old Testament tradition itself which point to peaceful relations between the Canaanite cities and the 'Israelite' groups which came into the country. Thus Josh. 9 mentions a treaty which the 'Israelites', probably the tribe of Benjamin, made with the Gibeonite tetrapolis. Although we know nothing further about its original content,[42] it probably dealt with

[42] The covenant-making tradition is used in the present context of Josh. 9.4–27 (9.1–3 belongs to the deuteronomistic framework) as an aetiology to explain the presence of Gibeonites as cultic personnel at an Israelite sanctuary (Gilgal? Gibeon? Jerusalem?). Even after the removal of the aetiological material, the story remains uneven on account of the large number of participants (on the 'Israelite' side there are Joshua, *ha-n^{e}śī'īm/n^{e}śī'ē hā-ʿēdā, hā-ʿēdā, b^{e}nē yiśrā'ēl/'īš yiśrā'ēl*). The fact of a treaty between *ha-ḥiwwī* and the *'īš yisrā'ēl* (perhaps originally **'īš binyāmīn*, cf. 9.7?) remains independent of the literary-critical and traditio-historical problems of the pericope and the evaluation of the role of Joshua in this context. Perhaps the Gibeonites actually intended a non-aggression pact (cf. 9.15, 18–22, 24, 26). Cf. the various opinions in M. Noth, *Josua*^{1}, 29–33; *Josua*^{2}, 53–59; K. Möhlenbrink, 'Die Landnahmesagen des Buches Josua', *ZAW* 56, 1938, 241–5; J. M. Grintz, '*B^{e}rīt ha-givʿōnīm*', *Zion* 26, 1961, 69–84; M. Haran, *Ha-givʿōnīm, ha-n^{e}tīnīm w^e-ʿavdē š^{e}lōmō* (*Hisṭōryā šel qibūṣ k^{e}naʿanī bīhūdā*) (*Y^{e}hūdā wīrūšālayim. Ha-kinūs hā-'arṣī ha-š^{e}nēm-ʿāśār līdiʿat hā-'āreṣ*, Jerusalem, 1957, 37–45) = 'The Gibeonites, the Nethinim and the Sons of Solomon's Servants', *VT* 11, 1961, 159–69; *Ha-givʿōnīm – m^{e}qōmām b^e-maʿ^{a}reḵet kibūš hā-'āreṣ ū-v^e-tōl^{e}dōt yiśrā'ēl* (*ʿIyūnīm b^e-sefer y^{e}hōšūaʿ. Diyūnē ha-ḥūg la-miqrā' b^e-vēt Dāwīd ben-Gūriyōn dīn w^e-ḥešbōn mālē'* [*Pirsūmē ha-ḥevrā l^e-ḥeqer ha-miqrā' b^e-yisrā'ēl* 9, Jerusalem 1960] 101–26); J. Dus, 'Gibeon – eine Kultstätte des Šmš und die Stadt des benjaminitischen Schicksals', *VT* 10, 1960, 370–94; J. Liver, 'The Literary History of Joshua IX', *JSS* 8, 1963, 227–43; Schunck, *Benjamin*, 38f.; F.Ch. Fensham, 'The Treaty between Israel and the Gibeonites', *BA* 27, 1964, 96–100; J. M. Grintz, 'The Treaty of Joshua with the Gibeonites', *JAOS* 86, 1966, 113–26. On the site of Gibeon see above n. 30, and on the *n^{e}śī'īm* who appear in Josh. 9 see M. Noth, *Das System der zwölf Stämme Israels* (BWANT IV 1, 1930), 151–62; H. Gese, *Der Verfassungsentwurf des*

delimiting the rights of use with regard to pastureland and water, analogous, for example, with Gen. 26, and perhaps also with agreements in respect of trade, the rights of intermarriage and mutual military support. The special position of Gibeon as a result of this treaty can be seen to remain effective right into the monarchical period.[43] A similar kind of assessment must be made of the attempt, reported in Gen. 34, on the part of the city of Shechem to enter into closer relationships with the tribes of Simeon and Levi. This narrative is stylized in the usual fashion and reads like a *novelle* with individuals as the protagonists. It presupposes, as Alt shows, that the two tribes, who seem to have had their original home in the heart of the Negeb,[44] have, in the course of changing their pastures, penetrated the district of Shechem. Astonishingly enough, an offer of alliance is made by the Canaanites, but the plan is unsuccessful; Simeon and Levi, rather, take the city in a sudden attack, kill the inhabitants and burn it to the ground, whereupon, certainly under pressure from the indigenous population (cf. Gen. 34.30), they withdraw southwards, perhaps back to their former territories, and never appear again in central Palestine; at a later date, Shechem belongs to Manasseh. The reason for this violent end to friendly relations is said, in the narrative as we have it, to be the rape of Dinah, the 'sister' of Simeon and Levi, by the son of the city prince, an incident whose background in tribal history is extremely obscure. Finally, in the case of the tribe

---

Ezechiel (Kap. 40–48) traditionsgeschichtlich untersucht (BHTh 25, 1957), 120; E. A. Speiser, 'Background and Function of the Biblical Nāśī'', *CBQ* 25, 1963, 111–17.

43 II Sam. 21.2b.

44 Even if the Simeonite list of places in Josh. 19.1–9 is correctly defined as an excerpt from Josh. 15.21b–32 (Josiah's Negeb district) (so Noth, *Josua*², 93, 113f.), there can still be no doubt that the region of Beersheba represents the old territory of the tribe of Simeon (which for a long time did not achieve permanent settlement); cf. Judg. 1.17 and A. Alt, 'Judas Gaue unter Josia' (1925), *Kl.Schr.* II, 285 and n.4. For Levi one can possibly accept a territory still further south, perhaps in the oasis-region of Kadesh-barnea (*'ēn qdēs*, *'ēn el-qdērāt*, *'ēn el-qṣēme*). On the distinction between the so-called 'secular' tribe of Levi and the levitical priesthood see, besides G. Fohrer, *RGG*³ IV (1960), 336f. *s.v.* Levi und Leviten (lit.), below n.139. In Gen. 49.5–7 allusion is made to the event which lies at the basis of Gen. 34; on this cf. also M. J. Dahood, 'MKRTYHM in Genesis 49.5', *CBQ* 23, 1961, 54–56, whose explanation of the word *mkrtyhm* as 'their circumcision knives' seems to me to overload the *novelle*-like structure of the tradition in Gen. 34.

of Manasseh, one must even accept the fact that Canaanite cities,[45] as is clear from the genealogies (Num. 26.29–34), were accepted into the alliance itself as 'clans' (*mišpāḥōt*). From the point of view of the conquest tradition this occurrence is astonishing. Alt explains it in terms of settlement history by suggesting that the tribe of Manasseh, which originated from the split in the 'house of Joseph', was crowded into living closely with Canaanite cities by the upsurge of his 'brother' Ephraim and, on grounds of self-preservation, was forced into forming an alliance with these cities. In this case, too, there is never any mention of hostile encounters; unless one accepts that the traditions referring to such encounters have been lost, then the conclusion is unavoidable that here too, as in the case of Benjamin and the Gibeonites, treaties of union were made.

8. If one accepts as fundamentally correct this picture of the settlement of tribes who were later to form Israel, it must then be asked how there arose the traditions, in Josh. 1–12 and partly also in Judg. 1, of a military conquest of the country either by individual actions on the part of tribes or tribal groups or by the twelve-tribe confederacy under a common leader, to what these traditions refer and also how one is to assess the role of Joshua in the settlement and in the early history of Israel generally. Alt has expounded his view of these matters in his lecture on 'Joshua'[46] delivered to the Old Testament conference in Göttingen in 1936. According to Alt, what we have in Josh. 2–11 was not originally a continuous narrative of the Israelite settlement. It is, rather, a series of indivi-

[45] In the primary form Shechem (*tell balāṭa*) Num. 26.31 and probably Hepher (*tell ibšar*?) 26.32. Amongst the 'daughters of Zelophehad' (26.33), who in Noth's view belong to an expansion of the text, Tirzah at least (north *tell el-fārʿa*) is an old city; the same may be true of the others (Mahlah, Noah, Hoglah, Milcah). Of these, Hoglah (45.1; 47.1), Noah (50.1) and Shechem (44.1) occur alongside other Manassite clan names (Abiezer 13.1f.; 28.1; Helek 22.1f.; 23.1; 24.1; 26.1; 27.1; Semida 3.2; 29.1?; 30.1; 31.1; 32.1; 33.1f.; 34.1; 35.1; 36.1; 37.1; 38.1f.; 39.1; 40; 63.2; Asriel [*śr'l*; cf. F. M. Cross Jr., *BASOR* 165, 1962, 36 n.10] 42.1; 48.1) in the so-called 'crown property ostraca' from Samaria (G. A. Reisner, C. S. Fisher and D. G. Lyon, *Harvard Excavations at Samaria 1908–1910* I, Cambridge, Mass., 1924, 239–43) as the names of administrative units. Cf. M. Noth, 'Das Krongut der israelitischen Könige und seine Verwaltung', *ZDPV* 50, 1927, 231–40; *Das System der zwölf Stämme Israels*, 124–30; 'Der Beitrag der samarischen Ostraka zur Lösung topographischer Fragen', *PJ* 28, 1932, 58f. Cf. also M. Weippert, *ZDPV* 80, 1964, 191 n.249.

[46] *Kl.Schr.* I, 176–92.

dual narratives which neither present a coherent historical picture as a whole nor describe the occupation of the whole of Palestine by 'Israel'. The one conclusion follows from the nature of the material which forms Josh. 2–11 as individual narratives,[47] the other from the geographical territory covered by these narratives: up to Josh. 10 they range along a line from the Jordan valley at Jericho as far as Gibeon. The 'digressions' into the later Judaean south (10.28ff.) and the Galilean north (11.1–15) are reported in very 'general' terms in a style different from that of Josh. 2–10.1ff. The centre of Palestine, the Samarian hill country, is not mentioned at all in the tradition, since the short pericope 8.30–35 is no substitute for a settlement tradition. The lists of conquered kings in Josh. 12 and more especially the description of tribal territories in 13–19 afford the first complete territorial picture that is even to some extent self-contained. A methodologically correct treatment of this complex must first of all, according to Alt, eliminate those elements which belong to the deuteronomistic reworking of it, thereby removing not only the conception of a unified military conquest of the land under Joshua but also the conception of a complete occupation of Palestine and of a division by Joshua of the whole territory among the Israelite tribes. The individual narratives which remain must then be analysed each on its own merits. The first thing that emerges from this is that, contrary to first impressions, these narratives do not belong to the class of 'hero-narratives' with Joshua as the protagonist; the narrative elements which might give such an impression are shown to be secondary insertions (Josh. 1; 3.7; 4.14; 6.27). Much more frequently, the narratives culminate in the formula '(as it is) to this day' (4.9; 6.25; 7.27; 8.28f.; 9.27; 10.27), thus showing that they are 'aetiological sagas of the most explicit type' which 'with regard to specific striking phenomena of the present explain their point of origin as due to events in the past' and thus 'attempt to answer in each case

[47] At this point, attention should be drawn to the fact that the authors discussed in this chapter, in contrast to the so-called 'recent' and 'most recent documentary hypothesis', do not usually admit the existence of the classical 'Pentateuchal' sources beyond Num. 36 (so especially Noth) or at the most beyond Josh. 24. As is well known, Noth, on the basis of his analysis of the book of Joshua, developed the hypothesis of the 'deuteronomistic history' which extended from Deut. to Kings; see M. Noth, *Überlieferungsgeschichtliche Studien: Die sammelnden und bearbeitenden Geschichtswerke im Alten Testament* (Tübingen ²1957), 3–110, 211–16; *Josua*², 6, 9.

the great question asked by children in all ages, "Why?" '.[48] Phenomena in need of explanation are, for example, the twelve stones of the sanctuary at Gilgal (Josh. 2f.), the naming of a specific locality at or near Gilgal as *gibʿat hāʿarālōt*, 'the hill of the foreskins' (5.2ff.), the *tell* of Jericho as a site with a curse upon it as well as the Canaanite tribe of Rahab which dwelt there 'in Israel' (Josh. 2; 6), a striking heap of stones in the plain of Achor near Jericho (Josh. 7), the great *tell* of Ai with a heap of stones in what was still recognizable as the opening of the city gate (Josh. 8.1–29), the employment of citizens of the Canaanite town of Gibeon in the cult personnel of an Israelite sanctuary, probably that of Gilgal (Josh. 9), and the five trees standing in front of a cave which was blocked with stones near the Judaean town of Makkedah (Josh. 10.16ff.). These aetiologies, like those of the 'Pentateuch', provide natural explanations of phenomena in or near their place of origin and are, therefore, traditions which are localized in a particular place. The individual places lie close together – Gilgal (probably, in spite of the difficult archaeological situation, near *ḵẖirbet el-mefjir*),[49] Jericho (*tell es-sulṭān* near *erīḥā*), the plain of Achor (near

[48] The quotations all *op. cit.*, 182f. – On the background of this 'children's question' cf. J. A. Soggin, 'Kultätiologische Sagen und Katachese im Hexateuch', *VT* 10, 1960, 341–7; one must however, beware of carelessly extending Soggin's impressively argued fixing of this question in the catechism in the case of Ex. 12.26ff.; 13.14ff.; Deut. 6.20ff.; Josh. 4.6ff., 21ff. to the aetiological settlement tradition as a whole.

[49] That Gilgal is to be located in the region of *ḵẖirbet el-mefjir* seems to me as good as certain on the basis both of the data provided by the sources (see below on Bächli) and of the results of Muilenburg's soundings (J. Muilenburg, 'The Site of Ancient Gilgal', *BASOR* 140, 1955, 11–27) in spite of the disagreement of F.-M. Abel, 'Galgala qui est aussi le Dodécalithon', *Mémorial J. Chaine* (Bibliothèque de la Faculté Catholique de Théologie de Lyon 5, Lyon 1950), 29–34, 298, and O. Bächli, 'Zur Lage des alten Gilgal', *ZDPV* 83, 1967, 64–71. It is true that the ruins which A. M. Schneider, 'Das byzantinische Gilgal', *ZDPV* 54, 1931, 50–59, held to be the remains of Byzantine *Γαλγαλα* are, according to D. C. Baramki's excavations, part of an (unfinished) Umayyad castle which Baramki, on the evidence of a Kufic inscription, would attribute to the Caliph Hišām (724–43) but which Hamilton would rather attribute to his nephew al-Walīd b. Yazīd (743); see D. C. Baramki, 'Excavations at Khirbet el Mefjer, III', *QDAP* 8, 1939, 53; R. W. Hamilton, *Khirbat al Mafjar, an Arabian Mansion in the Jordan Valley* (Oxford 1959), 7, 104f., 231f., 346. A few pillars with 'Maltese crosses' which were found in the ruins of the castle and which can be regarded as re-used Byzantine pillars, can hardly come from the church of the *Δωδεκάλιθον* which appears on the mosaic map from *mādebā* (P. Palmer and H. Guthe, *Die Mosaikkarte von Madeba* I [Leipzig 1906], plate 1; M. Avi-Yonah, *The Madaba Mosaic Map with Introduction and Commentary* [Jerusalem 1954], plate 1; cf. also the photo in

Jericho),[50] on the hill of Ai (*et-tell* between *bētīn* and *dēr dubwān*) – and their aetiologies are so bound up with Gilgal that we must, according to Alt, regard the sanctuary at Gilgal as the place where the aetiologies of this whole complex were localized and as the place where the combining of the individual local traditions took place. Since, in the narratives of Josh. 2–9, only Benjaminite

---

H. Donner and H. Cüppers, *ZDPV* 83, 1967, plate 12 above left) but which did not survive the Persian assault of the seventh century, since the pilgrim Willibald saw there only a small wooden church (cf. Avi-Yonah, *op. cit.*, 37[a]). The reason why the excavators were unable to find any trace of a pre-Umayyad level must be that Hišām (or Walīd) either utilized the ruins of the Byzantine church in his building operations or else built to one side of them. Iron Age Gilgal will have to be located, with Muilenburg, on one of the surrounding *telāl*, perhaps, in fact, on his *tell* II. The older rivals of *khirbet el-mefjir* (on this cf. *KBw* 218f.; Abel, *op. cit.*; Noth, *Josua*², 25; Muilenburg, *op. cit.*, 13–15) scarcely correspond to the data provided by the sources. On *khirbet el-mefjir* cf. also A. Alt, *PJ* 27, 1931, 46–49 (based on Schneider). I cannot accept the new theory of Bächli (*op. cit.* 70f.) that Gilgal is to be located on the *telāl mitlib*; both surface finds and the results of excavations (on the former cf. S. Mittmann in Bächli, *op. cit.*, 70; on the latter *ZDPV* 80, 1964, 192 No. 50) reveal only late Byzantine evidence, the map from *mādebā* can also be cited in support of *khirbet el-mefjir* and *mizrāḥ* in Josh. 4.19 cannot be pressed as if it could have only the exact geographical sense of 'east'; rather, in the ancient world 'east' can also include both 'north' (*khirbet el-mefjir*!) and 'south-east'. In addition, the information given by Eusebius (*On.* 46.19; 66.5 Klostermann) that Gilgal is pointed out as lying two miles (3 km.) away from Byzantine Jericho (*erīḥā*) exactly fits *khirbet el-mefjir* – which, moreover, lies close to the road that runs from Jericho north-south along the right bank of the Jordan – but not the *telāl mitlib* which lie about a mile (1.5 km.) north-east of *erīḥā*.

[50] The site of the valley of Achor is disputed. M. Noth (*Josua*¹, 60; *Josua*², 88) identified it with the region round *en-nebī mūsā*. With reference to Hos. 2.17 (EW 15) H. W. Wolff, 'Die Ebene Achor', *ZDPV* 70, 1954, 76–81 suggested the *wādī en-nuwē'ime* north-west of Jericho which also represents the 'Valley of Achor' of Jewish and Christian tradition (cf. J. T. Milik, *ADAJ* 4/5, 1960, 143), a suggestion with which, however, the information given in Josh. 15.7, where the valley of Achor appears as a point on the northern frontier of Judah between Beth-arabah (near *'ēn el-ġarabe*) and the ascent of Adummim (*ṭal'at ed-damm*), cannot exactly be harmonized. One must, therefore, look for it south of the *wādī el-qelṭ*. Noth's most recent suggestion, *buqē'a* (*ZDPV* 71, 1955, 42–55; cf. J. T. Milik and F. M. Cross Jr., 'Explorations in the Judaean Buqê'ah', *BASOR* 142, 1956, 5–17), fits the archaeological situation very well and also corresponds with Josh. 15.7 (cf. Milik and Cross, *op. cit.*, 17 n.32; S. Schulz, 'Chirbet ḳumrān, 'ēn feschcha und die buḳē'a', *ZDPV* 76, 1960, 59f.). Against the doubts of H. W. Wolff, *Dodekapropheton I: Hosea* (BKAT 14.1, 1961), 51f., one may perhaps ask whether Hos. 2.17 (15), where Wolff's suggestion fitted perfectly, is not perhaps thinking of a different place from Josh. 15.7 because of a loss of topographical knowledge over a period of time (having regard to the lateness of the tradition).

places occur, one will also need, with some justification, to regard these traditions as Benjaminite. The fact that, in their present context, they are now transferred to the 'national' or 'all-Israelite' realm, is explained by Alt as due to the temporary role of Gilgal as the central sanctuary of the Israelite amphictyony, a role which is attested by the fact that the proclamations of Saul and David as king took place there (I Sam. 11.15; II Sam. 19.41ff.).[51]

9. The designation of the individual narratives of Josh. 2–9 as aetiological traditions has, in Alt's view, consequences for the historical use which can be made of them. Although the circumstances explained in such narratives certainly contain a considerable degree of historical reality, yet this assertion cannot be made *a priori* about the past event which is narrated to explain them. In the case of the narrative about the conquest and destruction of the town of Ai (Josh. 8.1–19) the judgment concerning historicity here must even be totally negative since the excavations of the ruins which are definitely to be identified with this place, *et-tell*,[52] have revealed a gap in occupation between the Early

[51] Cf. also I Sam. 10.8; 13.4, 7; 15.12, 21, 33 for the period of Saul, and A. Alt, 'Die Staatenbildung der Israeliten in Palästina' (1930), *Kl.Schr.* II, 21 with n.2 (ET 'The Formation of the Israelite State in Palestine' in *Essays in Old Testament History and Religion*, 193 and n.50); H.-J. Kraus, 'Gilgal. Ein Beitrag zur Kultusgeschichte Israels', *VT* 1, 1951, 185, 191–4, 199; M. Noth, *Josua*², 33. On the 'amphictyony' see below, nn.125f.

[52] Since E. Robinson, *Palästina und die südlich angrenzenden Länder* II (Halle/S. 1841), 562–4, the alternative *et-tell*: *k̲h̲irbet ḥayyān* has dominated the discussion on the site of Ai (review in W. F. Albright, *AASOR* 4, 1922/23, 141–9; J. M. Grintz, *Bibl* 42, 1961, 201–6). The compromise solution finally arrived at and generally accepted and based, in part, on the archaeological discoveries at both places, located what appeared to be the Late Bronze Age Ai at *et-tell* and the subsequent (?) Iron Age settlement (*hā-ʿay* Ezra 2.28; Neh. 7.32; *ʿayyā* Neh. 11.31; I Chron. 7.28; *ʿayyāt* Isa. 10.28; perhaps *hā-ʿawwīm* Josh. 18.23) at *k̲h̲irbet ḥayyān*. But after the archaeological discoveries of 1964 (J. A. Callaway, *BASOR* 178, 1965, 16 n.4; B. T. Dahlberg, *BA* 28, 1965, 28; H. Donner, *ZDPV* 81, 1965, 16–18) *k̲h̲irbet ḥayyān* must be completely excluded since the strata there only begin in the early Arabic period. On the archaeological finds from *et-tell* see below n.53. Later expeditions have shown that at *k̲h̲irbet ḥayyān* we are dealing primarily with the site of a Byzantine monastery including a church and farm buildings (J. A. Callaway, orally). On the basis of a note attributed to Rabbi Berechiah (fourth century AD) in Midrash Ex. R. XXXII that the distance between Jericho and Ai was three Roman miles, B.-Z. Luria, '*Meqōmāh šel hā-ʿay*' ('*Iyūnīm be-sefer yehōšūaʿ*, 1960 [see above, n.42], 12–41) seeks to locate Ai on *k̲h̲irbet bēt jaber et-taḥtānī* or on the *telāl abū el-ʿalāʾiq*, against which is the fact that the biblical sources definitely locate Ai in the hills and not in the Arabah. Luria's uncritical handling of the biblical texts and the late date of the redaction of the Midrash

Bronze Age and Iron Age I,[53] so that the saga which linked the great heap of ruins with the Israelite settlement and therefore with the destruction of a Late Bronze Age settlement is wrong by more than a thousand years.[54]

10. These suggestions of Alt's have been elaborated especially by Martin Noth in a series of essays and in the two editions of his commentary on the Book of Joshua. While Alt[55] treated the problem of the conquest and destruction of Jericho very cautiously and, in view of the attempts of the archaeologist of the day, J. Garstang, to work from the exact dating of the 'latest' wall (which at that time was held to be Late Bronze Age) to a precise beginning of the settlement under Joshua,[56] indicated only briefly that, on the basis of the biblical account, a complete destruction of the town at the point of transition between the Late Bronze Age and the Iron Age was not to be expected, Noth provided a thoroughly aetiological exposition of the traditions of Josh. 2 and 6. This can be ascertained most clearly in the case of Josh. 6,[57] where the narrative leads up to the destruction of the town walls by Yahweh with the liturgical 'co-operation' of the 'Israelites' processing round the walls uttering war cries. The presupposition of this narrative is that at the time of the (first) narrator Jericho was in ruins, a condition which this very story is intended to

---

(eleventh to twelfth century; cf. L. Zunz, *Die gottesdienstlichen Vorträge der Juden,* Berlin ²1892, 256–8; H. L. Strack, *Introduction to the Talmud and Midrash,* New York and Philadelphia 1959, 215) detract from the value of his theory. Similarly the arguments of J. M. Grintz, ' " 'Ai which is beside Beth-Aven": A Re-examination of the Identity of 'Ai', *Bibl* 42, 1961, 201–16, are insufficient to refute the equation Ai = *et-tell.*

53 The settlement gap established in her excavations by J. Marquet-Krause, *Les Fouilles de 'Ay (Et-Tell) 1933–1935, entreprises par le Baron Edmond de Rothschild: La résurrection d'une grande cité biblique* (BAH 45, 1949), esp. p. 23, has been confirmed by the American investigations of 1964; cf. J. A. Callaway, 'The 1964 'Ai (Et-Tell) Excavations', *BASOR* 178, 1965, 37f.; L. Sabourin, *CBQ* 27, 1965, 50; B. T. Dahlberg, 'Archaeological News from Jordan: Ai (et-Tell)', *BA* 28, 1965, 26–30.

54 A. Alt, *PJ* 30, 1934, 10 n.2; 'Josua' (*Kl.Schr.* I), 185.

55 *Op. cit.*, 186.

56 On this see the summary in H. H. Rowley, *From Joseph to Joshua* (London ⁴1958), 12–17.

57 M. Noth, *Josua*¹, 3, 17–19; *Josua*², 21f., 40–43; 'Grundsätzliches zur geschichtlichen Deutung archäologischer Befunde auf dem Boden Palästinas', *PJ* 34, 1938, 14–16; 'Hat die Bibel doch recht?', *Festschrift für Günther Dehn* (Neukirchen 1957), 13f.; 'Der Beitrag der Archäologie zur Geschichte Israels', *SVT* 7, 1960, 274f.; cf. also the analysis in J. Maier, *Das altisraelitische Ladeheiligtum* (BZAW 93, 1965), 32–39.

explain. It follows, according to Noth, that in the long run we have no authentic tradition concerning the date and circumstances of the final destruction of Jericho in the pre-Israelite period, with the result that all attempts, based on the results of the various excavations, to reach certainty concerning the dating of the event recorded in Josh. 6 and, therefore, of the settlement, must necessarily fail. Noth finds a parallel tradition, likewise of the aetiological type, of which unfortunately only a fragment has been preserved, in the 'spy story' of Josh. 2 (with isolated details in 6.17b, 22, 23, 25a)[58] which is surely conditioned by the fact that 'to this day' there lived, probably on the site of Jericho, a Canaanite family called Rahab. In its original form the story must have had as its main point the fact that the prostitute Rahab, in whose house the Israelite spies lodged, delivered her town in some way into the hands of the attackers and so, when the town was taken, was spared.[59] Her house, in which her descendants, that same family of Rahab, perhaps still practised the profession[60] of their

[58] *Josua*^{1}, 3f., 9–11; *Josua*^{2}, 22f., 29–31; *PJ* 34, 14 n. 2. There is no proof in the Old Testament text for the interesting theory of J. A. Soggin, 'Giosuè 2 alla luce di un testo di Mari', *RSO* 39, 1964, 7–14.

[59] Comparative material on historical motifs in H. Windisch, 'Zur Rahabgeschichte (Zwei Parallelen aus der klassischen Literatur)', *ZAW* 37, 1917/18, 188–98; G. Hölscher, 'Zum Ursprung der Rahabsage', *ZAW* 38, 1919/20, 54–57.

[60] Noth's interpretation (*Josua*^{1}, 4; ^{2}, 23), tentatively discussed, of the expression which is not attested in the texts but which is deduced on the basis of traditio-historical analysis, **bēt rāḥāb* (or **bēt r*^{e}*ḥōb*) as an appellative for 'brothel', does not commend itself on linguistic grounds. Concerning the profession of the *'iššā zōnā* Rahab, opinion was already divided from an early period. In Josephus the spies enter a καταγώγιον (*Ant.* V 1.2, §§7, 8, 10, 13), according to T Rahab was a *pund*^{e}*qīt* (which, in turn, is explained in *Aruch* 122^{a} as *'iššā zōnā*), while G (γυνὴ πόρνη), V (*mulier meretrix*) and S (*'att*^{e}*tā zānītā*), like Heb. 11.31; James 2.25 (πόρνη) take her – correctly – to be a prostitute. Similarly divided were the Hebrew lexicographers who, towards the end of the eighteenth century, after lengthy discussion, turned to the opinion which prevails today; thus J. Simon(is), *Lexicon manuale Hebraicum et Chaldaicum* (Halle/S. ^{3}1793; ed. J. G. Eichhorn), 467f., 484; Ph.U. Moser, *Lexicon manuale Hebraicum et Chaldaicum* (Ulm 1795), 182; W. Gesenius, *Hebräisches und chaldäisches Handwörterbuch über das Alte Testament* (Leipzig ^{4}1834), 554^{a}; G. B. Winer, *Lexicon manuale Hebraicum et Chaldaicum in Veteris Testamenti libros ordine etymologico descriptum* (Leipzig 1828), 286; cf. on the other hand, however, J. Fürst, *Hebräisches und Chaldäisches Handwörterbuch über das Alte Testament I* (Leipzig ^{3}1876, ed. V. Ryssel), 351^{a}. Recently, D. J. Wiseman, *JSS* 9, 1964, 359 has reiterated the old explanation, adding to it a reference to Akk. *sābītu*. The two meanings are such that one does not necessarily exclude the other; according to *Aruch* the Targumic expression *pund*^{e}*qītā*, at least, has a double meaning.

eponymous ancestress, is to be seen among the ruins 'to this day'. If Noth's reconstruction of the narrative is correct (the part about the capture of the town has now been suppressed by Josh. 6), the aetiology is obvious. Noth finds a third aetiological narrative pertaining to Jericho in the fragmentary section 5.13–15[61] which tells of the appearance before Joshua *bîrîḥō* 'in (not 'by') Jericho' (5.13) of the 'commander of the army of Yahweh' and which presents the Israelite explanation of what was surely even in Canaanite times a sacred site in the region of the town of Jericho.[62]

11. Even in the middle of the thirties Noth[63] was able to base his judgment of the narrative of the conquest of the royal Canaanite town of Ai (Josh. 7.2–5a; 8.1–29) on the first results of the excavations carried out on *et-tell* by Judith (Marquet-) Krause.[64] In the course of these, as is well known, a large settlement gap was established between Early Bronze III and Iron I, without a single trace being found of the Late Bronze Age town presupposed by the biblical tradition. Against the various more or less tortuous attempts to establish a compromise between the Old Testament narrative and the archaeological facts,[65] Noth (as well as the excavator herself),[66] on the basis of the above-mentioned arguments of Alt, made it clear that even leaving aside the results of the excavations, Josh. 7f. had to be understood as an aetiological narrative which linked the prominent ruined site[67] with the settle-

[61] *Josua*[1], 4f.; [2], 23.

[62] One must ask at this point whether in this section we do not have a fragment of a tradition which belongs not to Jericho but to Gilgal, perhaps even the actual aetiology (discoverer saga) in Israelite dress of the Canaanite sanctuary there; the definition of the place *bîrîḥō* does not give the impression of being indissolubly linked to the context. On this cf. K. Galling, *BRL*, 197; 'Bethel und Gilgal', *ZDPV* 66, 1943, 142; H.-J. Kraus, 'Gilgal. Ein Beitrag zur Kultusgeschichte Israels', *VT* 1, 1951, 197; C. Keller, 'Über einige alttestamentliche Heiligtumslegenden', *ZAW* 68, 1956, 89f. F.-M. Abel, 'L'apparition du chef de l'armée de Yahveh à Josué (Jos. V, 13–15)', *Studia Anselmiana* 27/28, 1951, 109–13, thinks of *'ēn dōk*. Maier, *op. cit.*, 33f., supposes that the basically independent pericope (5.13f.; according to him 5.15 is an addition) became linked to the originally Benjaminite Rahab-narrative in the second stage of the formation of the tradition, the 'Ephraimite Joshua recension'.

[63] M. Noth, 'Bethel und Ai', *PJ* 31, 1935, 7–29; *Josua*[1], 19f., 23–28; *Josua*[2], 43, 47–51.

[64] See above, n. 53.

[65] See below ch. V, n. 2.

[66] J. Marquet-Krause, *Les fouilles de 'Ay (et-Tell) 1933–1935: La résurrection d'une grande cité biblique* (BAH 45, 1949), 24.

[67] In *ZDPV* 80, 1964, 185 I have, along similar lines, tried to trace the

ment of Benjamin and later, in an 'all-Israelite' extension, with that of 'Israel'. According to Alt and Noth the aetiology probably arose at the time of the minor Iron Age settlement which has been attested by the excavations and which is certainly Benjaminite,[68] in order to give historical support to the settlers' claims to possession (perhaps against the claims of the Ephraimite inhabitants of nearby Luz-Bethel). As starting points for this explanation there were perhaps the still recognizable burnt-out ruins of the Early Bronze town and – as far as details are concerned – a heap of stones in the ruins of the old town gate which could be pointed out as the grave of the executed Canaanite king and a nearby tree[69] which served as gallows for the criminal. That this conquest story arose within the short-lived Benjaminite settlement of Ai itself is indicated, according to Noth, by a series of topographical details in the account[70] which would be clear only to someone familiar with the locality. On the other hand, he finds it difficult to ascertain the origin of two prominent elements in the narrative, namely the failure of the first attempt to conquer the town, a failure which is explained in different ways (7.2–5a; 7.5b–26)[71] and the motif of

---

notices about the defeat of the king of Arad (Num. 21.1–3; cf. 33.40; Josh. 12.14) back to a lost aetiology of the extensive Early Bronze ruins of *tell ʿarād*. On this cf. now more precisely V. Fritz, 'Arad in der biblischen Überlieferung und in der Liste Schoschenks I.', *ZDPV* 82, 1966, 331–42, esp. 341f.

[68] The information given in Josh. 8.28 that Ai was made into a *tel ʿōlām* first became part of the tradition-complex, according to Noth (*PJ* 31, 27; *Josua*[1], 25; *Josua*[2], 47) when the short-lived Benjaminite settlement on *et-tell* already belonged to the distant past and had been forgotten. On the later subsequent settlements (?) see above, n. 52.

[69] Whether *ʿēṣ* in 8.29 means 'tree' or perhaps, rather, 'post' must remain open; linguistically both are possible. The same problem arises in connection with the five *ʿēṣîm* of 10.26f. In both cases a definite decision between the two would influence one's judgment of Noth's proposed aetiological explanations. – Impalement was particularly common with the Assyrians as a method of execution (intended to serve as a terrifying warning) for the most important political leaders of conquered cities.

[70] Cf. *PJ* 31, 24f. Whether one can translate *hammidbār* in 8.15, 20, 23 (?) by 'the pasturage (of Ai)' seems to me very questionable. Rather, by 'wilderness' is meant the eastern slope of the hill country to the west of the Jordan which lay in the path of the 'Israelites'' easterly direction of flight and which, in this area (east of *dēr dubwān*) certainly belonged to the wilderness region. As the routes of the flight one has to think of individual *awdiya* flowing into the *wādī er-rummamāne*.

[71] The narrative of Achan's theft has been used secondarily as the motivation for the initial 'Israelite' failure to take Ai. Originally it was probably a

ambush and pretended flight. The idea that the concept of an 'Israelite' ambush between Bethel and Ai developed in connection with certain topographical features of the terrain – either the great blocks of stone on the slope west of *et-tell*[72] or else the caves on both sides of the *wādī el-jāye* to the north-west[73] – apparently seemed so uncertain to Noth that, after advocating it in his 1935 paper on the basis of Sternberg and Garstang, he made no further reference to it in the two editions of his commentary on Joshua. For those who are unable to regard the narrative of Josh. 7f. as an account which is in its essentials historically exact, the matter is still undecided. However, the attempt at a solution recently presented by Roth[74] is worthy of consideration. He stresses the fact that in Judg. 19ff. the conquest of the Benjaminite town of Gibea is effected by means of the same stratagem and explains Josh. 8 as a partisan narrative whose purpose is to act as a polemic against the disgrace of Benjamin's defeat in the amphictyonic war by 'bringing to light the military strength and skill of Benjamin in its still distinctive tribal form'.[75]

12. For traditio-historical and historical analysis the situation in the pericope (Josh. 10) which could be entitled 'the battle at Gibeon and its consequences' (Noth) is not clear. As 10.1ff. shows, the redactor has understood the section as a sequel to the treaty between the 'Israelites' and the Gibeonite towns which he has reported earlier and which has already been discussed above.[76] Elliger[77] and Noth[78] are agreed that, in spite of that, the composition of Josh. 10 can be divided into the following sections:

Reubenite (?)-Judahite (see below pp. 43f. and n. 140) tradition localized in the valley of Achor (see above n. 50) which somehow at some time became linked with the Benjaminite tradition of the conquest of Jericho and was subsequently taken over into the Ai narrative by the 'collector' (Noth) when the Jericho pericope was linked to the Ai pericope. For the explanation (participation by Judahites in the cultic practices of the Benjaminite sanctuary at Gilgal?) cf. Noth, *Josua*[1], 19f.; *Josua*[2], 43.

[72] So J. Garstang, *The Foundations of Bible History: Joshua Judges* (London, 1931), 154.

[73] So G. Sternberg, 'Bethel', *ZDPV* 38, 1915, 14f.

[74] W. M. W. Roth, 'Hinterhalt und Scheinflucht. Der stammespolemische Hintergrund von Jos 8', *ZAW* 75, 1963, 296–303.

[75] Roth, *op. cit.*, 300.

[76] See above pp. 18ff. and n. 42.

[77] K. Elliger, 'Josua in Judäa', *PJ* 30, 1934, 47–71.

[78] M. Noth, 'Die fünf Könige in der Höhle von Makkeda', *PJ* 33, 1937, 22–36; *Josua*[1], 34–41; *Josua*[2], 60–67.

10.1–15,[79] the 'authentic story' (Elliger) or 'hero narrative'/'war narrative' (Noth) which records a battle between 'Amorite kings' and 'Israelites' at Gibeon and the pursuit of the defeated coalition by way of the ascent of Beth-horon as far as Azekah (*tell zakarīye*); 10.16–27, the aetiological narrative which is localized at a cave near Makkedah;[80] 10.28–39, the report of an 'Israelite' campaign under Joshua in southern Palestine which leads to the capture of the towns of Makkedah (secondary), Libnah,[81] Lachish,[82] Eglon,[83] Hebron and Debir;[84] 10.40–42 + 43, an appended summ-

[79] According to fairly general agreement 10.1–15 is composed, in turn, of the prose narrative (10.1–11), the quotation from the *sēper hayyāšār* together with its framework (10.12–14) and the editorial or later gloss (10.15). The largely apologetic literature on the subject of the so-called 'sun miracle' need not interest us here; on this cf. the critical remarks of B. J. Alfrink, 'Het "stil staan" van zon en maan in Jos. 10, 12–15', *StC* 24, 1949, 238–43 (lit.), 261–8; further: J. Schildenberger, 'Der Stillstand von Sonne und Mond in Josue 10, 12–14', *Oberrheinisches Pastoralblatt* 51, 1950, 311–21; J. de Fraine, 'De miraculo solari Josue, Jos. 10.12–15', *VD* 28, 1950, 227–36; H. van den Bussche, 'Het zogenaamd zonnewonder in Jos. 10, 12–15', *Collationes Gandavenses* 2.1, 1951, 48–53; G. Lambert, 'Josué à la bataille de Gabaon', *NRTh* 76, 1954, 374–91. The labour which has been expended on astronomical or physical 'explanations' of the 'sun miracle' is wasted effort. In Homer too Helios does not go down if the battle is going well for the Achaeans: *Iliad* II 411–18; XVIII 239–42. The passages show that this was a favourite topic in poetic descriptions of battle in the heroic age. Perhaps Judg. 5.20 should be included here.

[80] Not definitely identified. Elliger's proposal (*PJ* 30, 56f.), with Noth's qualified agreement (*PJ* 33, 33 n.4), of *bēt mak/qdūm* (spelling uncertain; the suggestion already in H. Holzinger, 'Das Buch Josua', *HSAT*³ I, 1909, 320 note m) at least delimits the region within which the place will need to be sought. No value can be attached to the slight similarity in the sound of the names.

[81] According to Elliger, *ZDPV* 57, 1934, 116; *PJ* 30, 58–62, probably *tell bornāṭ* (cf. also Noth, *PJ* 33, 34f.; *Josua*¹, 68, 118; *Josua*², 95f., 147; Schunck, *Benjamin*, 31 n.84), not *tell eṣ-ṣāfī* (so W. F. Albright, *AASOR* 2/3, 1923, 13f.; G. Beyer, *ZDPV* 54, 1934, 150–59; G. E. Wright, *JNES* 5, 1946, 110), which is identified, correctly in my opinion, by Elliger (*ZDPV* 57, 148–52; *PJ* 30, 60) with Gath.

[82] Since W. F. Albright, *ZAW* 47, 1929, 3 with n.2, generally and correctly identified with *tell ed-duwēr*.

[83] According to Elliger (*PJ* 30, 63–68) most probably *tell bēt mirsim*, an identification which should be seriously considered, since *tell bēt mirsim*, against Albright's frequently pronounced opinion and the present almost universal conviction, certainly cannot be identified with Kiriath-sepher/Debir (see below n.84). According to Noth (*PJ* 33, 33f.; *Josua*¹, 66f., 119; *Josua*², 95, 148), Eglon is, rather, *tell ʿēṭūn* on the *wādī el-jizāʾir*. Albright's proposal, suggested in various places but first in *BASOR* 15, 1924, 7f., *tell el-ḥesī* fits less well but cannot be entirely excluded.

[84] According to W. F. Albright, *BASOR* 15, 1924, 4f. *et al.*, *tell bēt mirsim*

ary[85] which affirms that the conquest of Palestine from Kadesh-barnea[86] in the far south to Gibeon[87] north of Jerusalem was accomplished under Joshua in a single campaign and which Noth attributes to the 'collector'.

According to Noth, the aetiology in 10.16–27 explains the phenomenon that the opening of a cave in the plain of Makkedah in the Shephelah was blocked by unusually large *stones*. An older, simpler form of the narrative would have described how once kings had hidden here from their pursuers after a military defeat, had been shut in by the victors' having rolled stones in front of the cave and had been starved to death. A variant would have made the further link with five *trees*[88] which stood in front of the cave: five defeated kings had been hanged here by the stronger party and their corpses had then been thrown into the cave[89] which had subsequently been blocked up with huge stones. Both Noth and Elliger stress the fact that this aetiological tradition originally

---

(which he himself excavated). Against this cf. Elliger, *PJ* 30, 63–65, who proposes *k̲h̲irbet zanūtā* and Noth, *JPOS* 15, 1935, 45–49, who proposes *k̲h̲irbet ṭarrāme*; neither of these sites is, however, pre-hellenistic. The most convincing is the siting of Debir on *k̲h̲irbet rabūḍ* by K. Galling, 'Zur Lokalisierung von Debir', *ZDPV* 70, 1954, 135–41, a site which fits well with Josh. 15.13–19 = Judg. 1.11–15 and which, as recent investigations have shown, represents a Late Bronze age site (Galling found only Iron Age traces, *op. cit.*, 141); cf. H. Donner, *ZDPV* 81, 1965, 24f.; Y. Aharoni cited by A. Kuschke, *ZDPV* 84, 1968, 86; also *Ḥᵃdāšōt 'arkē'ōlōgīyōt* 28, 1968, 30.

[85] 'Summaries' is the name which I give to sections such as 11.16–20, 21f., 23; 12.1–6, 7f. (9–24).

[86] To be sited most probably in the region of *ʿēn qdēs* and *ʿēn el-qdērāt*. Cf. H. C. Trumbull, *Kadesh-Barnea, Its Importance and Probable Site with the Story of a Hunt for it Including Studies of the Route of the Exodus and the Southern Boundary of the Holy Land* (New York 1884) (somewhat fanciful); H. Guthe, 'H. Clay Trumbull's Kadesh Barnea nach dem Englischen mitgetheilt und besprochen', *ZDPV* 8, 1885, 182–232; C. L. Woolley and T. E. Lawrence, 'The Wilderness of Zin (Archaeological Report)', *PEFA* 3, 1914/15, 69–71; P. Savignac, 'La région de ʿAïn-Qedeis', *RB* 31, 1922, 55–81; R. de Vaux, 'Nouvelles recherches dans la région de Cadès', *RB* 47, 1938, 89–93; but also Y. Aharoni cited in B. Rothenberg, *God's Wilderness: Discoveries in Sinai* (London 1961), 121–5, 137–42; H. Bar-Deroma, 'Kadesh-Barneʿa', *PEQ* 96, 1964, 101–34. On the excavations of 1956 at *tell* (*ʿēn*) *el-qdērāt* see M. Dothan, '*Mᵉṣūdat qādēš-barnēaʿ*' (*'Ēlāt. Ha-kinūs hā-'arṣī ha-šᵉmōnā-ʿāśār lidīʿat hā-'āreṣ* – Jerusalem 1963), 100–17 = 'The Fortress at Kadesh-Barnea', *IEJ* 15, 1965, 134–51; also M. Weippert, *ZDPV* 80, 1964, 189–92 (lit.).

[87] See above n. 30.

[88] See above n. 69.

[89] Perhaps the place where the narrative is localized really was a burial cave.

would have had nothing to do with the tradition about the battle at Gibeon; on the contrary, when one looks at it, the ideas contained in it are completely different from its present continuation in 10.29–39.[90] According to Noth, the Israelite inhabitants of the district would have regarded the kings (who perhaps at first were not named) as the rulers of the surrounding, formerly Canaanite towns, who earlier would have prevented the occupation of the land by the encroaching 'Israelites' and thereby have come to grief; on this view, 10.29ff. would have belonged, as far as content was concerned, to the Makkedah tradition. Admittedly, Noth achieves this connection between the two sections by dint of attributing to the editorial process the present names of the royal towns in 10.23 – Jerusalem, Hebron, Jarmuth, Lachish, Eglon – which correspond to those given in 10.1–15 and by substituting for them the place names from 10.29ff. Elliger adheres to the present text and is therefore forced to regard 10.29–39 as an independent tradition,[91] to which, on account of its schematic style and precise (uninventable?) details, he attributes historical worth: 'It seems to be a fact that the account which lies at the basis of Josh. 10.28ff. affords greater insight into the events of the settlement of the Calebites and the Kenizzites.'[92] Admittedly his reference to 14.6ff.; 15.13ff. = Judg. 1.10ff. is not very convincing, since there it is different events which are being described. Again, the stylistic argument can be used both for and against his interpretation: the stereotyped quality can, of course, actually be a 'characteristic of early historical writing', but, on the other hand, it could also be a means of covering up a lack of factual content with fictitious material. Thus, Elliger's hypothetical reconstruction of the whole too is built on a weak foundation: The Calebites and Kenizzites, having emerged from the wilderness of Sinai into the coastal plain, are supposed to have been pushed eastwards – perhaps by the king of Gezer[93] (10.33) – subsequently to have plundered those towns which were allied with him, Libnah,

[90] 10.28 is, as Elliger (*PJ* 30, 49, 52f.) and Noth (*PJ* 33, 26) perceived, secondary.

[91] So too Alfrink, *op. cit.* (see above n. 79), 243–50.

[92] Elliger, *op. cit.*, 70.

[93] According to Noth, 10.33 is an 'obscure addition' (*PJ* 33, 26 n. 2) or an 'intrusive addition' (*Josua*[1], 36; *Josua*[2], 63). The fact that no conquest of Gezer (*tell jezer*) is reported here corresponds exactly to Josh. 16.10; Judg. 1.29; I Kings 9.16.

Lachish and Eglon, and finally to have succeeded in settling in Hebron and Debir. However, those who are unable to agree with Noth's conjecture as to what was the original text in 10.23 and who are also doubtful as to Elliger's reconstruction[94] because of the reasons adduced for it, must find another explanation for 10.29–39. Admittedly this is difficult, unless one accepts the possibility of a fiction as indicated above, that is of a narrative constructed by someone who wanted to describe a conquest of the territory between Gibeon and Kadesh-barnea by Joshua (10.40–42) and in this way managed to bring his hero a little further than Azekah on the way to the famous oasis which lay far to the south. In answer to the objection which will immediately be raised, namely that the author could have extended his itinerary to Kadesh with less trouble from Debir, the argument can be adduced that in other places, too, the editorial methods in the book of Joshua are not always adequate to the intended goal and do not always produce the intended effect; meanwhile it is not clear why, if one accepts Kadesh as the goal, the route from Eglon had to make the detour up into the hill country to Hebron and back to Debir. And simply to suit the hypothesis one cannot attribute muddled geographical conceptions to the author who, after all, lived in the country. At this stage, therefore, the question must remain open.

13. Concerning Josh. 11.1–15, the report of a battle between 'Israel' under Joshua and a Canaanite coalition led by the king of Hazor (*tell el-qedaḥ*),[95] Alt has expressed himself in only very general terms.[96] He hesitates as to whether, in the lost original of the narrative, all the Israelite tribes were mentioned or only the Galilean ones or even, perhaps, only Naphtali whose territory lay closest to the place in question. However, he places the historical event behind the tradition in the period of 'territorial expansion' and interprets it as an attempt to gain access from the area to the south of Merom and Hazor to new territory for settlement further

[94] The judgment that 10.29–39 is determined by actual (communicational) geographical relationships is not affected by the dubiety as to the correctness of Elliger's reconstruction of the historical background (against Noth *PJ* 33, 33 n.6); cf. also I. Eph'al, '*Maʿareḵet givʿōn ū-vaʿyat masaʿ yehōšūaʿ li-drōm hā-'areṣ*' (*Hisṭōryā ṣevā'īt šel 'ereṣ-yisrā'ēl bīmē ha-miqrā*' – Jerusalem 1964), 86.

[95] We owe the identification to J. Garstang, 'The Site of Hazor', *AAA* 14, 1927, 35–42, and it has rightly won the day against older suggestions (on these see *KBw*, 244; P. Thomsen, *RLV* V, 1926, 231 *s.v.* Hazor §3).

[96] *Kl.Schr.* I, 134f.

north by breaking through the Canaanite encirclement.[97] According to Alt, the mention of king Jabin of Hazor in Judg. 4[98] would place the events described in Josh. 11.1–15 in a fairly late period. Noth, on the other hand, stresses the fact that the 'hero narrative' / 'war narrative' presupposes an 'event whose historical content can no longer be properly recognized but which comes from the period of the settlement or of the extension of Israelite occupation in the arable land',[99] an event in which Galilean tribes took a foremost part, probably Naphtali in particular under an unknown Naphtalite leader whom the 'collector' replaced by 'Joshua' when the tradition underwent 'all-Israelite' adaptation. The main protagonist is Jabin of Hazor, who – probably because of the impression he made on those who were ultimately victorious – appears secondarily also in Judg. 4, together with the king of Madon (*qarn ḥaṭṭīn*?)[100] probably as his most powerful neighbour, while

[97] On this see A.Alt, 'Galiläische Probleme: 1. Die Herkunft des Namens Galiläa' (1937), *Kl.Schr.* II, 363–74, esp. 371f.

[98] Jabin of Hazor certainly cannot be removed from the present form of Judg. 4 by a literary-critical operation; in spite of that he can have had nothing to do historically with the battle at the Kishon, especially since the Song of Deborah (Judg. 5) which stands much closer to the event does not mention him but envisages Sisera and the 'kings of Canaan', presumably the coalition (of vassals?) behind Sisera. I shall present my conception of Judg. 4.17 in greater detail elsewhere.

[99] Noth, *Josua*[1], 41–43; *Josua*[2], 67–69; the quotation from *Josua*[2], 67.

[100] Madon is attested only here (Josh. 11.1). The name *m*( )*-t-n* on the Egyptian stele-fragment from *tell el-ʿorēme* (*Urk.* IV, 1347) which Noth tentatively connects with it (*Josua*[1], 42; *Josua*[2], 68) is probably, as far as one can judge, Mitanni (cf. W. F. Albright and A. Rowe, *JEA* 14, 1928, 281–7). The city of Madon is usually identified, on the basis of the nearby *k̲h̲irbet midyan* (thus according to Dalman, not *k̲h̲irbet madīn*!), with the imposing *tell* of *qarn ḥaṭṭīn*; thus G. Dalman, *PJ* 10, 1914, 42; W. F. Albright, *AASOR* 6, 1926, 27; *BASOR* 29, 1928, 5f.; A. Alt, *PJ* 25, 1929, 50; F.-M. Abel, *Géographie de la Palestine* II (Paris 1938), 372, *et al.* Since G, both for Madon and for Merom, has *Μαρρων* = **mārōn*, Y. Aharoni, *Hitnaḥᵃlūt šivṭē yiśrāʾēl ba-gālīl hā-ʿelyōn* (Jerusalem 1957), 83, 91f.; *JNES* 19, 1960, 180, disputes the very existence of Madon and identifies *qarn ḥaṭṭīn* with the place mentioned several times in Egyptian sources 'Šamaš-Edom' (*ša-m-šu-ʾa/ʾi-tù-m*: variants: *ša-m-šu-ʾa/ʾi-tu4-m* city list of Tuthmosis III, no. 51; *š-m-šù-ʾa/ʾ-i-tu-m* stele of Amenophis II from *karnak*, *ZDPV* 69, 1953, plates 1 and 7 line 3; *š-m-šú-ʾa/ʾi-tu-m* the same stele from *mīt rahīne*, *ibid.*, plate 3 lines 3f.) and in addition with Adamah in Naphtali (Josh. 19.36) (so *JNES*, *loc. cit.*; in *Hitnaḥᵃlūt*, *loc. cit.*, Beth-shemesh in Naphtali [Josh. 19.38; Judg. 1.33] was also equated with both). Now E. Edel, *ZDPV* 69, 1953, 147 has, for sound reasons, located 'Šamaš-Edom' on the west bank of the Orontes a day's journey from Qatna (*el-mišrīfe*) so that at least Aharoni's identification of that place with *qarn ḥaṭṭīn* becomes questionable. Cf. W. Helck, *Die Beziehungen*

the kings of Shimron[101] and Achshaph,[102] who are also mentioned,

---

Ägyptens zu Vorderasien im 3. und 2. Jahrtausend v. Chr. (ÄgA 5, 1962), 127f. The whole discussion, of course, depends on whether the reference to the day in the first line of the stele from Memphis is original or must be attributed to a later restorer like the mention of 'year 7' which in the original certainly read 'year 2'. On this cf. Y. Aharoni, *JNES* 19, 177–81; S. Yeivin, *BO* 23, 1966, 25ᵃ; E. Edel in K. Galling (ed.), *Textbuch zur Geschichte Israels* (Tübingen ²1968), 29 n.1.

For the name *ḵḇirbet midyan/madīn* cf. the explanations which fit the identification theories of that time in Dalman, *op. cit.* and (those of B. Mazar and Y. Aharoni) in Aharoni, *Hitnaḥᵃlūt*, 83 n.80.

[101] Like Madon, Shimron is textually uncertain and has not been convincingly located. Usually the Shimron of Josh. 19.15 and that of our passage (11.1) and the Shimron-meron of 12.20 are equated and, on the basis of the form of the names in G (of which more shortly) identified with *ḵḇirbet simūnīye* (Simonias) above the northern edge of the plain of Jezreel (cf., e.g., *KBw*, 622; Aharoni, *Hitnaḥᵃlūt*, 93; *'Ereṣ-yiśrā'ēl bi-tqūfat ha-miqrā'. Gē'ōgrafyā hisṭōrit*, Jerusalem 1962, 354). In all three places G has Συμοων (Gᴬ, corrected as usual in accordance with a text corresponding to M, has on the other hand Σομερων, Σαμρων, Σεμρων) = **šum'ōn*/**šim'ōn* (Simeon).

A possibility which I considered in the course of my work but which I abandoned again, may at least be indicated here: If one separated the Shimron or *Simeon of Josh. 19.15 (= *ḵḇirbet simūnīye*) from the Shimron/*Simeon of Josh. 11.1 and from the Shimron/*Simeon-meron of 12.20, then according to the context of 11.1 (even if the mention of Shimron/*Simeon were secondary) one can happily locate the last two names, which, as emerges from the context of 12.20, designate the same place, in upper Galilee in the vicinity of Hazor (*tell el-qedaḥ*). If however there are two places in Galilee called Shimron/*Simeon, then the puzzling Shimron/*Simeon-meron can be read as **šim'ōn mērōn* (*šm'wn mrwn*) and understood as *Simeon near Meron (with a specifying addition analogous to *'ašᵗᵉrōt qarnayim* = Ashteroth near Karnaim in Gen. 14.5). If this interpretation were correct, then one could point for *Simeon near Meron to *ḵḇirbet šam'* which lies a little to the south of *mērōn* (near *ṣafed*). The decisive defect in this argument which led me to give up the hypothesis is that the visible ruins of *ḵḇirbet šam'* belong indubitably to the Roman period (cf. R. S. A. Macalister, 'Remains at Khurbet Shema', Near Safed', *PEFQS* 1907, 195–200), that the earliest pottery found there belongs to the Iron Age (Y. Aharoni, letter of 17 Jan. 1965) and that the whole site certainly does not give one the impression of a Late Bronze settlement (Aharoni, *ibid.*).

The suggestion of Alt (*Kl.Schr.* II, 376 n.2) which was approved by Noth (*Josua*², 72) that the (allegedly corrupt) place name Shimron-meron should be linked with *samsimuruna*, which is attested several times in Assyrian royal inscriptions, has such a weak philological basis that it does not require more detailed consideration.

[102] In the case of Achshaph too the site varies according to whether one reckons with one or two places of that name. Presumably the Achshaph of Josh. 19.25 lies in the plain of Acco; it is identical with the *'á-k-sap* of the city list of Tuthmosis III (no. 40), with the **Akšapu* of the Amarna letters (URU *ak-ša-pa* [gen.?], AO 7095.1; 7096.23 [*RA* 19, 1922, 99f.]) and with the *'-k-ša-pa* of the Pap.Anastasi I, 21.4; according to B. Mazar, *EM* I, 1950,

appear, from the fact that they have no names, to be additional here, probably introduced from 12.20, while the confused list of additional kings of Canaanite peoples,[103] which is inserted only loosely into the context and occurs again, but in a different order, in 9.1, must be considered as secondary. In his commentary,[104] Noth considered the notices about the capture of Hazor and other towns (11.10–15) to be the work of the 'collector' and in the last resort, although he does not use the expression, apparently an aetiology of the town of Hazor which – according to Garstang[105] – already lay in ruins at the beginning of the Israelite period. Alt[106] had already incidentally indicated the same possibility. Noth, however, in his more recent statements on the problem, concedes the point that the destruction of the town at the end of the thirteenth century BC, confirmed by the excavations of Yadin[107] at *tell el-*

280f. *s.v.* *'akšāf* = *tell harbaj*; according to J. Garstang, *The Foundations of Bible History: Joshua Judges* (London 1931), 354; W. F. Albright, *BASOR* 61, 1936, 24; 81, 1941, 19; 83, 1941, 33 = *tell kīsān*; cf. also Y. Aharoni, *Hitnaḥᵃlūt*, 93, 121f. Aharoni equates the Achshaph of Josh. 11.1; 12.20 with that of 19.25; so apparently also Noth, *Josua*¹, 89, who at any rate suggests the region of *jenīn* as the site. On the basis of Alt's disputable identification of *samsimuruna* and Shimron-meron (see above n. 101) Noth seeks, in an additional note in *Josua*¹, 111, and in *Josua*², 72, to locate the Achshaph of Josh. 11.1; 12.20 (to be distinguished from that in 19.25) in *ḫirbet iksāf* 9 km. (just over five miles) east of *mērōn*. This location, which had already been suggested by earlier writers (cf. E. Robinson, *Neuere biblische Forschungen in Palästina*, Halle/S. 1857, 70; *KBw*, 7 *s.v.*) is, however, open to debate especially if one rejects Alt's and Noth's equation of Shimron-meron and *mērōn* (see above, n. 101). Where the *'á-k/ku-sap-a* of Posener's 'execration texts' (E 11; see above n. 13) is to be located is uncertain; but in this case too one can think of the Achshaph in the plain of Acco.

103 Why one should mistrust the information that the Hivites lived at Hermon (so Noth, *Josua*¹, 42; *Josua*², 68) is not clear. Information given in secondary elements of the text need not necessarily be false! On Josh. 11.3 cf. Judg. 3.3 (according to Noth, *loc. cit.*, dependent on Josh. 11.3), but also II Sam. 24.7 and B. Maisler, *Untersuchungen zur alten Geschichte und Ethnographie Syriens und Palästinas* I (Arbeiten aus dem Orientalischen Seminar der Universität Giessen 2, Giessen 1930), 75.

104 *Josua*¹, 43; *Josua*², 69. 105 J. Garstang, *op. cit.*, 383.

106 'The present form of the tradition makes it difficult to judge Noth's view that it goes back to a hero-saga whose original hero has been secondarily suppressed by Joshua. It seems to me that its derivation from an aetiological saga (or rather from two, one each for the battle and the capture of the town) is not to be excluded.' A. Alt, *Kl.Schr.* I, 134 n. 5.

107 Summaries of preliminary reports in J. A. Soggin, *Protestantesimo* 17, 1962, 205 n. 21. Definitive publications: Y. Yadin and others, *Hazor I: An Account of the First Season of Excavations, 1955* (Jerusalem 1958); *Hazor II: An Account of the Second Season of Excavations, 1956* (Jerusalem 1960); *Hazor*

qedah, does admit of a link with the capture of it by 'Israelites' and thus with the event which stands behind Josh. 11.1–15.[108] He now dissociates himself explicitly, and correctly, from the classification of the narratives as an aetiology.[109]

14. From our presentation of the theories and hypotheses, emanating from the circle around Alt, concerning the settlement narratives of the book of Joshua (Josh. 2–11/12), we have hitherto excluded, as far as possible, any discussion of the role of Joshua himself in these traditions and in the actual historical course of the settlement. It is to this range of questions that we must now turn. If, on the one hand, we are dealing with individual Benjaminite traditions which have their original location in the southern Jordan valley around Gilgal and Jericho and in the hill country around Ai and Gibeon and which are, to a considerable extent, of an aetiological type and if, on the other hand, in the present state of the text every single 'digression' into the Judaean south (Josh. 10) and the Galilean north (Josh. 11) is reported, so that Ephraimite territory is touched only with the pursuit of the 'Amorite' kings after the battle at Gibeon, then the logical consequence is that the question must be asked what the *Ephraimite*[110] Joshua has to do with traditions which are, for the most part and originally perhaps entirely,[111] located outside the territory of his tribe. To put the

III/IV: An Account of the Third and Fourth Seasons of Excavations, 1957–58 (Jerusalem 1965).

108 M. Noth, 'Hat die Bibel doch recht?', *Festschrift für Günther Dehn* (Neukirchen 1957), 14f.; 'Der Beitrag der Archäologie zur Geschichte Israels', *SVT* 7, 1960, 273f.

109 *SVT* 7, 275 n. 1.

110 That Joshua was a figure of Ephraimite tradition admits of no doubt; this emerges conclusively from the tradition about his (hereditary land and) grave in Timnath-heres/serah in the hill country of Ephraim, Josh. (19.50;) 24.30; Judg. 2.8f., the modern *k̲ẖirbet tibne*. Cf. J. Jeremias, *Heiligengräber in Jesu Umwelt* (*Mt. 23, 29; Lk. 11, 47*). *Eine Untersuchung zur Volksreligion der Zeit Jesu* (Göttingen 1958), 46–48 (lit.). The Samaritan tradition of *kufr ḥāris* is secondary to this one and is a rival to the Jewish tradition of *k̲ẖirbet tibne*, Jeremias, *op. cit.*, 40–42.

111 This is my view since the tradition about the war of the Gibeonite coalition is so closely bound with Gibeon that one cannot locate its place of localization, namely the flight route suggested by the geographical conditions via the ascent of Beth-horon, in the Shephelah. Moreover, the supposition of Eph'al (*Ma'ᵃreḵet giv'ōn ūva'yat masa' yᵉhōšūa' li-drōm hā-'āreṣ – Hisṭōryā ṣᵉvā'īt šel 'ereṣ-yiśrā'ēl bīmē ha-miqrā'*, Jerusalem 1964, 82) that 'Joshua's' attack on the troops of the 'Amorite kings' was launched from the south and not from the east, thus cutting off for them the road back to Jerusalem, seems to me to be worthy of notice, although it cannot be verified from the text.

question, which is essentially a traditio-historical question, in this way is to answer it: nothing. But this complex problem has merited a more distinctive treatment, and in what follows we shall present the answer of traditio-historical investigation on the basis of the relevant pronouncements of Alt[112] and Noth.[113] At the outset, we can leave out of account those passages where Joshua appears in the 'Pentateuch' since it has been convincingly shown by (Möhlenbrink and) Noth[114] that the references to Joshua there belong to a later stage in the development of the tradition and are determined by the effort to provide the 'leader into Palestine' as the successor of the 'leader in the wilderness' (i.e. Moses) with close links with his great predecessor[115] and, in part, to pave the way for his prominent role in the book of Joshua as 'Israel's' military commander. We can also leave out of account the references to Joshua in the editorial passages in Josh. 1–11 which stem from the 'collector' and the Deuteronomist.[116] Since, as emerges from the pointed answer given above to the traditio-historical way of posing the question, the aetiological traditions do not need to be taken into account either, only a few passages remain to be looked at more closely. Thus, Alt[117] has stressed the importance of the non-aetiological war-narrative in Josh. 10.1–11, 12–14 in which the Ephraimite 'hero' Joshua is active in Ephraimite territory between Gibeon, which is claimed by Benjamin (Josh. 9 *et al.*), and the town of Aijalon, so that his exclusion from the tradition would have been contrary to the facts. Gibeon probably first of all found a place in the story in the framework which binds Josh. 10 and Josh. 9 together; originally it would only be a clash between Canaanites and the troops summoned in general levy by the tribe of Ephraim or by the 'house of Joseph' and, at that, only a single battle, not a campaign of conquest. Perhaps the inclusion of Beth-horon, which was later Ephraimite,[118] is to be connected with

[112] 'Josua' (1936), *Kl.Schr.* I, 186–92 *passim.*

[113] It is enough at this point to refer to *Josua*² *passim.*

[114] K. Möhlenbrink, 'Josua im Pentateuch', *ZAW* 59, 1942/3, 14–58; cf. M. Noth, *Überlieferungsgeschichte des Pentateuch* (Darmstadt ²1960), 192–4.

[115] On the deuteronomistic theory concerning the duties and the succession of Moses and Joshua see Noth, *Josua*², 27–29 (cf. Josh. 1.1f.).

[116] Cf. Alt, *op. cit.*, 179f.

[117] *Op. cit.*, 187f.

[118] Josh. 16.5 (*bēt ʿūr el-fōqā*). Lower Beth-horon (*bēt ʿūr et-taḥtā*) is one of the points which establish the frontier between Joseph/Ephraim and Benjamin, Josh. 16.3; 19.13. Cf. Josh. 21.22.

this. Since, in addition, the possibility that Benjaminites too – by reason of their treaty relationships with Gibeon? – took part in the undertaking cannot be excluded, it may perhaps be that from this point Joshua, the leader in the successful battle at Gibeon, has been incorporated in certain circumstances in the Benjaminite settlement tradition (Josh. 2–9). His authority, achieved through military success, may then have recommended him to the Israelite tribes as an arbitrator in inter-tribal disputes from which point his role in Josh. 17.14–18, where he is consulted by the 'house of Joseph' as an authority on frontier questions, naturally derives. In this connection, Alt points to Jephthah[119] who appears as both 'major' and 'minor judge', i.e. as charismatic military leader and as 'amphictyonic official'.[120] Finally, according to Josh. 24, Joshua could have played a decisive role in the setting up of the Israelite central sanctuary at Shechem[121] and, from there, have been adopted as the protagonist of the Benjaminite settlement tradition as this was interpreted along all-Israelite lines. In his commentary on Joshua Noth took up Alt's suggestions, modifying them only in the case of two insignificant details. In his view, too, Joshua has nothing to do with the aetiological sagas of Josh. 2–9.[122] Against Alt, however, he considers that the reference to Joshua in the

[119] Cf. on the one hand Judg. 11.1–12.6, on the other Judg. 12.7.

[120] The problem of the 'judges of Israel' cannot be examined here in detail. On it cf. among the more recent literature A.Alt, 'Die Ursprünge des israelitischen Rechts' (1934), *Kl.Schr.* I, ²1959, 300–2 (ET 'The Origins of Israelite Law' in *Essays in Old Testament History and Religion*, the present reference pp. 102f.); J. Dus, 'Die "Sufeten Israels"', *ArOr* 31, 1963, 444–69; K. Elliger, *RGG*³ V, 1961, 1095 *s.v.* 'Richter in Israel'; F. C. Fensham, 'The Judges and Ancient Israelite Jurisprudence', *Die Ou Testamentiese Werkgemeenskap in Suid-Afrika* 2, 1959, 15–22; C. H. J. de Geus, 'De richteren van Israël', *NThT* 20, 1965/66, 81–100; O. Grether, 'Die Bezeichnung "Richter" für die charismatischen Helden der Vorzeit', *ZAW* 57, 1939, 110–21; H. W. Hertzberg, 'Die kleinen Richter', *ThLZ* 79, 1954, 285–90; D. A. McKenzie, 'The Judge of Israel', *VT* 17, 1967, 118–21; L. M. Muntingh, 'The Period of the Judges', *Die Ou Testamentiese Werkgemeenskap in Suid-Afrika* 2, 1959, 29–34; M. Noth, 'Das Amt des Richters Israels', *Festschrift Alfred Bertholet* (Tübingen 1950), 404–17; W. Richter, 'Zu den "Richtern Israels"', *ZAW* 77, 1965, 40–71; A. van Selms, 'The Title "Judge"', *Die Ou Testamentiese Werkgemeenskap in Suid-Afrika* 2, 1959, 41–50; R. Smend, *Jahwekrieg und Stämmebund: Erwägungen zur ältesten Geschichte Israels* (FRLANT 84, 1963), 33–55; H. C. Thomson, 'Shophet and Mishpat in the Book of Judges', *GOST* 19, 1961/2, 74–85; W. Vollborn, 'Der Richter Israels', *Sammlung und Sendung: Festgabe für D. Heinrich Rendtorff* (Berlin, n.d. – 1958), 21–31.

[121] Cf. E. Kutsch, *RGG*³ VI (1962), 15 *s.v.* Sichem (lit.).

[122] *Josua*², 12, 21.

war narratives of Josh. 10.1–15; 11.1–11 is not original,[123] but supposes that there the figure of Joshua has suppressed older tribal 'heroes', thus in 11.1ff. some man or other from Naphtali. He is, however, 'from a traditio-historical point of view perhaps firmly rooted' in 17.14–18.[124] Decisive for the later interpretation of him in the tradition, however, was the role which he played, according to the tradition, in that event which was highly important and fundamental for the life of the tribes together, namely the 'assembly at Shechem', the solemn constitution of the Yahweh-amphictyony[125] of the twelve tribes (Josh. 24).[126] It is from here that his entry into the settlement traditions of Josh. 2–9, which were originally located in Benjamin, is most easily explained, in which respect it was to his further advantage that he belonged to the tribe of Ephraim which was neighbour to Benjamin.[127] In addition, in the narrative of the treaty making between 'Israel' and Gibeon, a narrative which, even in its literary form, is still fragmentary, one can discern a stage in the tradition where Joshua is missing. In Josh. 9.7 there appears, as one of the contracting partners, the collective *'īš yiśrā'ēl*; so too, in 9.11–13, a plurality of

[123] *Op. cit.*, 61, 67.

[124] *Op. cit.*, 106, with reference to Alt, *op. cit.*, 189ff.

[125] The increasing criticism of the theory that the ancient Israelite tribal confederacy was an amphictyony analogous to the Greek and Italian sacral confederacies (cf., e.g., H. M. Orlinsky, 'The Tribal System of Israel and Related Groups in the Period of the Judges', *OA* 1, 1962, 11–20) hardly affects Noth's original assessment (*Das System der zwölf Stämme Israels*, BWANT IV 1, 1930; *Geschichte Israels*, Göttingen ^{5}1963, 83–104 = *The History of Israel*, London ^{2}1960, 85–109). One cannot, of course, overlook the fact that the theory convincingly developed by Noth on the basis of earlier suggestions has been subject to all kinds of extensions which prove, on closer inspection, to be inappropriate. After due consideration of what is to be expected of an 'amphictyony' in the ancient world and what is not, one can cite especially the Etruscan 'amphictyony' at the grove of the goddess Voltumna (near Lake Bolsena) which reveals conditions of great antiquity. For the relevant summaries see in the first instance R. Smend, *Jahwekrieg und Stämmebund*.

[126] For Noth's standpoint cf. *Das System der zwölf Stämme Israels,* 66–75, 133–40; *Josua*^{1}, XII, 105–9; *Überlieferungsgeschichtliche Studien* (Tübingen ^{2}1957), 9 n.1; *Josua*^{2}, 15f., 135–40; *Geschichte Israels*^{5}, 89–92 = *History of Israel*^{2}, 90–95. Noth's chief witnesses are E. Sellin, 'Seit welcher Zeit verehrten die nordisraelitischen Stämme Jahwe?', *Oriental Studies Published in Commemoration of Paul Haupt* (Baltimore and Leipzig, 1926), 124–34; *Geschichte des israelitisch-jüdischen Volkes* I (Leipzig 1924), 98f.; A. Alt, 'Josua' (1936), *Kl.Schr.* I, 191f.; 'Die Wallfahrt von Sichem nach Bethel' (1938), *Kl.Schr.* I, 79–88.

[127] See above n. 110 and cf. Noth, *Josua*^{1}, XI; *Josua*^{2}, 12.

participants on the 'Israelite' side is presupposed. According to Noth, this is the original element in the narrative; Joshua has first been introduced by the 'collector' in his theoretical framework.[128]

15. If, according to Alt, the Israelite settlement was a peaceful process of laying claim to territory over a fairly long period, in other words the transition from being nomads with small cattle to being settled farmers in territories which had hitherto been either only partially occupied or not occupied at all – a process which, in the nature of things, took place in circumstances which were hardly spectacular – yet it is not to be accepted as a matter of course that this had, as its consequence, the formation of a detailed tradition of the occupation of the land. Just as certainly as Israel always knew that her roots lay outside the *'ereṣ yiśrā'ēl* and that she owed the 'beautiful' and 'good' land with all its abundance of 'milk and honey' exclusively to the goodness and faithfulness of her God, so, according to the analysis presented by Alt and Noth, actual events of occupation and settlement in the hill territories have left few deep impressions in the consciousness of the Israelite peasants. It will have been otherwise with the events of the period of 'territorial expansion', and it is, therefore, no surprise that the biblical 'settlement' traditions are full of battles waged by 'Israel' acting as a unit or by individual tribes against the towns of the Canaanites. Successes on the part of the immigrants, who were hardly equipped for such encounters, had a much greater claim to be celebrated in song by their contemporaries and to survive as narratives in the memory of later generations than the banalities of the conversion of woodland into arable land, the bringing of land under cultivation, sowing and harvesting and the commonplaces of pastoral life. For the beginnings of Israelite life in Palestine we are therefore entirely dependent on suppositions and *a posteriori* conclusions. What appears to be certain in the first place is the fact which was ascertained long before Alt, namely that we have to distinguish at least two waves of 'Israelite' immigration, the first of which is most probably to be connected with the so-called 'Leah tribes' and the second with the so-called 'Rachel tribes'.[129]

[128] *Josua*[1], 31; *Josua*[2], 55–57. Cf. also Möhlenbrink's distinction between an 'Israelite recension' and a 'Joshua recension', *ZAW* 56, 1938, 241–5 and above n. 42.

[129] For this theory which appears in numerous individual variant forms

Concerning the circumstances in which these two waves of immigration took place, we have almost no direct tradition. However, a few definite facts seem to emerge from the geographical division of the tribal territories.[130]

16. In his traditio-historical researches into the Israelite twelve-tribe system,[131] Noth has established that the group of six 'Leah tribes' which, according to Gen. 29.31ff.; 30.17ff., comprised Reuben, Simeon, Levi, Judah, Issachar and Zebulun, was not the product of artistic systematization but represented a historical reality, whatever judgment one may pass on the idea that they are descended from the same mother, Leah. This emerges from the fact that in the earliest references they appear, in stereotyped fashion, in this order[132] and from the fact that after the removal of the tribe of Levi from this circle the need was felt to preserve the number six by the addition of the 'Zilpah tribe' Gad in its place.[133] According to Noth, we have here a sacral tribal alliance, analogous to the 'amphictyonies' known from the Greek and Italian sphere,[134] which perhaps already bore the name Israel and to which reference is possibly made in some way by the mention of Israel on the victory stele of Merenptah from the year 1219.[135] From the information concerning the territories of the individual tribes, it appears that Judah was established in the hill country west of the Jordan to the south of Jerusalem (Josh. 15.1–12) and

---

detailed references cannot be given here; cf. H. H. Rowley, *From Joseph to Joshua* (London [4]1958), *passim* and 'Synthesis', p. 164.

On the problem of the 'Leah' and 'Rachel' tribes cf. *inter alia* C. Steuernagel, *Die Einwanderung der israelitischen Stämme in Kanaan* (Berlin 1901), 50–55; R. Kittel, *Geschichte des Volkes Israel* I (Stuttgart and Gotha [5, 6]1923), 297f., 299–305; S. Mowinckel, '"Rahelstämme" und "Leastämme"', *Von Ugarit nach Qumran* (BZAW 77, 1958), 129–50; S. Lehming, 'Die Erzählung von der Geburt der Jakobsöhne', *VT* 13, 1963, 74–81; R. Smend, *Jahwekrieg und Stämmebund,* 71–78; O. Eissfeldt, 'Jakob-Lea und Jakob-Rahel', *Gottes Wort und Gottes Land, Hans-Wilhelm Hertzberg zum 70. Geburtstag* (Göttingen 1965), 50–55.

[130] Where particular references are not given, what follows is a free exposition of M. Noth, *Geschichte Israels*[5], 54–82 = *History of Israel*[2], 53–84.

[131] *Das System der zwölf Stämme Israels,* 7–28, 34f., 75–85, 91f.

[132] Noth, *op. cit.*, 7–13.

[133] Noth, *ibid.*, 14–21.

[134] See above n. 125.

[135] Cairo 34025 vs. (see above ch. I n. 6), line 27. On the dating of the period of Merenptah's reign cf. most recently E. Hornung, *Untersuchungen zur Chronologie und Geschichte des Neuen Reiches* (ÄgA 11, 1964), 95f., 108.

had its centre in Bethlehem (*bēt laḥm*), while Zebulun and Issachar,[136] according to Josh. 19.10–16, 17–23, had settled on the southern edge of the Galilean hill country. With regard to Simeon and Levi, concerning whose territories there is no longer any authentic tradition, we know from Gen. 34 that they had at one time settled in the central Palestinian hill country in the neighbourhood of Shechem but could not maintain their position in the face of Canaanite pressure,[137] so that Simeon reappears later as a southern annexe of Judah[138] while every trace of the tribe of Levi has vanished.[139] Certain factors indicate that the tribe of Reuben, which, according to Josh. 13.15ff., is said to have settled east of the Jordan, once had a location west of the Jordan which is at

[136] On the settlement of the tribe of Issachar cf. A. Alt, 'Neues über Palästina aus dem Archiv Amenophis' IV.' (1924), *Kl.Schr.* III, 169–74; M. Noth, *Geschichte Israels*[5], 76f. = *History of Israel*[2], 78f. Along with W. Zimmerli, *GGA* 207, 1953, 7f.; J. Bright, *Early Israel in Recent History Writing*, 117f. and others I am unable to accept the theory of Noth (*op. cit.*, 76 = ET 78) which is linked with this, namely that the tribal name Issachar (surprisingly interpreted as 'labourer') is to be explained by the particular manner of its settlement; on the name, originally a hypocoristic personal name, cf. W. F. Albright, *JAOS* 74, 1954, 227f.

[137] See above pp. 18f.

[138] See above n. 44.

[139] See above n. 44. The so-called 'secular' tribe of Levi has originally nothing to do with the Levitical priesthood; the two entities were not equated until a considerable time after the disappearance of the tribe from history, and this disappearance was the necessary preliminary of the equation. The identification was helped by the similarity in sound and the etymological relationship between the name of the tribe and the appellative. Both are to be derived from the verbal root *LWI 'to be/become bound' (cf. Albright). The tribal name is a hypocoristic personal name and means something like 'client of the god X'; cf. the 'Amorite' personal names of the type *lawi-(la)*-GN in H. B. Huffmon, *Amorite Personal Names in the Mari Texts: A Structural and Lexical Study* (Baltimore 1965), 225f. *s.v.* LW' (lit.) and, e.g., the place name *ra-wi-'i-ri* = **lawi-'ili* 'client of (the god) El', No. 111 in the city list of Rameses III, Simons No. XXVII, Jirku No. XXII (J. Simons, *Handbook for the Study of Egyptian Topographical Lists Relating to Western Asia*, Leiden 1937, 165; A. Jirku, *Die ägyptischen Listen palästinensischer und syrischer Ortsnamen* [Klio Bh. 38, Leipzig 1937], 45) (the section in which the name occurs is, according to W. Helck, *Die Beziehungen Ägyptens zu Vorderasien im 3. und 2. Jahrtausend v. Chr.* [ÄgA 5, 1962], 252, copied from a lost list of Tuthmosis I) and the numerous personal names of the type *gr*-GN (on this J. Lewy, *HUCA* 28, 1957, 11; R. Borger, *ZDPV* 74, 1958, 129 and below ch. III 1, n. 132). On the priestly designation see W. F. Albright, *Archaeology and the Religion of Israel* (Baltimore 1953), 109f. and nn. 42f. to ch. IV on pp. 204f. and, for a criticism of the use of the Minaean material, R. de Vaux, '"Lévites" minéens et Lévites israélites', *Lex tua veritas: Festschrift für Hubert Junker* (Trier 1961), 265–73.

least still presupposed in Judg. 5.15b, 16. According to Noth, fragments of the tribe must have been absorbed both into Gad and into Judah, since the 'description' of Reubenite territory in Josh. 13.15–23 probably rests on a theoretical partitioning of the tribal territory of Gad[140] and since, on the other hand, the families of Carmi (cf. Num. 26.6 with Josh. 7.1, 18) and of Hezron (cf. Num. 26.6 with 26.21) are attributed both to the tribe of Judah and to the tribe of Reuben. Since in central Palestine, the original settlement area of these three tribes, we later find the so-called 'Rachel tribes' Joseph and Benjamin, it can definitely be assumed that the latter belong to a later wave of immigration, occupying the vacuum created by the breaking up of Reuben and the migration of Simeon and Levi. We have, however, no means of fixing more precisely the distance in time between these two occurrences or their place in the absolute chronology.[141]

17. Any attempt to determine more precisely the immigration route of the 'Leah tribes' will prove just as unsuccessful. Noth supposes that Issachar and Zebulun crossed the Jordan to Galilee from the northern part of Transjordan; but this supposition is based solely on their later location. The central Palestinian tribes and perhaps Judah also (cf. Judg. 1.16??) may have crossed the Jordan at Jericho and thus have come from southern Transjordan. Yet we can suppose with a certain amount of assurance that those tribes which were loosely connected with Judah and never achieved complete settlement,[142] namely the Calebites (centred on Hebron),[143] the Othnielites (centred on Debir),[144] the Kenites[145]

140 M. Noth, 'Studien zu den historisch-geographischen Dokumenten des Josuabuches', *ZDPV* 58, 1935, 239; *Josua*[1], 55; *Josua*[2], 83; H. W. Hertzberg, *Die Bücher Josua, Richter, Ruth* (ATD 9, [3]1965), 90. On the topography cf. also A. Kuschke, 'Historisch-topographische Beiträge zum Buche Josua', *Gottes Wort und Gottes Land: Hans-Wilhelm Hertzberg zum 70. Geburtstag* (Göttingen 1965), 90–94.

141 The general atribution of the main phase of the Israelite settlement to the thirteenth century naturally remains unaffected by this assertion.

142 Cf. the relatively frequent place names compounded with *ḥāṣēr* in the Negeb district of Judah and in Simeon: *ḥ^{a}ṣar-'addār* Num. 34.4 (Josh. 15.3 *ḥeṣrōn* and *'addār*); *ḥ^{a}ṣar-gaddā* Josh. 15.27; *ḥ^{a}ṣar-sūsā* Josh. 19.5 (*ḥ^{a}ṣar-sūsīm* I Chron. 4.31); *ḥ^{a}ṣar-šūʿāl* Josh. 15.28; 19.3; I Chron. 4.28; Neh. 11.27. Cf. also below pp. 115f. on the *ḫaṣirātum* and the *tarbaṣātum* of the 'Benjaminites' of Mari.

143 Josh. 15.13f.; cf. Judg. 1.10 ('Judah'; perhaps read *kālēb*?), and see below n. 147.

144 Josh. 15.15–19; Judg. 1.11–15. On Debir see above n. 84.

145 Kenites in alliance with the definitely nomadic Amalekites Judg. 1.16;

and the Jerahmeelites[146] reached the places where they lived from the south. In the case of Caleb this is quite clear from the basic form of the 'spy story' in Num. 13f. which is concerned with tribal history.[147] Thus, one must always reckon with the possibility that Judah too came from this direction. And if, according to Alt, Simeon and Levi were not permanently settled at Shechem but simply arrived there in the course of transhumance and, after their clash with the Shechemites, were driven back south into their proper territories, i.e. into the area of winter pasturage,[148] then the central Palestinian members of the 'Leah' group may well also have come from the Negeb. Whether one can then link with this the traditions about the 'Israelites' who emerged from Egypt having stayed in the neighbourhood of Kadesh-barnea, is uncertain.[149]

18. The 'Rachel' group, consisting of the 'house of Joseph' and the tribe of Benjamin (Gen. 30.22ff.; 35.16ff.), crossed the Jordan at Jericho, as the Benjaminite settlement tradition expressly states,[150] and moved up from there into the central Palestinian hill country. The 'house of Joseph' which, in our sources, always appears on Palestinian soil as two tribes, occupied the territory stretching from Bethel (*bētīn*) in the south to the southern edge of the plain of Jezreel in the north (cf. Josh. 16.1–3). The boundary between Ephraim and Manasseh, which cannot be examined here in detail,[151] runs a little to the south of the (Manassite) town of

---

I Sam. 15.6. 'Cities of the Kenites' are mentioned in I Sam. 30.29 as recipients of shares in the booty taken by David from the Amalekites. According to Judg. 4.11 the Kenite Heber pitches his tent in or near the plain of Megiddo and has a treaty relationship (*šālōm*) with 'Jabin the king of Hazor' (Sisera?; cf. above n.98).

146 Cf. I Sam. 27.10 ('Negeb of the Jerahmeelites'); 30.29 ('cities of the Jerahmeelites', recipients of a share of the booty taken by David from the Amalekites); I Chron. 2.3ff.

147 Cf. also Deut. 1.22–46; Josh. 14.6–15 and, besides J. Wellhausen, *Die Composition des Hexateuchs und der historischen Bücher des Alten Testaments* (Berlin [4]1963), 336–8, especially M. Noth, *Überlieferungsgeschichte des Pentateuch* (Darmstadt [2]1960), 143–9.

148 See above p.19 and n.44.

149 Cf. M. Noth, *op. cit.*, 181f.; *Geschichte Israels*[5], 123 n.3 = *History of Israel*[2], 130 n.3.

150 Cf. the Gilgal tradition Josh. 3f. which certainly is of an aetiological type but which need not therefore be regarded as simply unhistorical.

151 Cf. W. J. Phythian-Adams, 'The Boundary of Ephraim and Manasseh', *PEFQS* 1929, 228–41; K. Elliger, 'Die Grenze zwischen Ephraim und Manasse', *ZDPV* 53, 1930, 265–309; A. Fernández, 'Los limites de Efraim

Shechem (*tell balāṭa*). The history of the 'house of Joseph' and its settlement is particularly complex since we do not even know for certain whether it is a question of an original unit which later split up or of individual tribes which united to form a larger whole;[152] Noth accepts the former.[153] The difficulties are increased by the fact that in the oldest texts it is not Manasseh which appears alongside Ephraim but Machir (Judg. 5.14; cf. Josh. 17.1);[154] the main elements of this tribe appear later to have migrated east of the Jordan and to have settled in the territory north of the Jabbok. Its place west of the Jordan was taken by Manasseh which was formed perhaps by a union between those Machirites who remained behind and other elements, among which were individual Canaanite cities. The territory to the south of the Jabbok, Gilead proper, was colonized by Ephraim.[155]

2. THE ARCHAEOLOGICAL SOLUTION

1. The picture drawn by Alt and his followers of the course of the Israelite settlement has, from the outset, been subject to a very thorough criticism by William Foxwell Albright from the point of view both of the use and the limitations of the various methods and of the detailed results which have been achieved.[1] Albright

y Manasés', *Bibl* 14, 1933, 22–40; M. Noth, 'Studien zu den historisch-geographischen Dokumenten des Josuabuches', *ZDPV* 58, 1935, 201–15; F.-M. Abel, 'Tappouaḥ', *RB* 45, 1936, 103–12; K. Elliger, 'Tappuah', *PJ* 33, 1937, 7–22; 'Neues über die Grenze zwischen Ephraim und Manasse', *JPOS* 18, 1938, 7–16; E. Jenni, 'Historisch-topographische Untersuchungen zur Grenze zwischen Ephraim und Manasse', *ZDPV* 74, 1958, 35–40; E. Danelius, 'The Boundary of Ephraim and Manasseh in the Western Plain', *PEQ* 89, 1957, 55–67; 90, 1958, 32–43, 122–44; G. Wallis, 'Thaanath-Silo', *ZDPV* 77, 1961, 38–45; Y. Aharoni, *'Ereṣ-yiśrā'ēl bi-tqūfat ha-miqrā'. Gē'ōgrafyā hisṭōrīt* (Jerusalem 1962), 221f.

[152] Cf. K.-D. Schunck, *Benjamin: Untersuchungen zur Entstehung und Geschichte eines israelitischen Stammes* (BZAW 86, 1963), 13–18.

[153] *Das System der zwölf Stämme Israels*, 80f.; *Geschichte Israels*[5], 59 = *History of Israel*[2], 58f.

[154] On this cf. Noth, *Josua*[2], 101–3.

[155] On this whole subject cf. M. Noth, 'Beiträge zur Geschichte des Ostjordanlandes: 1. Das Land Gilead als Siedlungsgebiet israelitischer Sippen', *PJ* 37, 1941, 51–101.

[1] W. F. Albright, 'Archaeology and the Date of the Hebrew Conquest of Palestine', *BASOR* 58, 1935, 10–18; 'Further Light on the History of Israel from Lachish and Megiddo', *BASOR* 68, 1937, 22–26; 'The Israelite Conquest of Canaan in the Light of Archaeology', *BASOR* 74, 1939, 11–23; 'The

criticizes Alt and Noth especially for having paid too little attention in their work to the results of the archaeological investigations which flourished in Palestine after the first world war and for having reached one-sided and very limited conclusions by their preference for literary-critical and traditio-historical methods. Their historical evaluation of form-critical analysis takes too little account of the fact that 'all ancient literary composition had to conform to fixed patterns of oral delivery and formal styles of writing' so that the historicity of an event can never be proved or disproved on the basis of the framework in which it is handed down to us. The significance of aetiology for the stylization of Israel's early historical traditions cannot be contested, but there can be no *a priori* judgment as to whether a piece of information which exists in aetiological form rests on authentic historical tradition or, in *ad hoc* fashion, on a composite text: 'There must always be external evidence.'[2] For Albright it is this 'external evidence' which alone provides him with definite criteria for a judgment of the tradition, and it is this which is his particular aim and object within the framework of his studies on the problem of the Israelite settlement. 'External evidence' is provided by all that material with which extra-biblical sources illuminate biblical events: the written documents of the ancient East from Egypt, Mesopotamia, Asia Minor, Syria and Palestine itself, but above all the results of the Palestinian excavations which Albright has continually examined from the point of view of their significance for our problem.

2. By analysing the great excavations of the twenties and thirties which, on the basis of relatively exact methods, usually arrived at comparatively certain stratigraphic and chronological results, Albright established that in a series of sites the transition from the last phase of the Late Bronze Age to the first phase of the Early Iron Age was not continuous but was marked by devastating

---

Biblical Period' in L. Finkelstein (ed.), *The Jews – Their History, Culture and Religion* (New York 1949), 13–17; *The Biblical Period from Abraham to Ezra* (Harper Torchbook 102; New York and Evanston 1963), 24–34. The two editions of 'The Biblical Period' are abbreviated in what follows as BP^1 and BP^2. The work of S. E. Hardwich, *Change and Constancy in W. F. Albright's Treatment of Early Old Testament History and Religion 1918–1958* (Dissertation of New York University 1965 – typescript) is unfortunately not available to me.

[2] Both quotations *BASOR* 74, 12.

catastrophes and abrupt breaks in culture. Thus the latest Late Bronze Age settlements of *tell bēt mirsim* (according to Albright: Kiriath-sepher/Debir),[3] *tell ed-duwēr* (Lachish),[4] *bētīn* (Luz/Bethel)[5] and *tell el-qedaḥ* (Hazor)[6] were all destroyed, in the course of the thirteenth century BC, by terrible catastrophes whose traces are clearly visible in conflagration levels of ashes, charcoal and small burnt objects.[7] The rebuilding in the first Iron Age level then took place, either immediately or after a certain interval, in much poorer conditions with, as a rule, a cruder building technique and with domestic utensils of much less worth both from a constructional and from an artistic point of view.[8] Since, on the basis of considerations of principle as well as by the general consensus of opinion, the settlement of the Israelite tribes is also to be placed in this period, Albright did not hesitate to link the archaeologically confirmed destruction of cities in the thirteenth century with the 'Conquest of Palestine' under Joshua and to see in this the 'external evidence' for the campaigns of the immigrants reported in Josh. 2–11 (/12). Thus the thirteenth-century destruction level in *bētīn* paralleled the biblical account of the capture of Bethel by the 'house of Joseph' in Judg. 1.22–25,[9] that in *tell el-qedaḥ* the account in Josh. 11.10f., 13 of the conquest and destruction of Hazor by Joshua after his victory over king Jabin at the waters of Merom,[10]

[3] *Tell bēt mirsim* C: Albright, *BASOR* 58, 10; 74, 23; *BP*[1], 15f.; *The Archaeology of Palestine* (Pelican Book A 199; Harmondsworth [5]1960), 108; *BP*[2], 27.

[4] Albright, *BASOR* 58, 13f.; 68, 23f.; 74, 20–22; *BP*[1], 16; *BP*[2], 27.

[5] Albright, *BASOR* 58, 13, 15; *BP*[1], 15f.; *BP*[2], 27.

[6] Although Albright's assertion was first made on the basis of the results of Yadin's excavations at Hazor which were carried out in the fifties (cf. above ch. II 1, n. 107) and therefore, on a strict chronological basis, ought to be discussed elsewhere, I deal with it here along with the results of archaeological investigations in the twenties and thirties since this is where it belongs from the point of view of subject matter. (Albright, *BP*[2], 27f.)

[7] Similar grouping: P. D. Miller, *CBQ* 27, 1965, 260 and n. 20; H. Haag, 'Die Archäologie im Dienste der Bibel' in F. Leist (ed.), *SEINE Rede geschah zu mir: Einübung in das Alte Testament* (Munich 1965), 160.

[8] On the cultural decline between Late Bronze II and Iron I cf., e.g., G. E. Wright, *JBL* 60, 1941, 31f.; Albright, *Archaeology*[5], 119; for a criticism see below pp. 132f. with ch. IV 2, n. 15.

[9] Albright, *BASOR* 58, 15. This of course disregards the fact that Judg. 1.21ff. depicts a surprise attack on the city by cunning and treachery and knows nothing of its destruction by fire.

[10] Cf. Albright, *BP*[2], 102 n. 83; Y. Yadin, 'The Fourth Season of Excavation at Hazor', *BA* 22, 1959, 4, 10, 13f., 20; F. Maass, 'Hazor und das Problem der israelitischen Landnahme' in *Von Ugarit nach Qumran* (BZAW 77, 1958), 105–17; Schunck, *Benjamin*, 27.

and the conflagration levels of *tell ed-duwēr* (paralleled in Fosse Temple III) and *tell bēt mirsim* C have, if my understanding is correct, been linked with the reports of the capture and destruction of Lachish[11] and Debir[12] in Josh. 10.31f., 38f. With this approach, the archaeological situation gave rise to difficulties in the cases of *tell es-sulṭān* (Jericho) and *et-tell* (Ai). While, in the case of *tell es-sulṭān*, the excavations carried out by Sellin and Watzinger, using pre-1914 excavation methods which were not sufficiently developed even after the corrected chronology proposed by Watzinger in 1926,[13] did not commend themselves as an attempt at dating the capture of Jericho by Joshua and the Israelites as recorded in Josh. 6, the results of the excavations undertaken with much more advanced methods by Garstang[14] (from the early thirties) produced considerable difficulties for such an attempt. There was no sign of the Late Bronze Age city wall which figures so prominently in Josh. 6, nor, more particularly, was there any clearly recognizable settlement stratum at all from the latter part of the Late Bronze Age. Only the so-called 'Middle Palace',[15] of whose foundations a few layers of stones were preserved, could, on the basis of the pottery belonging to it, be designated as Late Bronze Age. According to Albright,[16] the pottery corresponds to that of Bethshan IX and VIII[17] and of Lachish Fosse Temple II[18] and belongs

[11] Cf. G. E. Wright, 'The Literary and Historical Problem of Joshua 10 and Judges 1', *JNES* 5, 1946, 111; Schunck, *op. cit.*, 35f.

[12] W. F. Albright, 'The Excavation of Tell Beit Mirsim II', *AASOR* 17, 1938, 78f.; cf. Wright, *op. cit.*, 111f.

[13] See above ch. I, n. 10.

[14] See the summary review in J. and J. B. E. Garstang, *The Story of Jericho* (London and Edinburgh ²1948).

[15] Garstang and Garstang, *op. cit.*, 123–8, 147f.; J. Garstang, 'The Story of Jericho: Further Light on the Biblical Narrative', *AJSL* 58, 1941, 368–72; reprinted in Garstang and Garstang, *op. cit.*, 177–80.

[16] *BASOR* 74, 19.

[17] Level IX is Rowe's 'Thotmes III Level', VIII the 'Pre-Amenophis III Level' which thus both belonged to the fifteenth century (A. Rowe, *The Topography and History of Beth-Shan, with Details of the Egyptian and Other Inscriptions Found on the Site,* [PPS 1, 1930], 7; *The Four Canaanite Temples at Beth-Shan: I. The Temples and Cult Objects* [PPS 2.1, 1940], IX; cf. C. F.-A. Schaeffer, *Stratigraphie comparée et chronologie de l'Asie Occidentale* [*III*ᵉ *et II*ᵉ *millénaires*], London 1948, 193f.). The reasons for dating them in the fourteenth century are given in W. F. Albright, *AASOR* 17, 1938, 76f.; on this cf. also B. Maisler, '*Ha-krōnōlōgiyā šel ha-miqdāšīm bᵉ-vet-šeʾān*', *BIES* 16.3/4, 1951, 16f., 19.

[18] O. Tufnell, C. H. Inge and L. Harding, *Lachish II* (*Tell ed Duweir*): *The Fosse Temple* (London 1940), 77ff. *passim*.

therefore to the fourteenth century. Since the series of names of Egyptian kings attested on scarabs found there breaks off at Amenophis III, the period of the latter's reign is to be regarded as the *terminus post quem* for the destruction of the Late Bronze city (?). Since, in addition, the discovery of a Mycenaean potsherd (although it was found outside a stratigraphic context) as well as a few local imitations of Mycenaean pottery types excludes, according to Albright,[19] a date before the middle of the fourteenth century and after the middle of the thirteenth, he arrived, in his paper of 1939, at the conclusion that Late Bronze Age Jericho must have fallen between *c.* 1375 and 1300 BC, at any rate in the fourteenth century,[20] so that an occupation of the city in the thirteenth century can in no sense be definitely proved.[21] The revision of the results of Garstang's excavations by G. E. Wright[22] and by Garstang himself[23] and the results of the new excavations undertaken with the most modern methods by K. M. Kenyon[24] led Albright most recently to accept that in the thirteenth century a city did stand on *tell es-sulṭān* but that the remains of it had almost entirely disappeared due to the effect of erosion in the long gap in occupation between the destruction by Joshua and the rebuilding by Hiel in the time of Ahab of Israel (I Kings 16.34), and this all the more easily since there had been only mud-brick walls.[25] Presumably the steeply sloping wall of the Middle Bronze period had continued in use as the city wall. For Albright the problem of Ai

[19] *BASOR* 58, 12; 74, 20; cf. Maisler, *op. cit.*, 19 supplement. On the finds in the latest attested stratum of Tomb 13 (J. Garstang, *AAA* 20, 1933, 15–21) cf. also A. J. B. Wace, 'Jericho Tomb 13', *ABSA* 37, 1936/7 (1940), 259–62 (fourteenth century).

[20] *BASOR* 58, 13; 74, 20; *BP*[1], 16.

[21] *BP*[1], 16.

[22] G. E. Wright, 'Two Misunderstood Items in the Exodus-Conquest Cycle', *BASOR* 86, 1942, 32–34.

[23] See above n. 15.

[24] Preliminary reports of the excavator: K. M. Kenyon, *PEQ* 84, 1952, 4–6, 62–82; 85, 1953, 81–95; 86, 1954, 45–63; 87, 1955, 108–17; 88, 1956, 67–82; 89, 1957, 101–7; 92, 1960, 88–108. Résumé: K. M. Kenyon, *Digging up Jericho* (London 1957). Definitive publications: K. M. Kenyon, *Excavations at Jericho: I. The Tombs Excavated in 1952–4* (London 1960); *II. The Tombs Excavated in 1955–8* (London 1965). Cf. also A. D. Tushingham, 'Excavations at Old Testament Jericho', *BA* 16, 1953, 46–67, as well as my bibliography in K. M. Kenyon, *Archäologie im Heiligen Land* (Neukirchen-Vluyn 1967), 299–301.

[25] W. F. Albright, *Archaeology*[5], 109; *BP*[2], 28f. The archaeologist herself says this: *PEQ* 84, 72; 86, 61; 92, 108; *Digging up Jericho*, 262f.

which he too correctly – in contrast, for example, to Grintz and Luria[26] – would situate on *et-tell* between *bētīn* and *dēr dubwān*, is somewhat different. We have already seen that on this site in the Early Bronze Age there was a large city with a strong outer wall, a palace and a temple but that the settlement there came to an end with a violent destruction as early as the twenty-sixth century BC and that the short-lived settlement on the *tell* in Iron Age I was not of the city type and soon disappeared. The obvious contradiction between the archaeological findings and the detailed account of the capture and destruction of the Canaanite royal city by Joshua and his Israelites in Josh. 7f. was solved by Albright's[27] accepting a transfer of the conquest tradition from nearby Luz/Bethel (*bētīn*), which, as we have already seen,[28] was definitely destroyed in the thirteenth century, to the 'ruin'[29] which lay in the fields belonging to the Ephraimite city, so that here too the historicity of the event described in the tradition recorded in Josh. 7f., a description which is stylized by the use of aetiological elements, could be defended in the face of the 'scepticism' of Alt, Noth and Lods.[30]

3. The 'Conquest of Palestine' reflected in the biblical settlement traditions of Josh. 1–12 and Judg. 1 and obvious from the archaeological evidence of the destruction of cities in the thirteenth century is also, in Albright's view, the final and decisive phase of a process which took place over a considerable period. Like Alt, Albright would regard the accounts of the battles of Jacob and his sons in the neighbourhood of Shechem (Gen. 34; 48.22; I Chron. 7.20ff.; Jub. 34)[31] as traditions about an earlier stage of the same process.[32] The settlement of later Israel had already begun there-

[26] See above ch. II 1, n.52.

[27] *BASOR* 74, 16f.; *BP*[1], 16; *BP*[2], 29f.

[28] See above p.48.

[29] It is generally and surely correctly held that *'ay* (later vocalized *'ī*: Jer. 26.18; Micah 1.6; 3.12; Ps. 79.1; Job 30.24) means 'ruin'.

[30] A. Alt, 'Das Institut im Jahre 1933', *PJ* 30, 1934, 10 n.2; 'Josua' (1936), *Kl.Schr.* I, 185; 'Erwägungen' (1939), *Kl.Schr.* I, 133; M. Noth, 'Bethel und Ai', *PJ* 31, 1935, 7–29; *Josua*[1], 23–27; *Josua*[2], 47–51; A. Lods, 'Les fouilles d'Aï et l'époque de l'entrée des Israélites en Palestine' in *Mélanges Franz Cumont* (Annuaire de l'Institut de Philologie et d'Histoire orientales et slaves 4, 1936), 847–57.

[31] According to W. F. Albright, *From the Stone Age to Christianity* (Anchor Book A 100; Garden City 1957), 277, I Chron. 7.20ff. is to be dated *c.* 400 BC, and the book of Jubilees probably in the third century BC.

[32] For what follows cf. *BASOR* 58, 1935, 14–18; *BP*[1], 16f.; *From the Stone Age to Christianity*, 276–81; *BP*[2], 26ff.

fore in the 'patriarchal period'. The traditions about the wanderings and activities of the 'patriarchs' in Palestine are then linked by Albright with the numerous reports concerning the activity of the *'apiru* in the fifteenth/fourteenth century in the same area, and he regards the 'patriarchs' (explicitly Abraham, at least, on the basis of Gen. 14.13) as belonging to this particular stratum of the population whom he considers to have been semi-nomads who transported merchandise on their donkey caravans.[33] They had, since the Middle Bronze Age (MB I), occupied the scarcely accessible mountainous regions to the west of the Jordan, so that the silence of the Amarna letters and of the Israelite settlement traditions about that region can be explained without any difficulty. They had, further, allied themselves with the 'Israelites' proper, members of the same profession and of the same race, when these latter returned from Egypt and burst into Palestine west of the Jordan. Albright also explains in this way how the later tradition could no longer differentiate the various groups. The *'apiru*/Israelites, united also by the religion of Moses, then gained the upper hand in the struggle for power within Palestine and either annexed the cities to their alliance by treaty,[34] subjection or absorption[35] or else annihilated them.[36]

4. According to G. Ernest Wright,[37] the deuteronomistic theory of the settlement is in agreement with the results of archaeology in so far as it considers that the Israelite occupation of the territory west of the Jordan took place in two stages. The destructions of Palestinian cities which have been established by excavation and which, as we saw above, Albright especially had in view, correspond to the Israelite campaigns under Joshua against the southern

[33] W. F. Albright, 'Abram the Hebrew: A New Archaeological Interpretation', *BASOR* 163, 1961, 36–54; on the *'apiru* especially pp. 53f. See above ch. I n.4 and below ch. III 1.

[34] Shechem, represented by the 'sons of Hamor' (cf. their god Baal-berith and the custom of the 'slaying of an ass' when a treaty is concluded with 'semi-nomads' in the region of Mari; see below ch. III 2, n.52) and Gibeon (Josh. 9).

[35] See above pp. 19f. and ch. II 1, n.45.

[36] According to Albright the custom of the 'ban' (*ḥerem*) which was usual in war played a prominent part in the encounters between the 'Hebrews' and the cities.

[37] For what follows cf. G. E. Wright, 'The Literary and Historical Problem of Joshua 10 and Judges 1', *JNES* 5, 1946, 105–14; *Biblical Archaeology* (Philadelphia and London ²1962), 69–85. Only direct quotation are provided with precise references.

part of central Palestine (Gilgal-Jericho-Bethel / 'Ai'-Gibeon),[38] against southern Palestine (Libnah-Lachish-Eglon-Hebron-Debir)[39] and against Galilee (Hazor),[40] which had the aim of decisively weakening the system of Canaanite city-states at strategically favourable points and of thus creating the necessary conditions for the settlement of the new arrivals in the country. Accordingly, Joshua's conquests involved only 'certain key Canaanite royal cities' and thus left untouched not only many cities but also a large number of the inhabitants of the country[41] with whom the Israelites subsequently had to come to terms and against whom they had to assert themselves. The second phase of the settlement then took place in numerous local conflicts during the 'period of the judges' and left its traces in the twelfth and eleventh century destruction levels of almost all of the Palestinian sites hitherto excavated. According to Wright, therefore, the Israelite settlement was not the peaceful infiltration into the thinly populated hill country, avoiding the area of the cities, by nomadic cattle breeders hungry for land which Noth and Albright, like Alt before them, suppose, but a planned conquest of the country by the twelve-tribe amphictyony under a unified leadership.

5. From this, it is already clear that Wright considers the settlement narrative in Josh. 1–12 to be 'essentially accurate'[42] and will admit modifications of it only in relatively insignificant details. He explains the contradictions between tradition and archaeological discovery, which are obvious in the case of Ai (Josh. 7f.) and probably exist also in the case of Jericho (Josh. 6), in the same way as Albright, and he is able here too to assert that there is agreement rather than contradiction. If, however, the picture presented in Josh. 1–12 is considered to be, on the whole, historically correct, the question is immediately raised as to how the traditions in Judg. 1 are to be assessed.[43] As is well known, the traditions gathered together in that chapter represent the settlement as a series of actions on the part of individual tribes or of several tribes acting in alliance and not, in clear contrast here to Josh. 1–12, as an

[38] Josh. 2.1–10.15.

[39] Josh. 10.16–39.

[40] Josh. 11.1–15.

[41] Cf. Deut. 7.22; Judg. 2.20–23. The quotation from *JNES* 5, 114.

[42] The quotation (*JNES* 5, 114) in Wright refers to the deuteronomistic theory of the settlement, but at the same time also in particular to Josh. 1–12.

[43] See especially *JNES* 5, 107–9.

undertaking on the part of Israel as a whole. Wright correctly points to the fact that in the amalgam of traditions in Judg. 1 there is reliable material side by side with highly dubious material, so that the first task must be the separation of these two groups of traditions. Thus, according to Wright, the report of the capture of Luz / Bethel by the 'house of Joseph' in Judg. 1.22–26 is certainly historically accurate, since it can easily be connected with the violent destruction of the city in the thirteenth century[44] which has been confirmed by the excavations at *bētīn*. The narrative about the capture and destruction of Ai (Josh. 7f.) which, with Albright,[45] is to be connected with the same event is, on the contrary, less original and much less reliable. It was the deuteronomistic redactor who first inserted Judg. 1.22–26 after the death of Joshua and introduced the Joseph tribe as the conqueror of Bethel because the city was later Ephraimite. Even the list of unconquered cities in 1.27–33 can be regarded as historically reliable information if it is read in the light of the deuteronomistic theory of the settlement the correctness of which has been proved.[46] According to Wright, there are, of course, more questions concerning the group of traditions in Judg. 1.1–21. The notice concerning the defeat of a king Adoni-bezek,[47] whose residence might perhaps have been Jerusalem (cf. 1.7?), at the city of Bezek, is perhaps a scarcely reliable variant of Josh. 10.1ff. if one reads, instead of the suspect name Adoni-bezek, rather Adoni-zedek.[48] The conquest of Jerusalem mentioned in 1.8 after the victory over Adoni-bezek/-zedek can, from all that we know, have been at the most an isolated and short-lived event of the thirteenth or the twelfth century, since the city figures in 1.21 as having remained unconquered, and not until the time of David was it, in fact, deprived of its independence and subjected to his rule.[49] The notice concerning the conquest of the

[44] Cf. above p.48 and n.5.

[45] Cf. above p.51 and n.27.

[46] One could, of course, ask here how Wright would define the historical place of the so-called 'negative list of possessions'; he is however silent on this question.

[47] On the new explanation of the pericope in P. Welten, 'Bezeq', *ZDPV* 81, 1965, 141, 143–6, see below p.146 and ch. V n.5.

[48] The harmonizing of Judg. 1.5ff. and Josh. 10.1ff. is found as early as G where, however, the king Adoni-zedek of Josh. 10 is changed to the Adoni-bezek of Judg. 1.

[49] II Sam. 5.6–9. On David's action cf. A. Alt, 'Jerusalems Aufstieg' (1925), *Kl.Schr.* III, 253–5.

(later Philistine) cities of Gaza, Ashkelon and Ekron by the tribe of Judah could also be regarded as a further, temporary success on the part of the Judaeans if passages such as 1.19; Josh. 13.2f.; 10.40ff.; 11.22 did not advise against such a conception. Finally, in 1.10ff., there is enumerated a series of individual conquests on the part of Judah and its annexed tribes which, of course, in the case of Hebron and Debir, seems to contradict Josh. 10.36ff. But here the two-phase theory provides the solution: Josh. 10.36ff. records the 'sweeping conquest' which, according to the deuteronomist and Wright, was undertaken by Joshua, while Judg. 1.10–15 belongs to the second phase of the settlement, to the consolidation undertaken by the individual tribes in the territory allotted to them, to what, according to Alt,[50] one could call 'territorial expansion'.

3. THE SOCIOLOGICAL SOLUTION

1. The fact that the 'schools' of Alt (II 1) and Albright (II 2) could, with the same source material and, in the main, on the basis of the same methodology, develop such fundamentally divergent views of the historical course of events involved in the Israelite settlement forces us, in the opinion of George E. Mendenhall,[1] to make a new and thorough examination of the foundations of research in this field, that is, to submit the 'ideal model' which has been utilized in all scientific work on the problem hitherto to a critical examination. As foundation stones of this model, that is,

[50] See above pp. 5f. and A. Alt, 'Erwägungen über die Landnahme der Israeliten in Palästina' (1939), *Kl.Schr.* I, 137ff.

[1] G. E. Mendenhall, 'The Hebrew Conquest of Palestine', *BA* 25, 1962, 66–87. Once again in what follows I give specific references only for direct quotations. Since Mendenhall's article is very condensed and gives relatively few detailed references, I have added, where it seemed necessary and where it was possible, references to sources and literature.

as the implicit or explicit presuppositions of the reconstructions attempted so far, Mendenhall lists the following:[2]

(*a*) The Israelites came from territories outside Palestine shortly before or in the course of the 'conquest'.
(*b*) The Israelites were 'nomads' or (in the more recent literature) 'semi-nomads' who, during or after the 'conquest', appropriated land and became sedentary agriculturalists.
(*c*) Israelite solidarity was based on an ethnic relationship which was also the (principal) reason for the opposition to the Canaanite way of life.

According to Mendenhall these theses are all in need of revision. While (*a*) and (*c*) have at least a general basis in the biblical tradition, (*b*), that is, the acceptance of a 'nomadic' origin for the Israelites, is 'entirely in the face of both biblical and extra-biblical evidence'.[3]

2. In the Late Bronze Age there were certainly – according to Mendenhall – genuine nomads like, for example, the *sutû*,[4] but, like the present-day bedouin, they did not have an important role either politically or socially.[5] The shepherds who moved around in the border regions between desert and cultivated land in the course of transhumance must, meanwhile, be sharply differentiated from nomads proper. They belong with the farmers of the cultivated land and are essentially village-dwellers who, on account of the limited extent of cultivable land, have had to take to raising cattle. The Cain-Abel narrative in Gen. 4 presupposes this kind of close relationship between farmers and shepherds, and the Jacob stories clearly show, as do extra-biblical references to shepherds in the ancient Near East, that the latter were members of a city or village community. Thus Jacob is a shepherd who moves about with the herds of Laban who has a settled home in Haran, as Jacob himself has later in Beersheba with his sons grazing *his* herds from there as far as Dothan (*tell dōtān*) (Gen. 37.12–17). It is also a mistake, according to Mendenhall, to consider the Israelite tribal organization, along with its genealogical system, as an indication of nomadic origins; this is, rather, a widespread characteristic of

[2] *Op. cit.*, 67.
[3] *Ibid.*
[4] See below ch. III 1 n. 20.
[5] C. D. Matthews, 'Beduin Life in Contemporary Arabia', *RSO* 35, 1960, 32f. (quoted in Mendenhall).

non-city cultures.[6] In addition, in any event, Mendenhall considers a Bronze Age 'tribe' very difficult to define. His final description regards it as 'a larger unit of society which transcended the immediate environment of an individual, normally a village, upon which the village could rely for aid against attack too strong for it to cope with unaided',[7] a unit, therefore, which was held together not by the fact of its descent from a common – even if, perhaps, fictitious – ancestor but by a complex of social feelings nourished by the experiences of the individual in childhood and adulthood and by the voluntary and involuntary intentions of upbringing, a complex of feelings which one could, in the language of recent sociology, call 'we feelings'.[8] The tribal identity thus achieved Mendenhall sees as called in question and neutralized by the process of urbanization, so that the sharp contrast is not between the farmer and the shepherd, as the older hypotheses suggested, but between the city-dweller and the country-dweller.[9] This assertion is fundamental to his understanding of the 'settlement' of the Israelites.

3. No doubt the conditions of a city community, in the ancient

[6] On this, reference should be made to the basic studies of G. P. Murdock, *Social Structure* (New York 1949) (cf. Mendenhall, *op. cit.*, 69 and n. 11) and of C. Lévi-Strauss, *Les structures élémentaires de la parenté* (Paris 1949; ET *The Elementary Structures of Kinship*, London 1969, a translation of the revised French edition of 1967). Mendenhall's argument certainly corresponds to the more recent insights of the ethno-sociological study of 'primitive' communities but does not, of course, affect Alt's and Noth's theories about the settlement since according to them the 'Israelite' tribes first developed after they had become sedentary in Palestine. The patriarchal narratives in Genesis which seem to me to indicate that the ancestors of the later Israelites were full nomads of the Middle and Late Bronze Ages, also indicate that then, as now among the Arabian bedouin, the *cellule sociale* is not the 'tribe' but the *ahl* (on this cf. T. Ashkenazi, 'La tribu arabe: ses éléments', *Anthropos* 41–44, 1946–49, 662–6). Mendenhall's argument therefore is rather *for* the origin of the later Israelites in a nomadic milieu.

[7] Mendenhall, *op. cit.*, 70.

[8] Cf. the distinction between 'in-group' and 'out-group' and the designation of 'we feelings' as a constituent of the 'in-group' as opposed to the 'others' in W. G. Sumner, *Folkways: A Study of the Sociological Importance of Usages, Manners, Customs, Mores, and Morals* (1906, reprinted New York 1959), 12f., §§ 13f.

[9] Cf., e.g., the contrast *ša libbālim* (crasis from *ša libbi ālim*; cf. GAG § 64e): *ša ṣērim* – 'city dweller': 'country dweller' in the omen interpretation Louvre AO 7030.23f. (J. Nougayrol, *RA* 40, 1945–47, 90): *šumma* . . .: *ša ṣe-ri-im i-ru-ba-am-ma ša li-ib-ba-li-im ū-ši-iṣ-ṣi* 'If . . . (there follows the description of the phenomena in the oracle liver): the country dweller forces his way in (*scil.* to the city), he forces the city dweller out.' Cf. also *CAD* 16/Ṣ, 148[a].

world as today, had the consequence that individuals or whole groups were opposed to the community, refused to participate in it and removed themselves from it. This withdrawal[10] by individuals and groups led to the formation of a class of men whom the legalistic city community had to regard as 'outlaws'.[11] According to Mendenhall this is precisely what the term *ʿapiru* means.[12] It is, therefore, highly significant when the Hebrew bible uses the terms 'Israelites' (*bᵉnē yiśrāʾēl*) and 'Hebrews' (*ʿibrīm*) = *ʿapiru* as virtually synonymous.[13] For the Israelites could be called 'Hebrews' (*ʿapiru*) only from the point of view of a legitimate political community from which they had isolated themselves. In the nature of things that was the Canaanite system of city states with its feudal set-up. This, then, can only mean that the Israelites, like the *ʿapiru* of the Amarna age, were not immigrants from outside, but elements of the autochthonous population of Palestine[14] who had cut themselves free from their responsbilities towards the community in which they lived and had set up in opposition to the system of government which was established in the country. There was, therefore, no statistically significant invasion, no real change of population, which might have been connected with expulsion and genocide. What was driven out and exterminated was, of necessity, only the feudal stratum of kings and military nobility in the cities, those who represented the old order. What in fact occurred was a

[10] What is meant is withdrawal from community work and from community solidarity, an attitude which can turn into opposition and resistance.

[11] The word 'outlaw' does not occur in Mendenhall but seems to me to fit very well what is meant: 'a person excluded from the benefits of the law or deprived of its protections', cf. *The Dictionary of English Law* II (London 1959), 1279 *s.vv.* 'outlaw', 'outlawry'; *Corpus Iuris Secundum* LXVII (Brooklyn 1950), 538ᵇ *s.v.* 'outlaw'; *Funk and Wagnalls Standard Dictionary of the English Language, International Edition, Combined with Britannica World Language Dictionary* I (Chicago and New York 1962), 897ᵃ; figuratively 'a lawless vagabond', 'one banished or ostracized by society; a social outcast', cf. H. C. Wyld, *The Universal Dictionary of the English Language* (London ¹³1960), 813ᵃ. In older English and American law one became an 'outlaw' 'by sentence of outlawry' (in England this was formally repealed in 1879 and 1938). The strictly juridical meaning is to be excluded from our sociological use of the term.

[12] Cf. above ch. I n.4 and below ch. III 1.

[13] On this cf., e.g., H. Weinheimer, 'Hebräer und Israeliten', *ZAW* 29, 1909, 275, and our detailed discussion below pp. 82f.

[14] According to I. Mendelsohn, *JBL* 63, 1944, 434, a similar theory had already been presented by S. I. Feigin, *Mis-sitrē hē-ʿāvār: meḥqārīm ba-miqrā ū-bᵉ-histōrīyā ʿattīqā* (New York 1943) (unavailable to me).

peasants' revolt against the excessive oppression of the plains by the city states, a revolt similar, *mutatis mutandis*, to the great German Peasants' Revolt in the sixteenth century,[15] even if, unlike it, it was more successful. The tribes which later became the members of the Israelite confederacy arose out of the local action groups of those who took measures against the intolerable political system in the country.

4. The impetus which produced this revolt and first established a united front for action on the part of the *ʿapiru* was of a religious,[16] not primarily a political nature even although its effects included all aspects of life and culminated in the overthrow of the existing political system of the country. This impetus emanated from a group of people, probably of Palestinian origin, who had been pressed into forced labour in Egypt and who, under the leadership of Moses, had succeeded in escaping from slavery. Since, at first, there was no community available to protect and support them, they entered, under the name of 'Israel', into a treaty relationship with a god, Yahweh, whom they had seen active in the saving events of their flight from Egypt. The treaty ('covenant', *b^erīt*) also included certain norms of inter-personal relationships such as the demand for absolute loyalty on the part both of the individual and the community towards the divine lord of the covenant[17] and, in this way, transcended tribal religion from the

[15] Although there is no reference to this in Mendenhall, this or a similar event seems to be in his mind in his conception of the settlement. On the social prerequisites and aims of the European peasants' revolts such as the German Peasants' Revolt of 1525/26 in particular, cf. C. P. Loomis and J. A. Beegle, *Rural Social Systems. A Textbook in Rural Sociology and Anthropology* (New York 1950), 616–22, and more especially G. Franz, *Der deutsche Bauernkrieg* (Darmstadt [4]1956), *passim*. Mendenhall's 'model' of the settlement would correspond to the progressive democratic peasant uprisings (Franz: 'fight for divine right') and not to the conservative ones (Franz: 'fight for the ancient right').

[16] This, too, fits at least partly the German Peasants' Revolt; cf., e.g., the 'twelve articles' of the Swabian peasants and on this Franz, *op. cit.*, 122–7.

[17] In this connection Mendenhall is surely referring to the formal relationship of content and type which is supposed by him and others to exist between the state treaties of the Hittite New Kingdom and the Israelite conception of the Yahweh covenant (*b^erīt*); amongst the enormous literature on this subject cf. G. E. Mendenhall, *Law and Covenant in Israel and the Ancient Near East* (New York 1955); K. Baltzer, *Das Bundesformular* (WMANT 4, 1960); D. J. McCarthy, *Treaty and Covenant: A Study in Form in the Ancient Oriental Documents and in the Old Testament* (AnBibl 21, 1963). There are good critical presentations of the many ramifications of the debate in: D. J. McCarthy, 'Covenant in the Old Testament: The Present State of Inquiry', *CBQ* 27, 1965, 217–40 (an expanded German version *Der Gottesbund im Alten*

very beginning by constituting a general human community which surpassed all boundaries of groups and 'tribes'. The demand for absolute loyalty towards the god provided, at the same time, a reason for the rejection of all religious, economic and political duties towards an autonomous political system and thus made the new faith attractive to all those who suffered under the oppression of the city kings and who strove for freedom from their yoke. The identification of their own fate with the experiences of the refugees from the 'house of bondage' in Egypt was obvious in this case and thus – according to Mendenhall – early Yahwism must have developed a powerful missionary force[18] which alone explains the swift successes of the 'Israelite' revolt against the old system and the rapid increase of 'Hebrews' or 'Israelites' from approximately seventy families at the exodus[19] to approximately a quarter of a million in the middle of the following (twelfth) century,[20] an increase which is attributable not to natural propagation alone, but above all to the conversion of indigenous population groups.

5. The revolt began east of the Jordan with the termination of the rule of the kings Sihon of Heshbon (*ḥesbān*) and Og of Bashan[21] by the Moses group and the native population. Since, as

---

Testament, Stuttgarter Bibelstudien 13, Stuttgart 1966); F. Nötscher, 'Bundesformular und "Amtsschimmel": Ein kritischer Überblick', *BZ* NF 9, 1965, 181–214. I think that the analogies which have been observed have revealed the genuine treaty character of the *b^erīt* – in contrast, e.g., to the view of J. Begrich, 'Berīt: Ein Beitrag zur Erfassung einer alttestamentlichen Denkform' (1944), *Gesammelte Studien zum Alten Testament* (ThB 21, 1964), 55–66; many of the consequences deduced from this are, however, grossly exaggerated.

[18] On this cf. also W. F. Albright, *The Biblical Period from Abraham to Ezra* (1963), 31. One should also note that in this work, which presents his last word to date on the problems dealt with in this book, Albright explicitly states his agreement with Mendenhall's results (which at that time had still not been published). This would mean a certain revision of the presentation of his views given above in ch. II 2, but Albright has intimated that he will deal with this subject himself and publication of this is still awaited.

[19] Referred to in Gen. 46.27; Ex. 1.5? Or Ex. 24.1, 9?

[20] Mendenhall (*op. cit.*, 79f.) gives no references for the figures 'seventy' and 'a quarter of a million'. Even with the help of the conclusions of his article 'The Census Lists of Numbers 1 and 26' *JBL* 77, 1958, 52–66, I have been unable to find any basis for the second figure.

[21] Since the recolonization of Transjordan begins, according to the discoveries of N. Glueck (cf. the résumé in *The Other Side of the Jordan*, New Haven 1940, 146f.), in the thirteenth century after a long settlement gap, the reigns of Sihon and Og cannot have lasted long before they were terminated by the 'Israelites'. Mendenhall supposes that both had come from the north

is clear from the Old Testament itself,[22] there existed close ethnic ties between the land east of the Jordan and that to the west, it was inevitable that the movement of revolt should spread quickly across the Jordan. Hastily formed coalitions of city kings[23] were unable to withstand the *élan* of the social revolution and were defeated. The cities were reduced to ashes, and later some of them were resettled. Others, such as Lachish (*tell ed-duwēr*), could not be held by the rebels, probably because of the intervention of the superior power of Egypt. Mendenhall assumes that the 'Palestine expedition' of Pharaoh Merenptah,[24] to which allusion is supposed

---

and had established a rule based on military force over the new population who had recently arrived from the west and the north. The participation of this subject people in their downfall, which Mendenhall postulates, would therefore be easily understood.

22 For the traces of the presence of the tribe of Reuben west of the Jordan cf. above pp. 43f. and ch. II 1 n. 140; on the connection between Gilead and Ephraim and Machir ('half-Manasseh') and Manasseh cf. above p. 46 and ch. II 1 n. 155.

23 Josh. 9.1f.; 10.1ff.; 11.1ff.

24 This campaign probably never took place, but has been wrongly deduced from the phraseology of the so-called 'victory hymn' of the 'Israel stele' (see above ch. I n. 6); cf., e.g., B. É. Naville, 'Did Menephtah Invade Syria?' *JEA* 2, 1915, 195–201; J. v. Beckerath, *Tanis und Theben: Zur Geschichte der Ramessidenzeit in Ägypten* (ÄgF 16, 1951), 66f. There, if one translates lines 26–28 in accordance with the rules of Egyptian syntax, there is scarcely even a mention of a Palestine expedition on the part of Merenptah:

The princes are overthrown while they say *šulmu*,
None lifts his head any more under the nine bows.
After Taḥ( )nu has been destroyed, Ḫatti is peaceful,
Canaan was plundered with (?) all the wicked,
Ashkelon was removed, Gezer was seized,
Jenoam was annihilated,
Israel is wretched and has no seed,
Ḫurru has become widowed for Egypt,
Every single country is at peace,
Everyone who roams about is subdued
By the king of Upper and Lower Egypt, *B3-n-Rʿ-mry-ỉmn*, the son of Rēʿ,
Merenptah-*ḥtp.w-ḥr-m3ʿ.t*, who is endowed with life like Rēʿ every day.

Once it has been realized that the *śḏm-n-f* form in *fḫ-n ta-ḥ-nu* line 26 indicates a period of time earlier than the following statements (on this cf. A. H. Gardiner, *Egyptian Grammar*, London ^{3}1957, 330 §414. 2), it follows that with *ḫt ḥtp(.w)* a series of parallel sentences begins which describe the effects of the defeat by the Libyans of powerful Syria-Palestinian enemies in extremely conventional terms (cf. J. H. Breasted, *Ancient Records of Egypt* III, New York ^{2}1962, 257f., §§603–5) which are all explications of the sentence *t3.w nb.w dmḏ(.w) śt m ḥtpw* 'every single country is at peace' and may not, therefore, be interpreted as the report of a campaign. The correct translation (without philological justification) is found also in É. Drioton, 'La date de l'Exode',

to be made in his so-called 'Israel stele',[25] was mainly intended to quell or suppress the peasants' revolt which was, of course, counter to Egyptian interests as well. In central Palestine, for which, as is well known, there is no 'settlement' tradition,[26] Mendenhall supposes the revolt to have occurred without any very significant military events. Since, however, the kings of Aphek, Hepher, Tappuah and Tirzah appear in the list in Josh. 12,[27] it can be assumed that the defeat of the ruling classes in this area was relatively quickly successful and led to the same result as east of the Jordan and in what later became Benjaminite territory.[28] The victorious population of Hepher and Tirzah then appear, appropriately, among the Manasseh clans.[29]

RHPhR 35, 1955, 44. To make the point doubly certain one might point out that the place name *ma'yan mē neptōaḥ* Josh. 15.9; 18.15, even if it really goes back to the name Merenptah (so F. Calice, *OLZ* 6, 1903, 224) offers no proof of a campaign on the part of the Pharaoh: such well stations were usually named after the ruler under whom they were opened up; cf., e.g., the dedicatory inscription of *kanā'is* B 6 (S. Schott, *Kanais: Der Tempel Sethos' I. im Wâdi Mia*, NAG 1961: 6, 143 and plate 19) and Schott, *loc. cit.*, 134f. Cf. generally W. Spiegelberg, *ZÄS* 65, 1930, 57f.

[25] See above ch. I n.6.

[26] But see Albright's view above pp.51f. and ch. II 2 n.31.

[27] Josh. 12.17f., 24.

[28] Mendenhall (*op. cit.*, 83) leaves open the solution of the problems of the conquest of Jericho and Ai which is reported in the Benjaminite settlement tradition.

[29] See above pp.19f. and ch. II 1 n.45.

III

TOPICS IN THE DEBATE

1. *ʿAPIRU* AND HEBREWS

1. Mendenhall's bold counter-suggestion to the prevailing settlement theories (II 3) hangs, on closer inspection, by a slender thread, namely his identification, taken by him as self-evident and basically presupposed, of the '*ḫab/piru*' attested in ancient Near Eastern texts since the days of the old Assyrian trading colonies in Asia Minor[1] with the biblical 'Hebrews' (*ʿibrīm*) who, for their part, are equated just as questionably with the 'Israelites' (*b^enē yiśrāʾēl*). If Mendenhall's sociologically based equation is correct, then we need concern ourselves no further with the question whether the 'Israelites' before the settlement in Palestine were 'nomads' or 'semi-nomads'. This question would be answered in the negative, for the '*ḫab/piru*', according to the unanimous testimony of all the texts in which they appear, were not a population group of a 'nomadic' or 'semi-nomadic' type.[2] For the time being, therefore, the nomad question can be completely excluded from our discussion. Much more important is the question whether too much is not being demanded of the equation '*ḫab/piru*' = *ʿibrīm* (achieved, in my opinion, primarily on linguistic[3] or even emotive[4]

[1] In what follows the texts relating to the *ḫab/piru* are cited by their number in the collection by J. Bottéro, *Le problème des Ḫabiru à la 4e Rencontre Assyriologique Internationale* (Cahiers de la Société Asiatique 12, Paris 1954) (abbrev. Bott.). The Ur-III-texts which mention a noun ^LÚ^SA.GAZ and a verb SA.GAZ (Bott. 1–4) are not relevant to the *ḫab/piru* problem. The earliest definite references are then to be found in the text of Bott. 5 from Aliṣar.

[2] This has, however, recently been maintained by M. Astour, 'Les étrangers à Ugarit et le statut juridique des Ḫabiru', *RA* 53, 1959, 75f., without, however, as he himself admits, being able to provide any definite evidence. Similarly for Mari A. Finet, *Syria* 41, 1964, 140–42.

[3] See below pp. 74–82.

[4] The Anglo-Saxon habit of saying 'Hebrews' for 'Israelites' (on this cf. J. Lewy, *HUCA* 28, 1957, 1f.) certainly plays an unconscious role in the identifications of Albright (see above pp. 51f.) and Mendenhall.

grounds) if it is required to bear the weight of a detailed hypothesis of the Israelite settlement as a great, victorious peasants' revolt against the feudal system of the ruling classes of the cities. In criticizing Mendenhall's hypotheses, therefore, we must give a definition of the term '*ḫab/piru*' which is faithful to the textual material available, then compare this term with that of 'Hebrew' (*'ibrī*) in the Old Testament and discuss the evidence, both of linguistic usage and of the content of the terms, for and against their identification.

2. This problem has kept scholarship busy ever since the discovery of the *ḫa*-BI-*ru* in the letters of king ÌR-Ḫeba of Jerusalem[5] in the Amarna archives. In this connection we can refrain from examining individually all the theses and opinions produced since 1888[6] since the discoveries of the last decades have made many of the older positions no longer tenable. With the publication and uncovering of the rich finds of clay tablets from the ruins of the Hittite capital Ḫattuša (modern Boğazköy) the proof was produced, in the twenties, for Winckler's supposition[7] that the Sumeriogram SA.GAZ which, according to the lexicographical lists,[8] has the reading *ḫabbātu(m)* 'robbers' (and 'itinerant workers'), is to be read in the Akkadian (and Hittite) texts of the Hittite and Syro-Palestinian state offices usually, even if not exclusively, *ḫab/piru*. In the year 1939 it became clear beyond all doubt that the consonantal element of the word *ḫa*-BI-*ru*, which could not be unambiguously determined from the cuneiform script, had to be established as *'-p-r*,[9] whereby at least all etymologies dependent on the root *ḤBR[10] were excluded, and corresponding attempts with *'BR and the *'ibrīm*[11] became dubious. In what follows, therefore,

[5] Bott. 142–6 (VAB II 286–90).

The correct reading of the logographically written element of the king's name cannot be determined with any certainty; I therefore prefer to leave the Sumeriogram. For the reading **'Abdi-Ḫeba*, see F. Thureau-Dangin, 'Le nom du prince de Jérusalem au temps d'El-Amarna', *Cinquantenaire de l'École Biblique et Archéologique Française de Jérusalem (15 novembre 1890–15 novembre 1940): Mémorial Lagrange* (Paris 1940), 27f.

[6] A detailed, if incomplete review of the history of research is offered by Bottéro, *op. cit.*, v–xxxii.

[7] H. Winckler, *Geschichte Israels* I (Leipzig 1895), 18f.; *Altorientalische Forschungen* III (Leipzig 1901), 90–94.

[8] Bott. 177–9. [9] See above ch. I n. 4.

[10] Cf. Bottéro, *op. cit.*, vi, viii, xiii, xxf., xxiif.

[11] In the first instance, amongst others, H. Zimmern, *ZDPV* 13, 1890, 137 n. 5; C. R. Conder, *PEFQS* 1890, 327. Cf. further Bottéro, *op. cit.*, vi, viii, x,

we can always take as our basis the form *ʿ*apiru*[12] and examine the meaning of the word unencumbered by hypotheses which have been superseded because they are linguistically impossible.

3. It is nowadays fairly generally recognized that the ʿ*apiru* who appear in numerous places from Mesopotamia to Egypt via Asia Minor, Syria and Palestine in the period between approximately 2000 and 1200 BC are not a 'people',[13] that is a relatively unified entity with much in common linguistically, sociologically and culturally, but an 'international' class of men, a social stratum[14] which, in the stratified society of the Middle and Late Bronze Age, plays anything but a leading role.[15] I have already indicated above, in my exposition of Mendenhall's theory of the settlement, that the word ʿ*apiru* is best rendered by 'outlaw'. In our context the term[16] is to be taken primarily in a sociological sense, implying also, of course, legal distinctions. Applied to the ʿ*apiru* class, it designates, with a kind of loose dependence on the etymology of the English word, a person who, for some reason or another, stands outside the acknowledged social system and thereby dispenses with the legal protection which the community guarantees to all its members. This definition of the term ʿ*apiru* occasionally appeared in earlier discussions in one form or another,[17] and it is to the credit of

XI, XIV–XVI, XXI–XXVIII; W. F. Albright, 'Abram the Hebrew: A New Archaeological Interpretation', *BASOR* 163, 1961, 36–54; N. A. van Uchelen, *Abraham de Hebreeër: Een literair- en historisch-kritische studie naar aanleidning van Genesis 14:13* (Studia Semitica Neerlandica 5, Assen 1964). Sharply opposed to this R. Borger, 'Das Problem der ʿapīru ("Ḫabiru")', *ZDPV* 74, 1958, 121–32. Cf. also generally F. M. Th. de Liagre Böhl, 'Babel und Bibel II', *JEOL* 17, 1963 (1964), 137–40.

12 On the vowel quantities see below p. 81.

13 So A. Jirku, starting with *Die Wanderungen der Hebräer im 3. und 2. vorchristlichen Jahrtausend* (AO 24.2, Leipzig 1924), and most recently in *Geschichte Palästina-Syriens im orientalischen Altertum* (Aalen 1963), 96f.; A. Pohl, 'Einige Gedanken zur Ḫabiru-Frage', *WZKM* 54, 1957, 157–60.

14 So explicitly in the first instance J. Lewy, 'Ḫabiru und Hebräer', *OLZ* 30, 1927, 738–46, 825–33; then especially B. Landsberger, 'Ḫabiru und Lulaḫḫu', *KlF* I, 1930, 321–34; also E. Chiera, 'Ḫabiru and Hebrews', *AJSL* 49, 1933, 115–24; M. Noth, 'Erwägungen zur Hebräerfrage', *Festschrift Otto Procksch zum 60. Geburtstag* (Leipzig 1934), 99–112; J. Lewy, 'Ḫâbirû and Hebrews', *HUCA* 14, 1939, 587–623. A compromise position in A. Jepsen, 'Die Hebräer und ihr Recht', *AfO* 15, 1951, 54–68.

15 It is sufficient to refer to the ritual against '(evil) tongues', many of whose details are still obscure but in which the *lulaḫḫiēš* and the *ḫapiriēš* refer to the lower strata of Hittite society (Bott. 91; cf. A. Goetze in Bottéro, *op. cit.*, 80).

16 See above p. 58 and ch. II 3 n. 11.

17 Cf., e.g., Landsberger, Chiera, *opp. cit.* (above n. 14) and now also E. F.

Mendenhall[18] that he has defined it in this way within the context of his treatment of the Israelite settlement. In order to fit in with his conversion hypothesis, however, Mendenhall is obliged to lay too great an emphasis on the voluntary nature of the existence of the *ʿapiru*. It seems to me that entry into this category of classless individuals must normally, as the texts seem to indicate between the lines, have been experienced as a misfortune, just as in the few cases in which we can observe the process of exclusion from 'middle-class society' external pressure is the cause, not free choice. Thus, the later king Idrimi of Alalaḫ[19] is forced by a revolt on the part of the inhabitants of his father's royal city of Aleppo to leave the city along with his brothers and lead a wandering life among the bedouin (*sutû*)[20] and in the cities of Emar[21] and Ammiya.[22] In Ammiya 'in the land of Canaan' there gather about him people from his home states (Aleppo, Mugis,[23] ʿAma'u[24]), and with them

Campbell, Jr., *BA* 25, 1960, 15; M. B. Rowton, 'The Topological Factor in the *Ḫapiru* Problem', *Studies in Honor of Benno Landsberger on his Seventy-fifth Birthday, April 21, 1965* (AssSt 16, 1965), 375–87.

[18] 'The Hebrew Conquest of Palestine', *BA* 25, 1962, 71.

[19] S. Smith, *The Statue of Idri-mi* (Occasional Publications of the British School of Archaeology in Ankara 1, London 1949), 14–17.

[20] On the *sutû* (old form *su-ti-um*^{KI}) cf. W. F. Albright, *JBL* 63, 1944, 220 n. 89; *BASOR* 118, 1950, 16 n. 18; F. M. Th. Böhl, *BO* 8, 1951, 54 n. 29; Bottéro, *op. cit.*, 41, n. 1; É. Dhorme in Bottéro, *op. cit.*, 114 and n. 2; *ARMT* XV, 133 *s.v.* Sutû; D. O. Edzard, *Die 'zweite Zwischenzeit' Babyloniens* (Wiesbaden 1957), 32, 108, 155; J.-R. Kupper, *Les nomades en Mésopotamie au temps des rois de Mari* (Bibliothèque de la Faculté de Philosophie et Lettres de l'Université de Liège 142, Paris 1957), 83–145; J. M. Grintz, *'Ereṣ hā-ʿivrīm* (*ʿOz lᵉ-Dāwīd: Qoveṣ meḥqārīm bi-TNK mugaš lᵉ-Dāwīd ben-Guryōn bi-mlōt lō šivʿīm wᵉ-ševaʿ šānīm* [*Pirsūmē ha-ḥevrā lᵉ-ḥēqer ha-miqrā' bᵉ-yiśrā'ēl* 15, Jerusalem 1964], 92–102).

[21] Cf. especially A. Goetze, 'The Syrian Town of Emar', *BASOR* 147, 1957, 22–27; J.-R. Kupper, 'Notes géographiques: 2. Sur un passage mentionnant Emâr', *RA* 52, 1958, 37; W. W. Hallo, 'The Road to Emar', *JCS* 18, 1964, 77, 81; A. Goetze, 'Remarks on the Old Babylonian Itinerary', *ibid.*, 115f., 119.

[22] Cf. S. Smith, *op. cit.*, 73.

[23] *Mugiš*(*ḫe*), Ug. *mgšḫ*, is the Hurrian form of the name of the state of Alalaḫ; cf. M. Liverani, *Storia di Ugarit nell'età degli archivi politici* (Studi Semitici 6, Rome 1962), 39 n. 50; M. Weippert, *GGA* 216, 1964, 185 n. 18; M. Dietrich and O. Loretz, *WO* 3.3, 1966, 213f.; R. Degen, *WO* 4.1, 1967, 55 and n. 29. The original place name *Mugiš* belongs to the non-Semitic and non-Hurrian group of toponyms in *-iš* such as *Karkamiš*, *Lākīš* etc. Against my supposition, *loc. cit.*, the sibilant is **š*, not **ṯ*. On the history of the state of Mugiš-Alalaḫ cf. now H. Klengel, *Geschichte Syriens im 2. Jahrtausend v.u.Z.: I. Nordsyrien* (VIO 40, 1965), 203–57.

[24] Cf. W. F. Albright, 'Some Important Recent Discoveries: Alphabetic Origins and the Idrimi Statue', *BASOR* 118, 1950, 15f., n. 13.

he prepares his return to power. Before the description of the mobilization of his expeditionary force he summarizes, in his autobiography, the preceding period of flight[25] as follows: *a-na li-bi* ERÍN.MEŠ LÚSA.GAZ *a-na* MU.7.KÁM.MEŠ *aš-ba-ku* 'amongst the *'apiru*-people[26] I remained for seven years', i.e., 'for seven years I was an *'apiru*'. That he was not an *'apiru* of his own free will is self-evident. Similarly a slave who, in spite of his position at the bottom end of the class system of the Late Bronze Age, is still endowed with certain rights, can break away from ties which he finds unbearable and seek his fortune as an *'apiru* (*a-na lìb-bi* LÚSA.GAZ *ir-ru-ub*),[27] at least in theory; for it is this very possibility which the ruling classes are trying to exclude by international treaty: LUGAL GAL *ú-ul a-la-qí-šu a-na* LUGAL KUR *ú-ga-ri-it ú-tá-ar-šu* 'I, the great king, will not take him in, but will send him back to the land of Ugarit'.[28] Now it is already clear that the basic position of the *'apiru* as an outlaw makes the securing of his life his most pressing problem. He can seek his livelihood outside and in opposition to the 'civic' order as a freebooter and highwayman[29] with all the risks involved in this way of life, or else he can endeavour to associate himself with the class system in a suitable fashion, that is, he can legally enter into the service of recognized members of this system. Thus we find *'apiru* in the service of kings,[30] private individuals[31] and perhaps even

[25] Text: S. Smith, *op. cit.*, 16:27f.; Bott. 37. Without at the moment being able to provide definite proof, I believe that the passage quoted sums up lines 3–26. The following description of the oracle which is linguistically difficult and is probably corrupt, perhaps introduces the narrative of the return (lines 30ff.) and at least describes the end of the hero's seven-year period of *'apiru* existence but not his activity during that period.

[26] For this interpretation of ERÍN.MEŠ = *ṣābū* see B. Landsberger in Bottéro, *op. cit.*, 201; R. Borger, *Babylonisch-assyrische Lesestücke* (Rome 1963), LXXVIII^{b}; *CAD* 16/Ṣ, 46ff. *s.v. ṣābu;* P. Artzi, *RA* 58, 1964, 163 n.4.

[27] RS 17.238, 11–19, the quotation line 16 (*PRU* IV, 108); Bott. 161.

[28] *Loc. cit.*, lines 17–19. The extradition of refugees is usually agreed upon in state treaties of this kind; cf. V. Korošec, *Hethitische Staatsverträge. Ein Beitrag zu ihrer juristischen Würdigung* (LRS 60, 1931), 80f. (to be amplified in certain details on the basis of recent discoveries, especially those from Ugarit).

[29] Bott. 6, 8; guerilla warfare Bott. 20, 25, 26 (?), 27 (?), 28, 36(?), 162. On the Amarna texts which are usually included here too see below pp. 71–4.

[30] Bott. 5, 18, 29, 64, 161. The distribution of rations, which is done by the state (supplied from crown property), probably belongs here: Bott. 9–16, 35, 48(?), 67–69; E. Cassin, 'Nouveaux documents sur les Ḫabiru', *JA* 246, 1958, 226–9 nos.1–6 (Nuzu). Clothes: Cassin, *op. cit.*, 228f. nos.7, 8.

[31] Attested only in Nuzu: Bott. 49–66.

temples.[32] The kings usually seem to have demanded military service of them, perhaps giving them positions to some extent as military colonists,[33] evidence for which exists in the cases of Larsa,[34] Mari,[35] Nuzu(?),[36] Ḫattuša[37] and Alalaḫ,[38] and particularly clearly in a letter of king Biriyawaza[39] of Upe (a state of Damascus) from the Amarna archives:[40] *a-nu-ma a-na-ku qa-du* ERÍN.MEŠ-*ya ù* ^{GIŠ}GIGIR.MEŠ-*ya ù qa-du* ŠEŠ.MEŠ-*ya ù qa-du* LÚ.MEŠ SA.GAZ.MEŠ-*ya ù qa-du* LÚ.MEŠ *su-te-ya a-na pa-ni* ERÍN.MEŠ *pi-ṭá-te a-di a-šar yi-qa-bu* ^{I}LUGAL EN-*ya* '. . . I shall (be) there with my infantry and chariot troops and with my brothers and with my *ʿapiru*-people and with my bedouin (*sutû*) at the head of the archers where the king, my lord, commands (me).' We see here that among the conscripted troops with which a fairly important Syrian vassal promises to join his overlord's army, the bedouin (*sutû*) and the *ʿapiru* are listed alongside Egyptian (ERÍN.MEŠ *pí-ṭá-te*)[41] and native troops. We do not know whether the *ʿapiru* made themselves available for such service in every case of their own free will. The indication given by Itūr-Asdu in a letter to his lord Zimri-Lim of Mari, that he had 'brought together' or 'organized' the *ʿapiru* (LÚ.MEŠ *ḫa-pí-ri a-ka-ṣa-a*[*r* . . .)[42] and the existence of the office of an UGULA

[32] In a fragmentary context Bott. 74:
600 ^{LÚ}SA.GAZ *ša* DINGIR É[
600 ^{LÚ}SA.GAZ *ša* MIN *ša*[

[33] Thus, e.g., in the lists from Alalaḫ Bott. 38, 40–42 where ERÍN.MEŠ ^{LÚ}SA.GAZ EN TUKUL.MEŠ/^{GIŠ}TUKUL '*ʿapiru*-people who own weapons' are listed along with the places where they live.

[34] Bott. 16: AGA.ÚS.MEŠ(*rēdû*) ^{LÚ}*ḫa-pí-ri*. On the position of the *rēdû* cf. G. Evans, 'An Old Babylonian Soldier: Notes on the Archive of Ubarrum', *JCS* 14, 1960, 34–42.

[35] Bott. 18, 21, 22, 24.

[36] Cassin, *op. cit.*, 229 no. 9 (HSS XV 62, 1–4) where the statement ^{LÚ}*ḫa-apí-ra-tu*$_4$ *ša la e-man-tuḫ*$^{!}$*-lu*$^{!}$ presupposes the fact that *ʿapiru* could also hold the office of *emantuḫlu* (= *rab ešri*) which was apparently a military rank in Nuzu; cf. E. A. Speiser, *JAOS* 59, 1939, 310f.; H. Lewy, *Or* NS 10, 1941, 202f.; E. Cassin, *op. cit.*, 234f. n.11; *JESHO* 5, 1962, 130 n. 2; *AHw* 211^{a}; M. Dietrich and O. Loretz, *WO* 3.3, 1966, 189 n.4.

[37] Bott. 72, 72′ (if the fragmentary context is correctly interpreted in Bottéro); *KUB* XXXVI 106 (H. Otten, *ZA* 52, 1957, 217–20).

[38] Bott. 38, 40–43, 46.

[39] Read instead of 'Namiawaza' by F. Thureau-Dangin, *RA* 37, 1940, 171.

[40] VAB II 195.24–32 (Bott. 132).

[41] ERÍN.MEŠ *pí-ṭá-te* corresponds to Eg. *pḏ.tyw*; cf. W. F. Albright and W. L. Moran, *JCS* 2, 1948, 246 n.16. In this case it is a question of a (probably small) Egyptian garrison probably in the royal city of Biriyawaza.

[42] Bott. 24.

(*wakil*) LÚSA.GAZ.MEŠ under the first dynasty of Babylon[43] both suggest that the kings who, understandably, had an interest in keeping a fairly strict control over this restless and always suspicious element, actively pursued a policy of 'barracking' the *ʿapiru*.[44] Only from Nuzu do we know of cases where *ʿapiru*-people of both sexes, in fixed contractual terms, give themselves 'of their own free will' (*ramān-šu* or *pī-šu u lišān-šu*), in so far as one can talk of 'freedom of will' at all under the given circumstances, into service as slaves (*ana wardūti/amūti*)[45] of a private individual, thus achieving legal protection as well as their livelihood. From these contracts it has often been wrongly concluded that the enslaving of themselves was the only characteristic of the *ʿapiru*.[46] It is, rather, one means among others by which he sought to ensure his life and his survival. The fact that he is outside the law emerges from the fact that the conditions of these contracts are scarcely favourable to him.[47] In many cases they seem to have been foreigners at Nuzu; at any rate, from time to time, there are mentioned *ʿapiru*-people from Asshur (LÚ*ḫapiru ša* KUR *aš-šu-ur*)[48] and from Akkad (LÚ*ḫ. ša* KUR *ak-ka₄-di/dì*)[49] and in one document the assertion is made about the people in question that they had 'arrived this year from Akkad' (*i-na* MU *an-ni-ti i-na/iš-tu* KUR *ak-ka₄-di a-li-ka₄*).[50] Similarly, at Mari, there appear *ʿapiru*-people from Jamudbal (LÚ.MEŠ *ya-mu-ud-ba-la-yú ḫa-pi-ru*).[51] On the other hand,

[43] Bott. 17.

[44] Nevertheless, we have from Boğazköy in the text Bo. 298/n = 756/f (*KBo* IX 73) the fragment of a treaty between a Hittite king and *ʿapiru*-people; cf. H. Otten, *ZA* 52, 1957, 220–23. The date formula in Bott. 36 from Alalaḫ is explained analogously by Otten, *op. cit.*, 223. According to the collation by M. Dietrich and O. Loretz (see *Theologische Revue* 65, 1969, 365), it does not contain the element ERÍN.MEŠ *ḫa-ʾ-pí-ru*, but, rather, ERÍN.MEŠ KI!-GA!-RU should be read.

[45] Cf. above n. 31. Once (Bott. 54), instead of this, there occurs [*a-na*(?) *kè*-] *el-lu?/zu?!-uḫ-lu-ti*; cf. J. Lewy, *HUCA* 14, 1939, 600f. n. 74. W. v. Soden, in *AHw* 284b *s.v. gelduḫlu/gelzuḫlu*, reconstructs our passage as follows: LÚ*ḫa-pí-ru* [*ša? ge?*-] *el-zu!?-uḫ-lu-ti*. According to this, the *ʿapiru* would be more accurately described by the vocational (?) description *kelzuḫlūtu*, but this does not correspond to the formula of the group of texts. Cf. also Dietrich-Loretz, *op. cit.*, 200.

[46] E. Chiera, 'Ḫabiru and Hebrews', *AJSL* 49, 1933, 115–24.

[47] Cf. E. Cassin in Bottéro, *op. cit.*, 65–69; Bottéro, *ibid.*, 70.

[48] Bott. 49, 50.

[49] Bott. 56, 63, 67.

[50] Bott. 56.

[51] Bott. 19. On Jamudbal/Emudbal cf. D. O. Edzard, *Die 'zweite Zwischenzeit' Babyloniens* (Wiesbaden 1957), 105f.; J.-R. Kupper, *Les nomades en*

another text from Mari speaks of 'indigenous *'apiru*-people' (*ṣa-bi-im ḫa-pí-ri* [gen.] *ša ma-a-tim*).[52] There is thus explicit confirmation in these passages of the point of view which is won from a thorough examination of a group of people scattered from Mesopotamia to Egypt, that there can be no question of an ethnic unity such as a 'nation' of *'apiru*. This, in turn, explains why, in the Hittite state treaties, the 'gods of the *'apiru*'[53] (along with the 'gods of the Lulaḫḫu')[54] are always mentioned in this summary form as the protective gods of the treaties alongside gods who are men-

---

Mésopotamie au temps des rois de Mari (Bibliothèque de la Faculté de Philosophie et Lettres de l'Université de Liège 142, Paris 1957), *passim* (see Index pp. 271ᵇ, 274ᵃ, *s.vv.* Emutbal, Iamutbal, Iamutbaléens); W. F. Albright, *BASOR* 163, 1961, 49f. n.67.

[52] Bott. 18. The interpretation of the expression *ša mātim* according to B. Landsberger in Bottéro, *op. cit.*, 204; *WO* 3.3, 1966, 260 n.56. Otherwise L. Oppenheim, *JNES* 11, 1953, 133: *mātum* = 'steppe'.

[53] Bott. 75–86 (Bott. 89, 90 are linguistically obscure). The question whether we are dealing with a god called 'Ḫabiru' with a plural determinative (*DINGIR.MEŠ*ḫa*-BI-*ru*: A. Jirku, 'Neues keilinschriftliches Material zum Alten Testament', *ZAW* 39, 1921, 156–8; *Die Wanderungen der Hebräer im dritten und zweiten vorchristlichen Jahrtausend* (1924), 18f.; 'GötterḪabiru oder Götter der Ḫabiru?', *ZAW* 44, 1926, 237–42) or 'gods of the "Ḫabiru"' (A. Gustavs, 'Der Gott Ḫabiru', *ZAW* 40, 1922, 314; 'Was heisst ilâni Ḫabiri?', *ZAW* 44, 1926, 25–38) is to be resolved along the lines of Gustavs: In two duplicates of the treaty between the Hittite king Šuppiluliuma and KURtiwaza (the exact reading of the name is not known: Mattiwaza? Šattiwaza? Kurtiwaza?) of Mitanni there correspond the forms DINGIR.MEŠ *nu*!-Ú!-*aḫ-ḫi* (Ú seems to me to be an error for LA) DINGIR.MEŠ *ša* LÚSA.GAZ (*KBo* I 2, v°. 27; Bott. 75; cf. *KBo* I 3+, v°. 4f.; Bott. 76) and DINGIR.MEŠ *lu-la-ḫi-i* DINGIR.MEŠ SA.GAZ (*KBo* I 1, v°. 50; Bott. 75). From this it is clear that in the Akkadian texts from Boğazköy **ilāni ša ḫapirī* or **ilāni ḫapirī* is to be read, and the form **ḫapirī* is to be understood as the plural of the oblique case (cf. Gustavs, *ZAW* 44, 28). The corresponding form in the Hittite texts is the gen.pl. *ḫapiriaš* in DINGIR.MEŠ *ḫa-pí-ri-ya-aš* (Bott. 82, 83; *ḫa-pí-ra-aš* Bott. 81). The variant form of this, *ḫapiriēš*, in DINGIR.MEŠ *ḫa-pí-ri-e-eš* (Bott. 84, 85?, 86), which is a nom.pl., is probably to be regarded with Gustavs (*op. cit.*, 31) and G. Neumann (letter of 4 June 1965) as an adjectival attribute (nom.pl. of **ḫapiriya-*) and the expression therefore to be translated as 'the 'apirite gods'. The replacement of the genitive by an adjective of belonging is not unknown elsewhere in the languages of ancient Asia Minor. The god D*ḫa*-BI-*ru* in the 'directory of gods' from Asshur (*KAV* 42 II 9; Bott. 167; R. Frankena, *Tākultu: De sacrale maaltijd in het Assyrische ritueel, met een overzicht over de in Assur vereerde goden,* Commentationes Orientales 2, Leiden 1954, 124: 60) which is hotly disputed in the discussion between Jirku and Gustavs, has been convincingly separated by W. v. Soden in Bottéro, *op. cit.*, 135, from the *'apiru* problems and explained as a neo-Assyrian form of the Bab. D*ḫāweru* ('spouse'; cf. *AHw* 338ᵇ).

[54] Literature on the *Lulaḫḫu* in Bottéro, *op. cit.*, 83 n.1.

tioned by name. It is, if the comparison may be allowed in respect of time and place, a question of a precautionary measure analogous to that of the Athenians who, in certain cases, dedicated altars ἀγνώστων θεῶν.[55] For the 'gods of the *ʿapiru*' are not a firmly defined group the members of which were known by name, not a definite pantheon, but the constantly changing totality of all deities of the most diverse origins who were worshipped by the individual members of the *ʿapiru* class. Each one of these gods whatever his name or wherever his home is to watch over the clauses of the treaty and, in a certain fashion, also guarantee the safety of the partners of the treaty from any possible intrigues on the part of his worshippers.

4. From the results achieved hitherto, it seems to me possible to determine also the character and the role of the *ʿapiru* mentioned in the Amarna letters[56] better than has generally been done till now. Mendenhall[57] is certainly right when he rejects the concept of a great *ʿapiru* invasion of Palestine and Syria in the Amarna period. The texts clearly state that city kings,[58] princes,[59] countries,[60] 'mayors' (*ḫazannūtu*),[61] cities (communities of citizens),[62]

[55] Cf. Pausanias I 1.4; V 14.8; Philostrat, *vita Apollonii*, 6.3; A. Deissmann, *Paulus: Eine kultur- and religionsgeschichtliche Skizze* (Tübingen 1911), 178–81; ET of 2nd ed., *Paul: A Study in Social and Religious History* (London 1926), 287–91; A. v. Harnack, *Marcion: Das Evangelium vom fremden Gott* (TuU 45 = III 15, ²1924), 2 top; E. Norden, *Agnostos Theos: Untersuchungen zur Formengeschichte religiöser Rede* (Darmstadt ⁴1956), 41ff., 117ff. However, for the ultimate background of the expression ἀγνώστος θεός cf. the name *kuišḫamaššani*- 'a certain (= anyone you like?) goddess' of a Luwian deity (Bo. 2311.8 in Liane Rost, *MIO* 8, 1961, 168) and on this G. Neumann, *MSS* 16, 1964, 51.

[56] Bott. 93–153.

[57] *Op. cit.*, 72f.

[58] VAB II 148.41–43 (Bott. 127); 185.9ff. (Bott. 129); 186.12ff. (Bott. 130); 254.32–35 (Bott. 138).

[59] VAB II 298.22–27 (Bott. 147).

[60] Mostly in the formula 'every country has joined the *ʿapiru*' (*ti-ni-pu-šu* or the like *ka-li* KUR.MEŠ *a-na* ᴸᵁ́⁽·ᴹᴱŠ⁾SA.GAZ): VAB II 73.32f. (Bott. 96); 74.35f. (Bott. 97); 76.34–37 (Bott. 99); 79.19f., 25f. (Bott. 101); 85.72f. (Bott. 105); 88.32–34 (Bott. 107); 89.31f. (Bott. 108); 111.19–21 (Bott. 114); 117.57f. (Bott. 118); 148.45 (Bott. 127); 272.14–17 (Bott. 139); 273.11–14 (Bott. 140); 290.12f., 23f. (Bott. 146).

[61] VAB II 73.28–30 (Bott. 96).

[62] VAB II 74.19–21 (Bott. 97); 76.34–37 (Bott. 99); 81.12f. (Bott. 102); 104.51–54 (Bott. 111); 116.37f. (Bott. 117); 127.20f. (Bott. 128); 207.19–21 (Bott. 134); 215.13–15 (Bott. 135). In the last two passages *ḫalāqu* + *ina* ᴸᵁ́GAZ.MEŠ/LÚ.MEŠ SA.GAZ ᴷᴵ must be interpreted as 'revolt among the *ʿapiru*'.

ḫupšu[63] belong to the *ʿapiru* or join up with them (*epēšu* N + *ana ḫapirī*).[64] The tenor of all the references – with the exception of three which will be discussed shortly – indicates that the writers of the letters, who remained faithful to the Egyptian crown or at least wished to appear faithful in their letters to the Pharaoh or to high officials, mean by *ʿapiru*, amongst whom they classify many of their colleagues (mostly their personal enemies), simply rebels against Egyptian sovereignty and are able, at the same time, to give to the term an additional pejorative sense similar to the way in which Rib-Hadda of Byblos calls SA.GAZ-people 'dogs' (UR.KU = *kalbu*, a singular in apposition to a plural noun)[65] or even a 'runaway dog' (UR *ḫal-qú*).[66] The rebel who rises against the Pharaoh and thereby attacks his sovereign's property, his lands and cities, is branded as a 'robber'; in actual fact, the scribes of the loyal or apparently loyal city kings also seem to have had this meaning in mind (and sometimes also the reading *ḫabbātu*?)[67] when they made use of the Sumeriogram SA.GAZ for *ʿapiru*. In this connection, one has of course to make exception of the text VAB II 195.24–32

[63] VAB II 118.37 (Bott. 119). On the class of *ḫupšu* cf. W. F. Albright, 'Canaanite Ḥofšî, "Free", in the Amarna Tablets', *JPOS* 4, 1924, 169f.; J. Pedersen, 'Note on Hebrew Ḥofšī', *JPOS* 6, 1926, 103–5; W. F. Albright, 'Canaanite Ḫapši and Hebrew Ḥofšî Again', *ibid.*, 106–8; 'The North Canaanite Poems of Al'êyân Baʿal and the "Gracious Gods"', *JPOS* 14, 1934, 131 n. 162; A. Alt, 'Eine syrische Bevölkerungsklasse im ramessidischen Ägypten', *ZÄS* 75, 1939, 16–20; I. Mendelsohn, 'The Canaanite Term for "Free Proletarian"', *BASOR* 83, 1941, 36–39; E. R. Lacheman, 'Note on the Word Ḫupšu at Nuzi', *BASOR* 86, 1942, 36f.; R. T. O'Callaghan, *Aram Naharaim: A Contribution to the History of Upper Mesopotamia in the Second Millennium* B.C. (AnOr 26, 1948), 67 and n.2; J. Gray, 'Feudalism in Ugarit and Early Israel', *ZAW* 64, 1952, 52–55; I. Mendelsohn, 'New Light on the Ḫupšu', *BASOR* 139, 1955, 9–11; H. J. Stoebe, 'Die Goliathperikope 1. Sam. XVII 1–XVIII 5 und die Textform der Septuaginta', *VT* 6, 1956, 403f.; P. Grelot, 'Ḥofšī (Ps. LXXXVIII 6)', *VT* 14, 1964, 256–63; M. Dietrich and O. Loretz, *WO* 5.1, 1969, 57–93.

[64] Cf. *AHw* 229ᵃ *s.v. epēšu* N 12; E. F. Campbell, Jr., 'The Amarna Letters and The Amarna Period', *BA* 23, 1960, 15; *The Chronology of the Amarna Letters with Special Reference to the Hypothetical Co-regency of Amenophis III and Akhenaten* (Baltimore 1964), 86 n.48. Cf. above n.60.

[65] VAB II 91.5 (Bott. 110): ᴸᵁ́GAZ.ME[Š] UR.KU.

[66] VAB II 67.16 (Bott. 93).

[67] Cf. the logographic form ᴸᵁ́SA.GAZ.MEŠ^{tu_4}, whose phonetic complement -tu_4 (TUM) fits only *ḫabbātu*(*m*) but not *ḫapiru*, in VAB II 299.26 (Bott. 148) and the wordplay (?) LÚ.MEŠ *ḫa-pí-ru ḫa-bat gáb-bi* KUR.HÁ LUGAL VAB II 286.56 (Bott. 142). Rowton, *op. cit.* (above n.17), 386 n.69, suggests with some justification that SA.GAZ/*ḫabbātu* perhaps not only meant 'bandit' but was also the correct Babylonian equivalent for the West Semitic *ʿapiru*.

(Bott. 132) which we have discussed above; it is in accordance with the tone of other archives when it speaks of the *ʿapiru* as a population group some of whose members were in military service. When Abimilku of Tyre reports to the Pharaoh that 'the king of Hazor has left his city and has joined the *ʿapiru*' (LUGAL URU*ḫa-ṣu-ra i-te-zi-ib* URU?-*šu ù it-ta-ṣ* [*a*] -*ab it-ti* LÚSA.GAZ),[68] one might at first think that the ruler of this important Galilean city had abandoned his seat of government and gone over to the *ʿapiru* who were in control of the lowlands. Yet what must be intended here too is that, perhaps along with the population of the city (*i-pu-uš* KUR LUGAL *a-na* LÚSA.GAZ),[69] he has joined the movement of rebellion against Egyptian supremacy. Thus, there remains finally the text VAB II 318.10–15 (Bott. 152) in which a king by the name of Dagan-takala, whose place of residence is unknown, asks the Pharaoh 'to rescue' him 'from the hand of the *ʿapiru*-people, the robbers and the bedouin' (*iš-tu* ŠUqa-ti LÚ.MEŠ SA.GA. A[Z.M]EŠ LU.MEŠ *ḫa-ba-ti ù* LÚ.MEŠ *šu-ti-i ù še-zi-ba-an-* [*ni*][70] LUGAL GAL *be-li-y*[*a*]). Yet here too one can explain, even if not with absolute certainty, the *ʿapiru* as rebels against the ruling power and its representatives in the country and the *ḫabbātū* as normal robbers of whom, in such uncertain times, there may well have been a greater number than usual.[71] The development in meaning to 'traitors' which is attested for *ʿapiru* in the Amarna letters can easily be derived from the definition of the term given above as 'outlaw', in so far as the rebel, although of course of his own free

[68] VAB II 148.41–43 (Bott. 127).

[69] *Ibid.*, 45.

[70] The form expressed here as *u šēzibanni* is usually explained as imp.sing. with 1st sing. suffix (E. Ebeling, *Das Verbum der El-Amarna-Briefe*, BAss 8.2, 1910, 64; Knudtzon, translation of the passage) like *še-zi-ba-an-ni* VAB II 318.8, 14, or, with 1st plur. suffix, *še-ez-zi-bá-an-na-ši-* 62.30. This is not certain since the conjunction *u* before the word is difficult; it could at the most be explained as a so-called 'pleonastic waw' or 'waw apodoseos' (on this cf. A. Finet, *RA* 46, 1952, 23f.). Perhaps however the form is to be taken as *ušēzibanni* (*ù-še-zi-ba-an-ni*) and interpreted as a precative wrongly formed (correctly: **lu-še-zi-ba-an-ni* = *lūšēzibanni*) and wrongly written (one would rather see, if anything, **ú-še-zi-ba-an-ni*) whose form has been influenced by that of the North-west Semitic jussive. Cf. the preterite forms *ú-še*$_x$(ŠI)-*zu-bu-ni* and *ú-še-zi-ba-an-ni* 3rd masc. sing. preterite subj. with 1st sing. suffix VAB II 74.33, 44.

[71] The *ghazū* of the bedouin is also favoured by the weakness of the central power. Cf. the complaint – the details are obscure – of King Japaḫu (**yapaʿu*) of Gezer about attacks by [L]Ú.MEŠ KUR*s*[*u*?]-*te*MEŠ VAB II 297.11–16 (on this and the parallel passage 292., 44–8 see *CAD* 6/Ḫ, 214 *s.v. ḫubbulu* B).

will and with hostile intent, stands outside the legitimate, existing political order.[72]

5. Even if Mendenhall is right so far, yet our observation of the fact that local kings and their followers took part in the rebellion, shows us beyond all shadow of a doubt that the *ʿapiru* revolt in the Amarna period was not an uprising on the part of the oppressed population of the plains against the ruling feudal classes of the cities and is certainly not to be understood on the basis of a comparison with the great German Peasants' Revolt of 1525/26. It now seems justified to ask at this point in what measure the other parts of Mendenhall's historical reconstruction of the Israelite settlement are tenable. In this respect we must first of all submit to examination the identification that is maintained of *ʿapiru*-people with the 'Hebrews' (*ʿibrīm*). I have already drawn attention to the fact that the establishment of the precise phonetic structure of the word *ḫa*-BI-*ru* as *ʿapiru* gives rise to doubts as to the connection with the Hebrew word *ʿibrī*. In answer to this it is usually asserted[73] that examples are known in other cases of a change between *b* and *p* within the Semitic languages.[74] The additional

[72] The statements of P. Artzi, ' "Vox Populi" in the el-Amarna Tablets', *RA* 58, 1964, 165f., which became available to me after I had concluded this section, agree in many points with my own on the meaning of the term *ʿapiru* in the Amarna letters; cf. also E. F. Campbell Jr., *op. cit.* (above n. 64).

[73] On this question cf. on the one hand R. Borger, *op. cit.*, 126–8 who, correctly, warns against a naïve adoption of the identification *ʿapiru*/Hebrews, even if I cannot share his strongly negative position (*op. cit.*, 132), as I show above, and on the other hand A. Jirku, *Geschichte Palästina-Syriens im orientalischen Altertum* (Aalen 1963), 96 n. 125: 'The change between *b* and *p* in the various written forms of the name Habiru cannot fail to provide difficulties for those who are unaware to what extent we can establish again and again the same phenomenon in the writing of proper names in Syria-Palestine.' One must emphasize, however, that the impression of the lack of orthographic (and phonetic?) rules in the treatment of the voiced stop/voiceless stop opposition in the Akkadian cuneiform texts from the area of Asia Minor-Syria-Palestine rests on two factors: (1) the lack of knowledge of the standard Babylonian orthography on the part of the Hittite and Syrian scribes and (2) unsatisfactory methods of transcription particularly on the part of older Assyriologists who were unable to do justice to texts in 'barbarized Akkadian' since they hesitated to accept unusual values (which resulted partly from [1]) and for the most part inserted the most frequent. In alphabetic systems of writing which are able to differentiate clearly and unambiguously between voiced and voiceless stops the apparently regular change can be observed only in a few cases where usually a phonetic reason (substitution of phonemes or graphemes in foreign words and names) can be given for it.

[74] Cf. generally C. Brockelmann, *Grundriss der vergleichenden Grammatik der semitischen Sprachen* I (Berlin 1908, reprint Hildesheim 1961), 154 §54eζ, 157

argument[75] that we actually have three Middle Babylonian examples of the word where the spelling – *ḫa*-BIR-*a-a*[76] in Middle Babylonian can be read only as *ḫa-bir-a-a* and not as **ḫa-pìr-a-a*[77] – clearly testifies to the pronunciation with *-b-* and where, moreover, the word reveals the ending corresponding to the *nisba* ending of Hebrew *ʿibrī*, has been convincingly refuted by R. Borger[78] who explains the questionable word *ḫabirāy-* as the gentilic of the city of *ḫa-bi-ri*KI[79] and correctly rejects any connection with the *ʿapiru* in the case both of the name of the city and of the adjective derived from it. It cannot, however, be denied that the Semitic languages know, to a limited extent, the sound shift *b/p*. In the following table I give a few examples which are certain and which could be supplemented by others of variable worth.[80]

---

§55f, 161 §58bγδ, 164 §58gβ, hη, 166 §§58iζ, 59aα, 169 §59eαγ, 170 §59fγ; *GAG* §27d; J. Aistleitner, *Untersuchungen zur Grammatik des Ugaritischen* (BSA 100.6, 1954) 11f., §§11, 12; P. Fronzaroli, *La fonetica ugaritica* (Sussidi eruditi 7, Rome 1955), 50f. §33d, 52 §35ab, 53f. §36; C. H. Gordon, *Ugaritic Manual* (AnOr 35, 1955), 28 §5, 25; G. Garbini, *Il semitico di nord-ovest* (Istituto universitario orientale di Napoli, Quaderni della sezione linguistica degli annali, 1, Naples 1960), 19–26 *passim*; M. Dahood, *Proverbs and Northwest Semitic Philology* (SPIB 113, 1963), 10f., 20, 24, 32f., 43 and n. 1. A considerable proportion of the examples cited there must be regarded as uncertain or unfounded. Cf. also the criticism of Garbini in E. Y. Kutscher, 'Contemporary Studies in North-Western Semitic', *JSS* 10, 1965, 22–24.

[75] Cf. B. Landsberger, *ZA* 35, 1924, 213f. n. 1.

[76] Bott. 165, 165′, 166.

[77] W. v. Soden, *Das akkadische Syllabar* (AnOr 27, 1948), 73 no. 237; Borger, *op. cit.*, 126. For this reason the form '*ḫāpiraja*' (with BIR = *pìr*) in *CAD* 6/Ḫ,84ᵃ is, to say the least, precipitate. At this point Rowton, *op. cit.* (above n. 17), 384 n. 61 turns against Borger.

[78] *Op. cit.*, 126. On the divine name D*ḫa*-BI-*ru* KAV 42 II 9, which, according to the rules of neo-Assyrian orthography, should very probably not be read as *D*ḫa-pi-ru*, see above n. 53.

[79] Bott. 35 (Susa): *ḫa*-BI-*ri*KI among nothing but place names.

[80] The reference to the Semitic word for 'iron' where the shift *b/p* appears in initial position (Garbini, *op. cit.*, 21): Ug. *brḏl*, Hebr. *barzel*: Akk. *parzillu*, Aram. *przl*(ʾ), OSArab. *frzn*, Arab. *firzilun* is also, of course, of no value, for this is a foreign word of unknown origin and uncertain phonetic structure, so that we cannot say for which foreign phoneme Sem. *b* or *p* has been substituted. The word could even come from a language which knew no difference between *b* and *p*. The Hittite word for 'iron' '*barzillu*' which is pursued by L. Köhler, *JSS* 1, 1956, 7, and again by R. Meyer, *Hebräische Grammatik, I. Einleitung, Schrift- und Lautlehre* (Sammlung Göschen 763/763ab, Berlin ³1966), 106 §24.4, does not exist; 'iron' is rather *ḫapalki-* (E. Laroche, *RHA* 15, fasc. 60, 1957, 9–15). Cf. also M. Ellenbogen, *Foreign Words in the Old Testament, their Origin and Etymology* (London 1962), 52f.; L. Deroy, 'L'expansion préhistorique du fer et les noms de ce métal en grec ancien et en

Forms with *b*	Forms with *p*
(*a*) *BḎR 'scatter' Hebr. *bzr* G 'scatter' (Dan. 11.24), D 'scatter' (Ps. 68.31); Aram. *bdr* (Chr.Pal. G and D, Bibl., Jewish,[81] Syr. D) 'scatter'; Arab. *bḏr* G 'sow, disseminate', D 'squander'.	Hebr. *pzr* D 'scatter, spread, disseminate' (N pass.); Jewish Aram. *pzr* (probably a Hebraism).
(*b*) *BQʿ 'split' Hebr., Jewish Aram. *bqʿ* 'split' and derivatives; Moab. *bqʿ hšḥrt* 'daybreak'.	Syr. *pqʿ* and derivatives, Mand. *fīqa* 'cleft'.
(*c*) BṮN Akk. *bašmu*, Ug. *bṯn*, Arab. *baṯanun* a type of snake.	Aram. *pitnā*, *patnā* (Syr.), Hebr. *peten* (Aramaism)[82] a type of snake.
(*d*) *DBŠ 'honey' Ug. *dbš*, Hebr. *d^{e}baš*, Aram. *d^{e}baš* (Bibl.), *debšā* (Syr.), *dwbšʾ* (Jewish), OSArab. *dbś*, Arab. *dibsun*, Eth. *debsä* (Gafat), *dims* (<**dibs*; Argobba), *dūs* (<**dbs*; Harari)[83] 'honey'.	Akk. *dišpu* (<**dipšu*) 'honey'.

latin', *Anadolu Araştirmalari* 2.1/2, 1965, 184–6. The Ugaritic word *prṯl* (*PRU* II, 1957, 1.7.19) associated with it by Ch. Virolleaud, *GLECS* 6, 1951–1954, 17f.; *PRU* II, 6 (cf. Garbini, *op. cit.*, 21) is of unknown meaning and has nothing to do with it.

[81] Also *bzr*, probably a Hebraism. Cf. also M. Wagner, *Die lexikalischen und grammatikalischen Aramaismen im alttestamentlichen Hebräisch* (BZAW 96, 1966), 33 no. 37.

[82] Cf. G. Garbini, 'Considerazioni sulla parola ebraica peten', *RivBibl* 6, 1958, 263–5; *Il semitico di nord-ovest*, 23, 33f.; Wagner, *op. cit.*, 97 no. 242a.

[83] See W. Leslau, *Ethiopic and South-Arabic Contributions to the Hebrew Lexicon* (UCP 20, 1958), 16.

Forms with *b*	Forms with *p*
(*e*) *HB/PK 'turn'	
Akk. *abāku* 'bring away, lead away'.	Ug. *hpk* 'overthrow'; Hebr. *hpk*, Aram. *hpk*, *'pk* 'turn, overthrow'; Arab. *'fk* 'turn back, tell lies'.
(*f*) *KBŠ 'tread'[84]	
Amarna Akk. *kabāšu* (West Semitism), Hebr. *kbš* 'tread'; Aram. *kbš* 'tread down, force'; Chr.Pal. *kbš* D 'force'; Syr. *kbš* G and D 'oppress' (A caus.); Arab. *kbs* 'press down, fill up, attack'.	Hebr. *kpš* H 'press down' (Lam. 3.16); PBH *kpš* D *ibid.*, cf. PBH *kāpūš* 'turned in'.
(*g*) LBŠ 'be clothed'	
Akk. *labāšu*, Ug., Hebr., Aram. *lbš*, Arab. *lbs* 'be clothed' and derivatives (e.g. Ug. *lbš* 'garment').[85]	Ug. *lpš* (alongside *lbš*) 'garment'.
(*h*) *NBK 'well up'[86]	
Ug. *mbk nhrm*, Hebr. *nibkē yām* (Job 38.16, pausal form), *nibkē mayim* (Prov. 8.24), **mabbᵉkē mayim* (Job 28.18),[88]	Ug. *npk* 'spring' (‖*mqr*)[87]

[84] To what extent *KBS (Akk. *kabāsu*, Hebr. *kbs* 'to full') is to be linked with this must remain open; Arab. *kbs* could also belong to *KBS.

[85] On the basis of Akk. *libšu(m)/lubšu*, *lpš* is certainly to be regarded as a 'segholate'; in the case of *lbš* one might ask whether **lubūš-*, analogous to Akk. *lubūšu*, does not lie behind Hebr. *lᵉbūš*.

[86] On nn. 87–89 cf. W. F. Albright, *Archaeology and the Religion of Israel* (Baltimore 1953), 194f. n. III 7; G. M. Landes, *BASOR* 144, 1956, 30–37.

[87] Probably **napk-* or **nipk-*; cf. Hebr. **nēbek* in *nibkē yām* (pausal form).

[88] Prov. 8.24 M *ma'yānōt nikbaddē māyim* (pausal form) 'springs heavy with water' does not make much sense; on the basis of Ug. *npk* 'spring', cf. Job. 28.11 (; 38.16), it is better to read as proposed above. In G (*πρὸ τοῦ προελθεῖν τὰς πηγὰς τῶν ὑδάτων*) *nikbaddē* is certainly not envisaged. The text in Job 28.11a is difficult. In view of Ug. *mbk* (in *mbk nhrm* = **mabbikī naharēmi*) one should vocalize **mabbᵉkē nᵉhārōt*; what ḤBŠ D (no other occurrence of it with *min*) means in this context I do not know; perhaps the conjecture *ḤPŚ (cf. G) should be adopted so that it can be translated: 'the sources of the rivers he

Forms with *b*	Forms with *p*
Aram. *nbg*, Arab. *nbj* and derivatives.[89]	
(*i*) *NPŠ 'throat' Old Aram., Phoen. (both Zincirli), Hebr. (Arad)[90] *nbš* 'soul'.[91]	Akk. *napištu(m)*, Ug. *npš*, Hebr. *nepeš*, Aram. *napšā*, Phoen. *npš*, OSArab. *nfś*, Eth. *nafs*, Arab. *nafsun* 'throat, soul'.
(*k*) *NŠP 'blow' (trans. and intrans.) Hebr. (G; H caus.), Chr.Pal. (G; A caus.), Syr. (G and D) *nšb* 'blow' (intrans.) and derivatives.	Akk. *našāpu* (G and D; N pass.) 'blow away'; Hebr. *nšp* G 'blow' (trans.); Chr.Pal. *nšp* 'blow' (intrans.); Arab. *nsf* 'blow away, scatter'; cf. Syr. *na/ušpā* 'serpent'.
(*l*) *ʿRP[92] Hebr. *rōkēb bā-ʿ^{a}rābōt* (Ps. 68.5) 'he who rides upon the clouds' (divine epithet)[93]	Akk. *erēpu* 'cover oneself with clouds' (*erpu* 'clouded'),

seeks out' (I should not like, on this evidence alone, to accept the shift *b/p* in ḤBŠ/ḤPŚ). Cf. also J. A. Montgomery, *JAOS* 53, 1933, 111; G. R. Driver, *Canaanite Myths and Legends* (Old Testament Studies 3, Edinburgh 1956), 162[a] and n. 11 (the derivation from *BūK seems to me to be unfounded).

[89] Cf. GesB[17], 480[b] *s.v.* **nēbek*. The Aramaic and Arabic forms show partial regressive assimilation of the *k* to the *b* (>*g*).

[90] Ostrakon Arad 6005/1 v°. line 7 *bnbškm* for **b^{e}napš^{e}kem* or *b^{e}napšēkem*; see Y. Aharoni, *EI* 9, 1969, 10f. The same ostrakon also has *whbqydm* for **w^{e}hipqīdām* v°. lines 3f.

[91] Cf. Z. S. Harris, *Development of the Canaanite Dialects* (AOS 16, 1939), 71; J. Friedrich, *Phönizisch-punische Grammatik* (AnOr 32, 1951), 18 n. 2, 37 n. 2, 155; G. Garbini, 'Note aramaiche, 1. p > b in ya'udico', *Antonianum* 31, 1956, 310f.; 'Note aramaiche, 2. Una nuova iscrizione di Bar-Rkb', *Antonianum* 32, 1957, 427f.; 'Nuovo materiale per la grammatica del aramaico antico', *RSO* 34, 1959, 43f.; *Il semitico di nord-ovest,* 24f.

[92] Against the general consensus of opinion, Hebr. *ʿ^{a}rāpel*, Aram. *ʿrpyl'* do not belong here since ʿ in these words goes back to **ġ*, as Ug. *ġrpl* shows; on *ġrpl* cf. Ch. Virolleaud, *GLECS* 9, 1960–3, 51; O. Eissfeldt, 'Neue keilalphabetische Texte aus Ras Shamra-Ugarit', *SAB* 1965:6, 1965, 47.

[93] The pioneers of Hebrew lexicography followed Ibn Ezra in associating *ʿ^{a}rābōt* with *ʿ^{a}rābā* 'steppe' (cf., e.g., H. Opitz, *Novum Lexicon hebraeo-chaldaeo-biblicum*, Leipzig and Frankfurt [2]1705, 257[a]) with the delightful justification: '*nubes*, vel *coelum*, ob similitudinem, quae intercedit inter campestres terrae

Forms with *b*	Forms with *p*
	erpetu 'clouds'; Ug. *rkb ʿrpt* 'he who rides upon the clouds' (divine epithet).
(*m*) *PʿL 'do, make' Ug. *bʿl* 'do, make'.[94]	Hebr., Old Aram., Phoen, *pʿl*, OSArab., Arab. *fʿl* 'do, make' and derivatives, e.g. Syr. *pʿālā* 'work'.
(*n*) *PRG̱Ḫ̱Ṯ 'flea' Arab. *burg̱hūṯun* 'flea'.	Akk. *pu/irša'u, pur'usu*,[95] Ug. *prġṯ* (PN), Hebr. *parʿōš* (also PN), Syr. *purtaʿnā* 'flea'.
(*o*) *ŠPḤ Ug. *šbḥ* (= *špḥ*) 'posterity' (or the like).[96]	Ug. *špḥ* (= *šbḥ*) 'posterity'; Hebr. *mišpāḥā*, Phoen. *špḥ* 'family'.

locos, & inter amplissimam coeli planitiem, quam deus pro lubitu quasi permeat' (Ch. Stockius, *Clavis linguae sanctae Veteris Testamenti*, Leipzig ^{6}1753, 847). In BHK^{3}, *ad loc.*, the conjecture **beʿābōt* is proposed. Borger, *op. cit.*, 128, wishes to emend on the basis of Ug. to **baʿarāpōt*, supposing that the two expressions are at all comparable. J. A. Montgomery's scepticism at the interpretation of *rkb ʿrpt* as 'rider on the clouds' (*JAOS* 53, 1933, 118f.; 54, 1934, 60f.) has scarcely any justification, for *ʿrpt* = 'hall of pillars' on the basis of Phoen. *ʿrpt* (*DISO* 222, 16–18) does not fit the Ugaritic context. Garbini, *Il semitico di nord-ovest,* 23, also compares Hebr. *ʿarīpīm* (Isa. 5.30; meaning unknown).

94 According to M. Dahood, *Bibl* 44, 1963, 303; *Proverbs and Northwest Semitic Philology,* 10, BʿL 'do, make' also occurs in Hebrew as a dialect variant of PʿL; of his examples, however, only Eccles 8.8 is, in the long run, relevant, where *welō yemallēṭ rešaʿ 'et-bʿlyw* could be translated 'and wickedness will not deliver him who does it' (reading **bōʿalō*). F. Ellermeier (oral communication) would not, however, regard this suggested translation as of any worth.

95 Cf. B. Landsberger, *Die Fauna des alten Mesopotamien nach der 14. Tafel der Serie ḪAR.RA = ḫubullu* (Leipzig 1934), 126. In Old Akkadian, *B/Pirḫašum* (written BIR5-*ḫa-šum/sum/šu-um*, BI-*ir-ḫa-šum*!; see I. J. Gelb, *Glossary of Old Akkadian* [MAD III, 1957], 217 *s.v.* PR'5Š) is attested as a proper name where the reading with *b-* is possible as well as that with *p-* (on the treatment of the plosives in the cuneiform orthography of the Old Akkadian period cf. I. J. Gelb, *Old Akkadian Writing and Grammar* [MAD II, 1952], 19, 37f., 41f.); probably what is intended is **pir'āšum* (i.e. *pir*6- . . ./*pí-ir-* . . .).

96 *špḥ* and *šbḥ* alternate in parallel passages (*CTA* 14, 144 : 290). Cf. accordingly above n. 85.

It is not possible to determine a generally valid rule for this sound shift. It occurs in the initial position in our examples five times (*a*, *b*, *c*, *m*, *n*), in final position once or twice (*k*; perhaps *l*),[97] in an internal position between vowels two or three times (*e*, *f*; perhaps *l*), in an internal position as the middle consonant of a triliteral 'segholate' five times (*d*, *g*, *h*, *i*, *o*) and not exclusively in contact with *š*. This argues against the suggestion which is occasionally made in connection with the last mentioned group that the appearance of *p* instead of *b* is to be attributed to the partial assimilation of the voiced labial *b* to the voiceless *š*;[98] other voiceless consonants also enter into consideration (the voiceless pharyngal spirant *ḥ* in [*h*], the voiceless palatal plosive *k* in [*h*]. In actual fact it is not at all possible to speak of such a partial assimilation of the voiced consonant to the following voiceless consonant, for two groups among our examples are in contrast to each other in that in their case the process has occurred in opposite directions: *b* > *p* in (*d*), (*g*), (*h*): *p* > *b* in (*i*), (*o*). One can, therefore, only speak of an *oscillation* of the labial plosive before the following voiceless consonant.[99] This oscillation will have found expression in variations of the (quasi-phonetic) writing which have in turn become orthographically fixed, if at all, in different ways in individual languages, possibly by analogy with corresponding phonetic developments. If this hypothesis is approximately correct, then we have a possible analogous explanation of the change of the *p* of *ʿapiru* to the *b* of the sehgolate derivative *ʿibrī*. In this case we must, of course, notice that this can be only a possibility to prove which brings one close to a vicious circle and which must, therefore, be regarded with a corresponding caution. As has been affirmed several times above, we know that the consonantal component of the word *ḫa*-BI-*ru*, which turns out to be not an Akkadian but a

[97] The singular forms of Ug. *ʿrpt* and Hebr. *ʿarābōt* cannot be determined with any certainty. On the basis of Akk. *erpetu* one would envisage a feminine 'segholate'. Accordingly the Ugaritic word could have been **ʿarpatu* (or **ʿara/iptu*?), the Hebrew one **ʿarbā* or **ʿerbā*. However, a feminine without the feminine termination could also be possible, **ʿarpu* in Ugaritic, **ʿereb* or **ʿēreb* in Hebrew. The exact classification of the sound shift *b*/*p* here must therefore remain open.

[98] *GAG* §27d; A. Herdner, *Syria* 23, 1942/43, 136; Fronzaroli, *op. cit.*, 52 §35a.

[99] A personal experiment can show that usually an intermediate sound occurs which can be treated as either a voiceless or a voiced stop.

West Semitic word,[100] is ʿ-*p*-*r*[101] and that the vowels are -*a*- and -*i*- (possibly *-*e*-). We do not, however, know the vowel quantities. With the exception of a single case from Nuzu, which is hardly of any great importance,[102] the Akkadian occurrences never give any indication of the length of the vowels in the form of so-called '*plene*-writing'; that is, there are no forms such as *ḫa-a-pí-ru*, **ḫa-pí-i-ru* or **ḫa-a-pí-i-ru*.[103] That does not automatically mean that both vowels must therefore be regarded as short; rather, we can say only that the vowel quantities cannot with any certainty be determined from the orthography.[104] It comes, therefore, as no surprise that **ʿāb/piru*[105] and **ʿapīru*[106] and **ʿapiru*[107] have all been suggested. A decision on the question would perhaps be possible if a convincing etymology for *ʿapiru* could be found, but all the suggestions proposed so far seem to me to be unsatisfactory. This is also true of the suggestion made most recently by Borger (it has been proposed before) that the word is to be connected with Semitic *ʿPR = 'dust' and to be explained as an adjective of the form **faʿīl*, whence **ʿapīru* = 'dust covered'.[108] But this meaning cannot be incorporated in any very obvious way into the semantic range which we have already established for the word. If, however, as Borger suggests, the word is in fact originally an adjective – and Akkadian usage in some cases would lend complete support to

[100] Cf. W. v. Soden in Bottéro, *op. cit.*, 157–9; B. Landsberger, *ibid.*, 160; A. Goetze, *ibid.*, 162; J. Lewy, *ibid.*, 163; Borger, *op. cit.*, 130.

[101] See above ch. I n. 4.

[102] HSS XV 62. 3 (cf. E. Cassin, *JA* 246, 1958, 229 n. 9): ^{LÚ}*ḫa-a-pí-ra-tu*$_4$ nom. pl. (*ḫa/āpirātu*). On the plural form cf. *GAG* §61n.

[103] The Hittite forms *ḫa-a-pí-ri-ya-aš HT* 6 v. 18 (cf. Bottéro, *op. cit.*, 151 §Be) and *ḫa-a-pí-ri-an* Bott. 92b, f. prove nothing at all with regard to the arbitrary use of '*scriptio plena*' by the Hittites. The isolated form ^{LÚ}*ḫa-a-pí-ra-tu*$_4$ in Nuzu (see n. 102) must be judged similarly.

[104] On the indication of long vowels in medial position by '*scriptio plena*' see *GAG* §7e.

[105] B. Landsberger, *KlF* I (1930), 328f. (**ʿābiru*); *CAD* 6/Ḫ, 84f. *s.vv. ḫāpirāja, ḫāpiru;* J. Lewy, most recently *HUCA* 28, 1957, 8f. n. 13 (**ʿābiru*); M. P. Gray, *HUCA* 29, 1958, 170–3 (**ʿābiru*).

[106] R. Borger, *ZDPV* 74, 1958, 131f.; A. Alt and S. Moscati, *RGG*³ III (1959), 105 *s.v. Hebräer* (following Borger).

[107] A. Goetze in Bottéro, *op. cit.*, 163; W. F. Albright, *BASOR* 163, 1961, 53f. and nn. 77 and 78; *The Biblical Period from Abraham to Ezra* (Harper Torchbook 102, New York and Evanston 1963), 5, 98 n. 17.

[108] Borger, *op. cit.*, 130f., with reference to R. de Langhe, *Les textes de Ras Shamra-Ugarit et leurs rapports avec le milieu biblique de l'Ancien Testament* II (Gembloux and Paris 1945), 465; É. Dhorme, *RevHist* 211, 1954, 261; with reservations also Albright, *Biblical Period* (*op. cit.*), 5.

this suggestion[109] – then one could establish, irrespective of possible etymologies, the form **ʿapiru* (type **faʿil*). This is the only one of the possible nominal forms from which one can establish a connection with Hebrew *ʿibrī*. Nominal forms of the **faʿil* type have a tendency in the Semitic languages to develop into 'segholates' of the type **faʿl* and **fiʿl*.[110] In Akkadian this is quite normal,[111] but examples can also be found in the North-west Semitic languages[112] which are primarily involved here. We would, then, have the form **ʿapr-/ʿipr-* which can be lengthened by the *nisba*-ending *-ay-*, giving the form **ʿa/ipray*. According to the rule (?) of the oscillation of the labial which we suggested above we can add the form **ʿa/ibray* as a further development in the process. But this form in Massoretic Hebrew would be *ʿibrī*. In other words, the equation *ʿapiru* = Hebrews can certainly be substantiated with linguistic proofs. That in Hebrew the word has taken on the *nisba*-ending should no longer astonish us, for that ending serves not only for the formation of gentilic forms in the narrower sense, that is of designations of belonging to a people, tribe, clan, place or country, but also for the expression of belonging to all types of concrete and abstract classes.[113] There is, moreover, an exactly parallel form in the word *ḥopšī* as the Hebrew equivalent of the Akkadian *ḫupšu*.[114]

6. It is, of course, true that purely linguistic proofs are not sufficient to set this identification free of all doubt. So long as one

[109] Cf. B. Landsberger in Bottéro, *op. cit.*, 200. The possibility must also be admitted that *ḫapirū* in expressions such as *awīlū* (/LÚ.MEŠ) *ḫapirū* (/SA.GAZ) is a substantive in apposition (cf. *GAG* §134b) to *awīlū*.

[110] On this cf. C. Brockelmann, *Grundriss* I, 73 §42d, 337 §119d n., 339 §123a, 340 §124a; R. Körbert, *Or* NS 34, 1965, 42. On the change **faʿl-/*fiʿl-* cf. also Brockelmann, *op. cit.*, 148 §52g. An example: **malik-* > Akk. *malku* 'prince', Hebr. *melek* (< **malk-*) 'king', but Old Can. *milk-* (in proper names; cf., e.g., ᴵDINGIR-*mil-ku* RS 19.70, 8 (*PRU* IV, 294) = **Ilu-milku*; ᴹᴵNIN-*mi-i[l-ki]* RS 17.35, 7 (*PRU* IV, 123) = **Aḫāt-milki*); against this Arab. *malikun* 'king'. The situation is now complicated by the fact that for Ugaritic the vocalization **malk-* has been verified by *ma-al-ku*, *Ugaritica* V 1 130 III 13′; 137 II 32′. M. Dietrich and O. Loretz, *Theologische Revue* 65, 1969, 365 also point to the personal name *bi-it-ta-ma-al-ki* Alalaḫ 94, 18 (variant: *bi-it-ta*-LUGAL *ibid.*, 12).

[111] Cf. *GAG* §§12b, 55f.

[112] Cf. Brockelmann, *op. cit.*, 337 §§119a n., 119b.

[113] G. Beer-R.Meyer, *Hebräische Grammatik* I (Sammlung Göschen 763/763a, Berlin ²1952), 110, §41, 4. Parallels to the formation *ʿibrī* in W. F. Albright, *Archaeology and the Religion of Israel* (Baltimore 1953), 205 n. IV 43.

[114] See above n. 63.

argues along purely linguistic lines the danger is ever present of succumbing to the suggestion of the similarity in sound.[115] Rather, the equation can be regarded as sufficiently proved only when parallelism with regard to content appears probable. This of course at once raises a methodological problem.[116] If, leaving the *ʿapiru* aside, we look at the occurrences of *ʿibrīm* in the Old Testament, then we can safely say that the word *ʿibrī* is another designation for 'Israelite' and is to be treated as an ethnic term.[117] If, however, we take the *ʿapiru* into consideration, then in certain places there arise points of contact or, at least, possibilities of comparison, so that behind the immediate sense of the term *ʿibrī*, which in the last resort can be attributed to editorial modifications of the tradition which have occurred in the course of its history,[118] we seem to come upon an older, more original conception which would appear to bring us closer to historical reality. The unavoidable decision between the two methods of assessment is difficult to make. For if, with the intention of reaching as objective a judgment as possible, one that is free from preconceived ideas concerning identity or difference, we take into consideration only the Old Testament material, then we are in danger of making a wrong judgment, one that has been subjectively conditioned because we have not evaluated all the possible sources at our disposal. If, however, in our investigation, we take *ʿapiru* and *ʿibrīm* together, then this pre-judgment on our part very much influences our results from the outset. In what follows, therefore, the way of compromise can be followed only to the extent that, in following the second of these two possibilities, we are constantly aware of its limitations and of the one-sidedness of our assessment.[119] Finally,

[115] Cf. B. Landsberger, *ZA* 35, 1924, 213f.; in Bottéro, *op. cit.*, 161.

[116] Cf. M. P. Gray, 'The Ḫâbirū-Hebrew Problem in the Light of the Source Material Available at Present', *HUCA* 29, 1958, 136.

[117] This of course corresponds to the usage in the post-Old Testament period; cf. H. Parzen, 'The Problem of the Ibrim ("Hebrews") in the Bible', *AJSL* 49, 1933, 256f.; M. P. Gray, *op. cit.*, 188–93.

[118] If our explanation given above is correct, then it is obvious that in the law about the *ʿebed ʿibrī* in the 'Book of the Covenant' reference is to an *ʿapiru* in a situation such as we are familiar with from the Nuzu contracts (Ex. 21.2–6) while the deuteronomic development with its phrase 'your brother, the Hebrew' (Deut. 15.12; cf. Jer. 34.14) is referring to an Israelite who has sold himself into 'slavery' (*kī yimmākēr*). In Jer. 34.9 the 'brother' who is originally referred to as a 'Hebrew' (*hāʿibrī*) is specified as Judaean (*yᵉhūdī*) (see below p. 85 and n. 123).

[119] The vulnerability of the procedure must be particularly stressed *vis-à-*

it should not be forgotten that the whole *ʿapiru*-Hebrews problem arose from a misunderstanding of the role of the former in the Amarna letters.[120]

7. The term *ʿibrī(m)* is used thirty-three times in the Hebrew Old Testament; thirty-two of these references are laid out here in a systematic way:[121]

(*a*) *Laws* (see § 8)

Book of the Covenant	Ex. 21.2
Deuteronomy (dependent on B)	Deut. 15.12 (two instances)
Reference	Jer. 34.14, cf. 34.9

(*b*) *Exodus Narratives* (see § 10)

Story of Moses' birth	J Ex. 2.6, 7 ? Ex. 1.15, 16, 19
Emergence of Moses	J Ex. 2.11, 13
Plagues	J Ex. 3.18; 5.3; 7.16; 9.1, 13; 10.3

(*c*) *Joseph Story* (see § 10)
J? Gen. 39.14, 17; 43.32
E? Gen. 40.15; 41.12

(*d*) *Philistine Wars in the Time of Samuel and Saul and the Rise of David* (see § 9)
I Sam. 4.6, 9; 13.3, 19; 14.11, 21; 29.3

(*e*) *Unclassifiable* (*Late Texts*) (see § 11)
Gen. 14.13; Jonah 1.9

In five places *ʿibrī* is found as a designation of 'Israelites' in the mouth of Egyptians (Gen. 39.14, 17; 41.12; Ex. 1.16; 2.6), in six places in the mouth of Philistines (I Sam. 4.6, 9; 13.3, 19; 14.11; 29.3). The expression is used by 'Israelites' to describe themselves *vis-à-vis* Egyptians once in the Joseph story (Gen. 40.15), eight times in the exodus narratives (Ex. 1.19; 2.7; 3.18; 5.3; 7.16; 9.1,

---

vis M. P. Gray (*op. cit.*, 183) since the authoress considers that the separate examination of the terms *ʿapiru* and *ʿibrī* is 'unscientific' and recommends as objective and as a 'full investigation of the data' the method selected by us here only with reservation.

[120] A comparison was made between the activities of the *ʿapiru* of the Amarna letters and those of Joshua in Josh. 1–12; cf. Bottéro, *op. cit.*, VI.

[121] The corrupt passage I Sam. 13.7 is excluded here (cf. BHK[3] *ad loc.*).

13; 10.3) and once by the 'prophet' Jonah in his pathetic confession to the 'heathen' sailors (1.9). In narrative contexts the word occurs mostly in the same way in which it does in direct speech (Gen. 43.32; Ex. 1.15; 2.11, 13; I Sam. 14.21). Gen. 14.13, on the other hand, is an isolated case.

8. In the legal text of the 'Book of the Covenant' in Ex. 21.2–6 there is, at first glance, nothing which positively demands that the *ʿebed ʿibrī* (21.2) should refer to an 'Israelite slave'. In support of such an assertion one cannot, of course, adduce the fact that the enslavement of Israelites by Israelites was totally prohibited by Lev. 25.35–43[122] for we do not know whether both laws were ever valid simultaneously (if at all). In addition, the deuteronomic development of this law (Deut. 15. 12ff.), which must be discussed at the same time, as well as the reference to it in Jer. 34.9, 14 show that, at least at the time of the deuteronomic reformation, the reference was, and had to be, exclusively to Israelite (or, to be more precise, Judaean)[123] slaves. The possibility cannot, therefore, be excluded that Israelites too came under this law concerning the *ʿebed ʿibrī*. That, however, still does not mean that *ʿibrī* must be understood as an ethnic term with the sense of 'Israelite'. Rather do the various clauses of the text, as has been worked out especially by J. Lewy,[124] reveal such close points of contact with the conditions of the contracts from Nuzu, which have been dealt with above, between private individuals and the *ʿapiru*-people that the

[122] Against A. Jirku, ' "Hebräische" and "israelitische" Sklaven', *OLZ* 21, 1918, 81–83; M. P. Gray, *op. cit.*, 185.

[123] I see no reason for denying to Jeremiah the prophetic word (vv. 13ff.) in the somewhat difficult pericope Jer. 34.8–22. In v. 14, in the quotation, significantly, from the deuteronomic law, the 'Hebrew' is described as the 'brother' of those being addressed – in the circumstances of the time 'Judaeans'. This is clarified correctly in v. 9 by means of the later and not very well integrated gloss *bīhūdī ʾ*^{a}*ḥīhū* on *bām* (referred to *ʾet-ʿabdō w*^{e}*- . . . ʾet-šipḥātō hāʿibrī w*^{e}*hāʿibrīyā*); after deletion of the addition one ought to have the original text which, however, in the form *l*^{e}*biltī ʿ*^{a}*bod-bām ʾīš* is as awkwardly phrased as the corresponding formula *l*^{e}*biltī ʿ*^{a}*bod-bām ʿōd* in v. 10. It should also be noted that the difficulty of the words *miqqēṣ šebaʿ šānīm* in v. 14 arises from the fact that there the introduction to the *š*^{e}*miṭṭā*-law of Deut. 15 is briefly summarized along with an epitome of the law about the *ʿebed ʿibrī*. It seems that Jeremiah connected the practice of freeing slaves with the *š*^{e}*miṭṭā*. In literary-critical terms this observation means that the prophet had in front of him Deut. 15.1–18 essentially in its present form and sequence. Cf. also A. Weiser, *Das Buch des Propheten Jeremia* (ATD 20/21, ^{4}1960), 321f.

[124] 'Ḫābirū and Hebrews', *HUCA* 14, 1939, 587–623; 'A New Parallel between Ḫâbirū and Hebrews', *HUCA* 15, 1940, 47–58 (on this however see below n. 132); cf. M. P. Gray, *op. cit.*, 182–5.

conclusion suggests itself that in both instances the same group of people are being dealt with. In the first instance, the limiting of the period of 'slavery' to six years indicates that the *'ebed 'ibrī* does not have the status of a proper slave, a slave for life (*'ebed 'ōlām*, 21.5) but has bound himself, perhaps by a contract, for this period. This, of course, presupposes that the status was entered into voluntarily. Its 'voluntary nature' becomes obvious when the short-term slave can decide at the end of his six years whether he will become a slave for life or will go free. In the Nuzu contracts the voluntary aspect was always stated explicitly since it determined the legal status of the *'apiru*.[125] There, of course, no fixed period of service was laid down,[126] but the *wardūtu* could be dissolved by the short-term slave by means of a substitute or by payment of a certain sum of money.[127] There is no difference in principle between the Mitannian and the Israelite dissolution. If the *'ebed 'ibrī* opts for his freedom on the expiry of the six-year period, he leaves his master on the same personal terms as those in which he entered his service. That he receives no wages shows that he was forced by his previous situation to engage himself in less favourable conditions than someone who could become a 'hired servant' (*śākīr*).[128] This situation becomes understandable in the light of the definition of *'apiru* existence given above[129] as a condition of outlawry which made security of life necessary at any price. What he possessed beforehand he is allowed to take away with him. This applied to his wife whom he had brought into servitude with him. A wife who had been given to him by his master[130] remained the property of the master. Here, in any case,

[125] See above p. 69.

[126] The opinion of J. Lewy, *HUCA* 14, 609f.; M. P. Gray, *op. cit.*, 184, that the Nuzu contracts also presupposed a fixed period of service whose length was generally known and is therefore not specified, is not based on the texts and has arisen only from the tendency to make the regulations in Nuzu and in Israel appear as parallel as possible.

[127] On this cf. E. Cassin in Bottéro, *op. cit.*, 66–68.

[128] Cf. Deut. 15.18 where the difference from the point of view of the master is clearly brought out: 'It shall not seem hard to you, when you let him go free from you; for at half the cost of a hired servant he has served you six years.'

[129] See above pp. 65–7.

[130] The *wardūtu*-contracts from Nuzu (e.g. JEN 610, 611) adduced by J. Lewy, *HUCA* 15, 1940, 49, 52f., 56, as parallels do not refer, according to E. Cassin in Bottéro, *op. cit.*, 68, to *'apiru*-people and are to be explained along different lines. M. P. Gray's comparison of Ex. 12.4 and Bott. 63 (*op. cit.*, 184 and n. 356) is equally uncertain.

it was a question of a woman who was a slave for life and was the master's property. If the *ʿebed ʿibrī* wanted to keep her, then he had to take on her social standing and himself become a slave for life. In this case, the equation of the terms *ʿapiru* and *ʿibrī* with regard to their content could be accepted. It is, of course, otherwise in the later development of the law in Deut. 15.12–18. Here the 'Hebrew' is described as the 'brother' of the person addressed in the legal text and is, therefore, defined as an Israelite. If he is allowed to go free, he receives, as a consequence, a certain payment, the amount of which is left to the discretion of his master (15.13f.). He too has the possibility of becoming a slave for life out of 'love' for his master. This new interpretation of the law is presupposed in Jer. 34.9f., 14. There appears here the sense of *ʿibrī* which is attested later in Jonah 1.9 and which is predominant in texts later than the Old Testament[131] and which rests on the fact that at a certain period – probably at the beginning of the first century – the word *ʿapiru* is replaced by the words *gēr* and *tōšāb*.[132] This, of course, has no bearing on Ex. 21.2–6.

9. In the narratives about the Philistine wars, the expression occurs, as a rule, in the mouths of the Philistines as a designation, with a somewhat contemptible ring, of their opponents (I Sam. 4.6, 9; 13.3, 19; 14.11). One might ask why the Philistines could not equally well have talked about 'Israelites' if they wanted to use their enemies' name. Those who regard *ʿibrī* as an ethnic term[133] are unable to offer a suitable explanation of this. Yet this element of contempt which we have just noted and which is particularly clear in 14.11 perhaps provides a clue when we remember the way in which Rib-Hadda of Byblos described the *ʿapiru* of his time, the anti-Egyptian rebels, as 'dogs'.[134] In fact, there could, in the texts from Samuel, be a reflection of the meaning established by us for the *ʿapiru* of the Amarna letters, namely 'rebels against

[131] See above n. 117.

[132] From this there follows the parallelism of the terms noted by J. Lewy, *HUCA* 28, 1957, 11f. and R. Borger, *ZDPV* 74, 1958, 128–30. The social changes which are, in the long run, reflected in this, have still to be investigated. Cf. also similarly S. Yeivin, 'The Origin and the Disappearance of the *Khab/piru*', *Trudy dvadcat' pjatogo meždunarodnogo kongressa vostokovednov Moskva 9–16 avgusta 1960* I (Moscow 1962), 439–41.

[133] Cf., e.g., A. Jirku, *Die Wanderungen der Hebräer im dritten und zweiten vorchristlichen Jahrtausend* (AO 24.2, Leipzig 1924), 7f.

[134] See above p. 72.

the lawful ruling power'.[135] If Alt[136] is right with his supposition that after the final collapse of Egyptian rule in Palestine the Philistines regarded themselves as the rightful successors of the Pharaoh, the parallelism in the linguistic usage is not surprising, since the Philistines would regard any resistance to their expansion as rebellion against their right to rule. The case of 14.21 and 29.3 is, of course, different. In 14.21 the narrator speaks of *'ibrīm* who had hitherto been with the Philistines and who had gone over to the 'Israelites' after Saul's victory at Michmash. Since, here, the 'Hebrews' are clearly differentiated from the 'Israelites', there could lie behind this usage the original designation of *'apiru* as a particular social class; we have encountered *'apiru*-people in military service often enough.[137] It is more difficult to see what is meant in the case of 29.3, for David and his men, both in the wilderness of Judah and in Ziklag, were, in the second millennium sense of the word, *'apiru*-people who earned their living as highway robbers[138] and mercenaries,[139] and perhaps the term *'ibrīm* is meant in this sense here. But they were also 'Israelites', David a runaway 'servant of Saul'[140] suspected, not without reason, of collaboration with those who were 'rebelling' against the leadership of his former master. One could, therefore, think of this meaning of *'apiru* as well.

10. More difficult to evaluate are those passages in the Old Testament which designate the 'Israelites' in Egypt, both individuals such as Joseph and the totality of the 'descendants of Jacob', as *'ibrīm*. In this connection the Egyptian references to *'pr.w*[141] are usually cited, and we must, therefore, include a brief discussion of these at this point. We encounter *'pr.w* in the already familiar role of robbers and highwaymen in the 'smaller' stele of king Sethos I

135 See above pp. 72f.

136 'Ägyptische Tempel in Palästina und die Landnahme der Philister' (1944), *Kl.Schr.* I, 229f.

137 See above p. 68 with n. 33–40, 42f. According to B. Mazar, *The Philistines and the Rise of Israel and Tyre* (The Israel Academy of Sciences and Humanities, Proceedings, 1.7, Jerusalem 1964), 10 they are in fact 'auxiliary units from the native population'.

138 See above p. 67 and n. 29.

139 See above n. 137.

140 I Sam. 29.3f., 10.

141 Cf. J. A. Wilson, 'The 'Eperu of the Egyptian Inscriptions', *AJSL* 49, 1933, 275–80; G. Posener in Bottéro, *op. cit.*, 165–75 (Bott. 181–93); W. Helck, *Die Beziehungen Ägyptens zu Vorderasien im 3. und 2. Jahrtausend v. Chr.* (ÄgA 5, 1962), 526–31.

from Beth-shan (*tell el-ḥuṣn*) in the neighbourhood of that city (Bott. 184);[142] they are the object of an Egyptian punitive expedition. In this context they need occupy us no longer. In the *novelle*-type narrative of the siege of the city of Joppa (*yāfā*) by the historically well-known general of Tuthmosis III, *Ḏḥwty*, an *ʿpr* appears in a very obscure context (Bott. 185).[143] It is generally accepted that what is meant is a potential horse-thief[144] about whom the Maryannu (*mryn*)[145] are being warned, but it seems to me to be more correct, on the basis of the restoration of the fragment *mr*[most recently proposed by Helck,[146] namely *mr*[ʾ] 'groom'[147] (instead of *mr*[*yn*]), to see in the *ʿpr* a member of the *ʿapiru* class in the position of a slave either to the Egyptian general or to the prince of Joppa. This interpretation, too, fits well into the picture obtained so far from the various roles played by the *ʿapiru* and has no connection with the 'Israelites' or 'Hebrews' in Egypt. But how did the *ʿpr.w*, who, in all the Egyptian examples, prove to be Asiatics,[148] come to Egypt? The answer is given in the 'lists of booty' of the Asiatic campaign in the ninth year of Amenophis II on two duplicate steles of the king found in *mīt rahīne* (Memphis) and *karnak* (Thebes) respectively.[149] In the

[142] Publication: A. Rowe, *The Topography and History of Beth-Shan* (PPS 1, 1930), 29f. and plates 42–45. 1; cf. B. Grdseloff, *Une stèle scythopolitaine du roi Séthos Ier* (Études égyptiennes 2, Cairo, 1949); W. F. Albright, 'The Smaller Beth-Shan Stele of Sethos I', *BASOR* 125, 1952, 24–31; E. Edel in K. Galling, *Textbuch zur Geschichte Israels* (Tübingen 1950), 30 no. 14B. The reading of the place of residence of the *ʿpr.w* is partly uncertain, but *yr*[*dn*] (or rather with Grdseloff and Albright: *yr*[*mt*]) seems to me to be scarcely possible.

[143] Pap. Harris 500, v°. x + 1. 4f. (A. H. Gardiner, *Late Egyptian Stories*, Bibliotheca Aegyptiaca 1, Brussels 1932, 82: 6f.).

[144] Grdseloff, *op. cit.*, 25f.: 'sinon un *ʿpr* passera [près d'eux (*scil.* the horses) et] les [volera]'; cf. also the translation of Posener in Bottéro, *op. cit.*, 168 (Bott. 185); Helck, *op. cit.*, 526.

[145] Since H. Winckler, *OLZ* 13, 1910, 291, this is almost generally explained as a Hurrianized 'Aryan' word (cf. Sanskrit *márya-*); cf., e.g., W. F. Albright, 'Mitannian maryannu, "chariot warrior", and the Canaanite and Egyptian Equivalents', *AfO* 6, 1930/31, 217–21. Against this already A. Gustavs, *ZA* 36, 1925, 301f., and now, especially, A. Kammenhuber, *Die Arier im Vorderen Orient* (Heidelberg 1968), 220–23.

[146] *Op. cit.*, 523.

[147] On *m*( )*-rú-ʾù* (*mrʾ*) 'groom' cf. A. Alt, *ZAW* 58, 1940/1, 279; Helck, *op. cit.*, 560 n. 95.

[148] Cf. G. Posener in Bottéro, *op. cit.*, 175.

[149] On the stele from *karnak* see E. Edel, 'Die Stelen Amenophis' II aus Karnak und Memphis mit dem Bericht über die asiatischen Feldzüge des Königs', *ZDPV* 69, 1953, 98–113, where the earlier copies and discussions

Memphis version of the text, between '127 princes of *rṯnw*; 179 brothers of princes' and '15200 Bedouin (*šȝs.w*); 36300 Asiatics (*ḫȝr.w*); 15070 Nuḫašše(*ngs*)-people', there are mentioned, as prisoners of war, 3600 *ʿpr* (Bott. 183).[150] *ʿpr.w* as prisoners of war probably occur also in the *novelle*-like narrative of a campaign of Tuthmosis III in Asia which is found in Pap. Turin 1941, x+1.9 (Bott. 186), but the context is much too fragmentary for any very precise statements to be made on this basis. In this way, too, the *ʿpr.w* directly attested for Egypt in other places must have arrived in the land of the Nile where they were employed as agricultural labourers (Bott. 181, 182),[151] as members of an expedition of Rameses IV to the *wādī ḥammāmāt*, as quarry workers (and/) or soldiers (Bott. 190) and on building work of Rameses III (Bott. 187, 188). The *ʿpr.w* assigned by Rameses III to the temple of Atum at Heliopolis (the mention of them along with 'princes' and Maryannu would suggest that here too we are dealing with

are listed; restored text *ibid.,* plate 7. The stele from *mīt rahīne* is published in A. M. Badawy, 'Die neue historische Stele Amenophis' II', *ASAE* 42, 1943, 1–23; copy *ibid.,* plate 1; photographs in Edel, *op. cit.*, plates 3–5. A synoptic transcription and translation of both steles in Edel, *op. cit.*, 113–36.

[150] On the character of the lists of booty on both steles see Edel, *op. cit.*, 167–73. It is clear that the list of booty discussed here and belonging to the campaign of year 9 on the stele of *mīt rahīne* (lines 29–32; Edel, *op. cit.*, 123, 124, 135f.) does not belong to the campaign to which it is ascribed. Amenophis II did not go further than Galilee in his ninth year; the mention of people from Nuḫašše as prisoners from this limited campaign would therefore be very surprising. Moreover, we do not, of course, know how this list is to be classified historically. The large numbers of persons which exceed the figures of contingents of prisoners brought to Egypt at other times are explained by J. J. Janssen, 'Eine Beuteliste von Amenophis II. und das Problem der Sklaverei im alten Ägypten', *JEOL* 17, 1963 (1964), 141–7, by accepting that this is a census list, used secondarily, of Asiatic territories ruled by Egypt. But it seems to me that the figures are again too low for this. If we leave open the question as to when and in what circumstances these prisoners came into Pharaoh's hands, one could accept that they were, at least in part, requisitioned in Syria-Palestine itself for work on the royal domains (on this cf. Helck, *op. cit.*, 261f.) while only a small 'élite' were deported to Egypt.

[151] T. Säve-Söderbergh, 'The *ʿprw* as Vintagers in Egypt', *Orientalia Suecana* 1, 1952, 5–14. The reservations raised by G. Posener in Bottéro, *op. cit.*, 166f., especially on the basis of the writing of the word *ʿpr.w* with the sign *ʿpr* (Aa 20 in A. H. Gardiner, *Egyptian Grammar,* London ³1957, 542) in tomb 39, against the citing of the Theban tomb inscriptions (cf. similarly also Helck, *op. cit.*, 527) are not convincing, for we are sufficiently familiar with 'frivolous' ways in which the Egyptians wrote Asiatic foreign words which have a connection with Egyptian words of related or even very remote meaning. In this case the puzzle anyhow is fairly obvious. Cf. similarly Säve-Söderbergh, *op. cit.*, 6f. and n.4.

prisoners of war) were probably utilized for similar tasks (Bott. 189). From these passages it is clear that the *ʿpr.w* represent a group of men who have been brought by the Egyptians from Asia and have been called by their native Asiatic, i.e. North-west Semitic, designation. The class of *ʿapiru* is fundamentally foreign to the Egyptian social organization. If, therefore, one regards the Old Testament *ʿibrīm* who live in Egypt as *ʿapiru* and considers that the description in this sense is completely authentic, then one must accept that the 'Israelites' described in this way already belonged to the *ʿapiru* in their own land and have arrived in Egypt, in 'the house of bondage',[152] as the Pharaoh's prisoners of war or at any rate by means of force. This contradicts the narrative of the voluntary migration of Jacob and his sons to Egypt as this exists within the framework of the Joseph story (Gen. 46; 47.1–12), a narrative which describes the migrants as breeders of small cattle and 'semi-nomads'.[153] Even if one accepts that the present form of the Joseph story (which can scarcely be utilized as the historical event immediately preceding Ex. 1ff. and which is, in any case, of late date)[154] has suppressed older and perhaps deviant traditions about the immigration (?) of 'Israelites' into Egypt, one cannot positively assume that these lost traditions had presented the ancestors of the exodus generation as prisoners of war. This is in fact contradicted by the older formulations of the elements of tradition concerning the descent of the Jacob family to Egypt,[155] and the texts in Ex. 1ff. clearly show the aversion felt

[152] Cf. Ex. 20.2; Deut. 5.6. [153] Cf. Gen. 46.32–34; 47.3–6.

[154] On this cf. from the traditio-historical aspect M. Noth, *Überlieferungsgeschichte des Pentateuch* (Darmstadt ²1960), 226–32 and, from the aspect of history of subject-matter and of philology, J. Vergote, *Joseph en Égypte: Genèse chap. 37–50 à la lumière des études égyptologiques récentes* (Orientalia et Biblica Lovaniensia 3, Louvain 1959), 203–13 (at least for the 'editorial modernization' of the narrative; the hypothesis of the Mosaic origin of the original need not be discussed here); D. B. Redford, *VT* 15, 1965, 532 and n. 3 (see also below n. 162). One can – even against the most recent excellent treatment of the theme by L. Ruppert, *Die Josepherzählung der Genesis: Ein Beitrag zur Theologie der Pentateuchquellen* (StANT 11, 1965), 23f. and 29ff. *passim* – justifiably still ask the question whether the Joseph-*novelle* ever belonged within the context of the 'Pentateuchal sources' J and E or JE and whether it is not rather an originally independent even if stratified composition.

[155] Cf. G. v. Rad, 'Das formgeschichtliche Problem des Hexateuch' (1938), *Gesammelte Studien zum Alten Testament* (ThB 8, 1958), 11ff. (ET 'The Form-Critical Problem of the Hexateuch', *The Problem of the Hexateuch and Other Essays,* Edinburgh and London 1966, pp. 3ff.); Noth, *op. cit.*, 227.

by the 'semi-nomads' towards the forced labour[156] to which they had been compelled by the Egyptians and which they regarded as 'slavery'. One may always suppose that from the Egyptian point of view the distinction between labouring 'semi-nomads' (who, earlier, had always been referred to as *šꜣś.w*) and *ʿpr.w* as state or temple slaves had become blurred; but these are *ad hoc* speculations completely without significance for the historical appraisal of our material. The fact that, according to the Old Testament, the work done by the 'Hebrews' in Egypt coincides, in part, with that of the *ʿpr.w*[157] is no proof of the identity of the two groups; identical operations are also carried on by other peoples in cases where there is not the slightest question of identification with the *ʿapiru*/Hebrews. Consequently, even the two passages in letters from the time of Rameses III,[158] which are frequently compared with Ex. 1.11 (where we should note that it is 'Israelites' who are mentioned), can prove nothing. In this connection, too, explicit denial must be made of any connection[159] between the *'elōhē hāʿibrīm*, at whose command Moses appears before the Pharaoh in the plague narratives (Ex. 3.18; 5.3; 7.16; 9.1, 13; 10.3J) and the 'gods of the *ʿapiru*' of the Hittite treaties. On the basis of the explanation which we have given above of the expression *ilāni (ša) ḫapirī*,[160] such a connection is impossible, the more so since what is certainly meant by the 'God of the Hebrews' is *YHWH 'elōhē yiśrā'ēl*[161] and since the term *ʿibrīm* is used here in accordance with Yahwistic usage in the rest of these narratives. The same is surely true of the description of Joseph as an *ʿibrī* 'stolen' (Gen. 40.15) from the 'land of the Hebrews' (*'ereṣ hāʿibrīm*), a description which says nothing about his social status as *ʿebed* (39.17, 19; 41.12) but which, in accordance with later usage, apparently represents a pure ethnic form. This is quite unobjectionable if in the Joseph story we have

[156] See also below p.121 and ch. III 2 n.82 on *ARM* III, 38.19–22.

[157] Cf. M. P. Gray, *HUCA* 29, 1958, 177–80.

[158] Sample letter (school text): Pap. Leiden 348, v°. 6.6; E. Edel in K. Galling, *Textbuch zur Geschichte Israels* (Tübingen 1950), 30 no. 14D; Bott. 187. Identical formulation in Pap. Leiden 349 b 7; Bott. 188, which is a genuine letter in the view of J. Černý as reported by Posener on Bott. 188.

[159] Gray, *op. cit.*, 152f., 178. On Jirku's views see the literature cited in n.53 above.

[160] See above p.70 and n.53.

[161] Cf. the formulation *YHWH 'elōhē hāʿibrīm* in all the relevant passages except Ex. 5.3 and the contrast between Ex. 3.15 (directed at 'Israelites') and 3.18 (directed at Pharaoh).

to do, as we have supposed above, with a unit of a relatively late date and originally independent of the 'Pentateuchal sources' J and E.[162] We can sum up by stating that we can indicate no definitely convincing reason for the description of the 'Israelites' in Egypt as 'Hebrews' in certain parts of the Joseph story and of the exodus narratives. It may be, however, that the Yahwist already regarded the expression as an archaic ethnic term for his people.[163]

11. The last reference to *ʿibrī* which will be discussed here is Gen. 14.13. It cannot be the aim of this examination to discuss *in extenso* Gen. 14,[164] a chapter which has been much discussed and

[162] Cf. above p. 91 and n. 154.

On the expression *'ereṣ hāʿibrīm* cf. most recently D. B. Redford, 'The "Land of the Hebrews" in Gen. xl 15', *VT* 15, 1965, 529–32, who believes that he has found a corresponding Egyptian expression in the demotic papyrus D 6278–89 + 6698 + 10111 in the papyrus collection of the Austrian national library in Vienna (R. A. Parker, *A Vienna Demotic Papyrus on Eclipse- and Lunar-Omina*, Brown Egyptological Studies 2, Providence 1959). In text A of this papyrus which comes from the Roman period but which, according to Parker, goes back to an original probably from the Persian period, specific months, hours and sections of the sky are drawn up for, besides *kmy* = Egypt, the four countries *išwr* (*pꜣ tꜣ/tš pꜣ išwr* IIIb; IV 28 as well as *išwr* III 6 and *pꜣ tš išwr* IV 15) = Asshur = Mesopotamia, *ʿybr* (III 5, II 22 probably needs to be supplemented thus; variants: *ʿbr* II 27; *y[b]r* IV 9) = Hebr. *ʿēber* = Palestine, *pꜣ ʿymr* (II 30; IV 9, 17) = Amurru (ʿ instead of i is unobjectionable in demotic orthogrpahy) = Syria and *grṯy* (II 29, 30; III 3; pꜣ *grṯy* IV 29; *nꜣ grṯy* II 26) = Crete (cf. Parker, *op. cit.*, 6f.). According to Redford, the name *ʿybr* corresponds to the Hebrew expression *'ereṣ hāʿibrīm* Gen. 40.15 and is an indication of the late composition of the Joseph-*novelle*. If, in the interests of a more exact analogy, one were to read rather in the demotic text **pꜣ tꜣ/tš pꜣ/nꜣ ʿybr* or the like, then Redford's argument is completely tenable – but not his dating of the original form of the papyrus in the Saite period (*op. cit.*, 531) which cannot simply be deduced from the occurrence of the expressions *pꜣ nsw* 'the king' or *pꜣ nsw kmy* 'the king of Egypt' since these could be the transposing into Egyptian of the Akk. *šarru* (or LUGAL) from a possible Babylonian original – and would be additional support for our interpretation of *ʿibrī(m)* in the Joseph-*novelle*. The identification proposed by R. J. Williams, *JNES* 25, 1966, 69 n. 1, of *ʿybr* with Akk. *eber* (*nāri*) cannot be excluded but is not very likely since *ʿybr* would then be in too close a geographical proximity to *ʿymr*.

[163] It is questionable whether the Yahwist could still have understood the class term *ʿibrī/ʿapiru*, which he must have found to hand, in a sociological sense. See also above p. 87 and n. 132 on *gēr*.

[164] From the enormous literature I select what is not exclusively concerned with the so-called 'Melchizedek episode': W. F. Albright, 'A Revision of Early Hebrew Chronology', *JPOS* 1, 1921, 68–79; 'Shinar-Šanḡar and its Monarch Amraphel', *AJSL* 40, 1923, 125–33; 'The Jordan Valley in the Bronze Age', *AASOR* 6, 1926, 62–66; 'The Historical Background of Gen. XIV', *JSOR* 10, 1926, 231–69; 'A Third Revision of the Early Chronology of Western Asia', *BASOR* 88, 1942, 33–36; 'Abram the Hebrew: A New

debated and which still remains enigmatic. A few remarks are, however, necessary since for Albright,[165] for example, this chapter is central to his discussion both of the 'patriarch' Abraham and of the *'apiru*-people of the second millennium. It is well known that Gen. 14 cannot be attributed to any of the sources of the 'Pentateuch'. It stands like an outcrop of rock in the middle of the Abraham narratives with which it has, of course, certain features in common, but, on the whole, it depicts the 'patriarch' differently from the main line of the traditions. Opinions concerning the character and age of the chapter are, therefore, understandably varied. According to Eissfeldt,[166] it presupposes 'the already complete compilation L+J+E+B+D+H+P' since it is not only dependent on the 'L' narrative of Lot and Abraham (Gen. 12.6–8 +

Archaeological Interpretation', *BASOR* 163, 1961, 36–54; H. Asmussen, 'Genesis 14, ein politisches Flugblatt', *ZAW* 34, 1914, 36–41; I. Benzinger, 'Zur Quellenscheidung in Gen. 14', *Vom Alten Testament: Karl Marti zum 70. Geburtstage gewidmet* (BZAW 41, 1925), 21–27; F. M. Th. (de Liagre) Böhl, 'Die Könige von Genesis 14', *ZAW* 36, 1916, 65–73; 'Tud'alia I, Zeitgenosse Abrahams, um 1650 v.Chr.', *ZAW* 42, 1924, 148–53; 'Das Zeitalter Abrahams' (1930; [2]1931), *Opera Minora* (Groningen and Djakarta 1953), 43–48; 'King Ḫammurabi of Babylon in the Setting of his Time' (1946), *Opera Minora* (1953), 353f.; *RGG*[3] I (1957), 332f. *s.v.* Amraphel; E. Burrows, 'Notes on Hurrian', *JRAS* 1925, 283f.; F. Cornelius, 'Genesis XIV', *ZAW* 72, 1960, 1–7; C. H. Cornill, 'Genesis 14', *ZAW* 34, 1914, 150f.; A. Deimel, 'Amraphel, Rex Senaar . . . Thadal, Rex Gentium', *Bibl* 8, 1927, 350–57; É.Dhorme, 'Ḫammourabi-Amraphel', *RB* NS 5, 1908, 205–26; 'Abraham dans le cadre de l'histoire', *RB* 37, 1928, 367–85, 481–511; 40, 1931, 364–74, 503–18; J. C. L. Gibson, *JSS* 9, 1964, 362f. and n.10; N. Glueck, *The Other Side of the Jordan* (New Haven 1940), 114; F. Hommel, 'Zu Gen. 14 und insbesondere zu Arioch von Ellasar', *BZ* 15, 1920, 213–18; K. Jaritz, 'Wer ist Amrafel in Gen. 14?', *ZAW* 70, 1958, 255f.; P. Jensen, 'Genesis 14 und ein Ausschnitt aus den Res gestae des Aššur-bān-apli', *ZA* 42, 1934, 232–5; A. Jirku, 'Neues keilinschriftliches Material zum Alten Testament', *ZAW* 39, 1921, 152–6; 'Zum historischen Stil von Gen. 14', *ibid.*, 313f.; J. H. Kroeze, *Genesis Veertien. Een exegetisch-historische studie* (Hilversum 1937); J. Meinhold, *1. Mose 14* (BZAW 22, 1911); M. Noth, 'Arioch-Arriwuk', *VT* 1, 1951, 136–40; A. Parrot, *Abraham et son temps* (Cahiers d'Archéologie Biblique 14, Neuchâtel 1962), 76–86; W. T. Pilter, 'The Amorite Personal Names in Genesis 14', *PSBA* 35, 1913, 205–26; 36, 1914, 125–42; N. A. van Uchelen, *Abraham de Hebreeër. Een literair- en historisch-kritische studie naar aanleiding van Genesis 14:13* (Studia Semitica Neerlandica 5, Assen 1964); R. de Vaux, 'Les patriarches hébreux et les découvertes modernes', *RB* 55, 1948, 326–37; S. Yeivin, *Beʾēr-ševaʿ ʿīr hāʾāvōt* (*Meḥqārīm bᵉ-tōlᵉdōt yiśrāʾēl wᵉ-ʾarṣō*, Tel-Aviv 1959), 56–58.

165 *BASOR* 163, 1961, 49–54.

166 *Einleitung in das Alte Testament* (Tübingen [2]1956), 251f.; (Tübingen [3]1964), 280f. (ET *The Old Testament: An Introduction*, Oxford 1965, 211f.).

13.2, 5, 7–11a, 12bb–18) and of Sodom (Gen. 18f.) but also has all manner of linguistic peculiarities in common with P; on these grounds it is, therefore, a very late and certainly post-exilic section into which have been worked 'some information about warlike events in the remote past and perhaps a tradition concerning the pre-Israelite priesthood of Jerusalem'. According to Albright the contents of the section are very old, and the text is, in addition, 'strewn with indications of a very archaic verse tradition underlying its transmitted prose form';[167] he would like to date the events in the nineteenth century BC or a little later,[168] even if our knowledge does not (yet) extend to a more exact historical classification. Now, it cannot be doubted that the names of the protagonists have a Middle and Late Bronze Age colouring. It has often been pointed out that *tidʿal melek gōyīm* has the name of the Hittite king *Tudḫaliya*.[169] The name of Arioch (*'aryōk*) of Ellasar is encountered in the form *ar-ri-yú-uk* in the Mari texts (ARM II 63.3; 64.3)[170] and in Nuzu as ^{I}*a-ri-ú-uk-ki*.[171] Chedorlaomer (*kᵉdorlāʿōmer*) is a

[167] *Op. cit.*, 49. [168] *Op. cit.*, 49f.

[169] Recognized by A. H. Sayce, *ExpT* 19, 1908, 283; *OLZ* 13, 1910, 489–91; cf. F. M. Th. Böhl, *ZAW* 36, 1916, 68f.; 42, 1924, 148–53. In the Ugaritic alphabetic script the name appears as *tṯġl*, *PRU* II 69. 4; the word *tdġl*, *PRU* II 34. 9; 39. 21, hitherto associated with *tṯġl* as a variant, whose written form would correspond better to Hebr. *tdʿl*, has been recognized correctly by M. Dietrich and O. Loretz, *WO* 3.3, 1966, 201, as a vocational description of Hurrian origin (unexplained, with formative element *-uḫli*/*ḫuli-*, perhaps in Nuzu as ^{LÚ}*ti*! (ḪI)-*du-uḫ-l*[*i*] *RA* 56, 1962, 77 line 21). The correspondence Hitt-Hurr. *ḫ*: Ug. *ġ*: Hebr. ʿ is regular.

What *melek gōyīm* means I do not know. The association of the expression by F. Cornelius, *ZAW* 72, 1960, 3f., with Thieme's disputed interpretation of the 'Aryans' as the 'foreigners' (P. Thieme, *Der Fremdling im Rgveda*, AKM 23.2, 1938), and with the *ḥqꜣ.w ḫꜣś.wt* ('Hyksos'), along with the historical consequences deduced from this, is unfounded. The association with the *ummān manda* (A. H. Sayce, *JTVI* 29, 1897, 90) is old and rests primarily on the supposed correspondence in meaning of *ummānu* 'army, troop, people' and *gōyīm*.

[170] *Ar-ri*-PI-*uk* is probably to be read thus and not as *ar-ri-wu-uk*; only in this way can the Hebrew form be easily explained. The equation first of all in F. M. Th. Böhl, *JEOL* 2, 1945, 66; cf. R. de Vaux, *RB* 55, 1948, 333; Ch. F. Jean, *Studia Mariana* (DMOA 4, 1950), 98; H. Schmökel, *ThLZ* 75, 1950, 689; M. Noth, *VT* 1, 1951, 136–40; F. Cornelius, *ZAW* 72, 1960, 2. The old equation with a hypothetical name *^{I}ÈRI-*aku* (after ^{I}ÈRI-^{D}É-*a-ku* of the 'Spartoli texts') (cf. E. Schrader, *SAB* 1894, 279ff.) was already dismissed by F. M. Th. Böhl, *ZAW* 36, 1916, 67 and n. 4; his interpretation of the name at that time as **āryaka*-'Aryan, worthy of an Aryan' (*op. cit.*, 70 n. 1) was from the very beginning scarcely probable.

[171] I. J. Gelb, P. M. Purves and A. A. MacRae, *Nuzi Personal Names* (OIP 57, 1943), 30ᵃ.

good Elamite name (**Kuder-Lagamar*)[172] which suits a 'king of Elam', even if it has not hitherto been attested as the name either of a king or of a private individual. Finally, the name Amraphel (*'amrāpel*; G *Αμαρφαλ*), borne by the 'king of Shinar',[173] has a completely Mesopotamian ring, but cannot be connected with the name of the great Hammurapi[174] or with that of

[172] This identification is old and surely also correct; cf., e.g., P. Dhorme, *RB* NS 5, 1908, 209f.; F. M. Th. Böhl, *ZAW* 36, 1916, 67; *Opera Minora* (Groningen and Djakarta 1953), 46f. and 478 n. 39; W. Hinz, *Das Reich Elam* (UB 82, 1964), 9. The element *kdr-* corresponds to Elam. *kud.e.r* 'protector he/protectress she' (written *ku-te-er, ku-ti-ir, ku-ter*) in proper names such as ^{I}*kuder-*^{D}*humban*, ^{I}*kuder-*^{D}*nahhunde EKI*, 199. Since G has *Χοδολλογομορ* (variant *Χοδολλαγομορ*) it may be assumed that Hebr. *k*^{e}*dor-* goes back to **kodor-* and the latter to **kudur-*, with which may be compared Assyrian forms of the name Kuder-Nahhunde: ^{I}NÌ.KU(*kudur*)-^{D}*na-ḫu-un-du* Sennacherib V 1, 12 (*BAL*, 75); ^{I}*ku-dúr-na-an-ḫu-un-di* Assurbanipal Ann. 5 vs. 12. Both the Elamite and the Assyrian forms are surely attempts to reproduce what was pronounced as /**kudər*/ or /**kudr*/ (W. Hinz orally). In the case of the name of the goddess Lagamar (^{D}*la-ga*$_5$*-ma-ar*) one would have to establish the pronunciation /**lağamar*/ with dull a-vowels in order to arrive at the Hebr. *lāʿōmer* (theoretically *lāʿōmer* could be traced back to **laġumr*). Another possibility would be to derive *lāʿōmer* from the name of the god Nahhunde. In this case **lāʿōmed*$^{!}$ (error *d*/*r*) would have to be read and it would have to be assumed that initial *n* had become *l*-, that Hebr. -ʿ- went back to -**ġ*- standing for Elam. *-hh-* and that the nasal *-n-* had become *-m-* before *-d*. The vowels of the Hebrew form agree perfectly with the Elamite ones (*-e-* a parasitic vowel) and one acquires, in addition, the name of a king that is frequently attested (O. Rössler orally). This at first sight illuminating hypothesis, to which I refer with the friendly permission of Prof. Rössler, nevertheless has against it insuperable difficulties of the phonetic law: the shift *n*/*l*, as opposed to the shift *r*/*l* – cf. ^{D}*ruhurater EKI* 6h, 4; 7 IIb. 2, 3, 4; 11 C. 4, 5; 86.14, 16; VAB I, 180: 3,9 (in the proper name *tan-*^{D}*r.*) with ^{D}*luhurater* in the proper name ^{I}*kuk-*^{D}*l.* DP XXIII 318 vs. 5, 7 and ^{D}*lahuratel CT* XXV 11, 37; Šurpu II 162 or ^{D}*lagamar EKI* 34.6; 48.199; 69.28, 29 with ^{D}*lagamal EKI* 30.3 and R. Labat, *CILUP* 10, 1950/51, 28 §5 – is not attested in Elamite and the *ḫ* of the Elamite cuneiform texts (such as in Assyrian attempts at writing Elamite words and names) does not transcribe a velar spirant but rather a weak pharyngal spirant comparable to our *h* (cf. Labat, *op. cit.*, 28 §3) which cannot therefore be reproduced by Sem. **ġ* > Hebr. ʿ.

[173] *Šinʿār* is usually identified with *šanḫar*(*a*). On this cf. W. F. Albright, 'Shinar-Šanğar and its Monarch Amraphel', *AJSL* 40, 1923/24, 125–33.

[174] The equation already in E. Schrader, *SAB* 1887, 600f.; cf. Dhorme, *op. cit.*, 205–26; W. T. Pilter, *PSBA* 35, 1913, 171–86, 244f. It is, however, phonetically impossible since we would expect a Hebrew form corresponding to Ugaritic *ʿmrpi* (Ch. Virolleaud, *JA* 243, 1955, 133f.). The more recent attempt by Cornelius, *ZAW* 72, 1960, 2 and n. 4, to support the equation on grounds of historical 'probability' is linguistically and factually untenable. For to call the deified Ḫammurapi **ʿammu-rāpi'-'il*(*u*) (= *'amrāpel*!) would be odd, nor can it be supported by Babylonian proper names whose theophorous element is the name of a ruler – e.g. ^{D}*bur-*^{D}SUEN-*ì-lí* BIN VII 59.11; 60.12, 17;

Amud-pî-el[175] of Qatna or even with the country of Jamudbal/Emudbal.[176] Even the names of the Palestinian opponents of the coalition are, as Albright[177] has shown, to be attributed, from the point of view of their type, to the second millennium and, in spite of apparent textual corruption (or deliberate alteration?), can be associated with the group of so-called 'Amorite' names.[178] Is, then, the mention of 'Abraham the Hebrew' to be looked at in the light of the archaic use of names in this narrative? Albright answers this question in a positive way and sees, therefore, in Abraham an

---

215 (seal); ᴰ*ri-im-*ᴰSUEN-*ì-li* YOS VIII 118.16; *ḫa-am-mu-ra-pi-ì-li* J. J. Stamm, *Die akkadische Namengebung* (MVAeG 44, 1939), 372. Against the equation also Böhl, *ZAW* 36, 66f.; *Opera Minora,* 354.

175 Böhl, *Opera Minora,* 353f.; on the contrary *ibid.*, 478 n.34; cf. K. Jaritz, *ZAW* 70, 1958, 255f. Other proposals by Böhl, which admittedly are not very illuminating, can be found in *ZAW* 36, 69 and n.5; *Opera Minora,* 45.

176 W. F. Albright, *BASOR* 163, 1961, 49. I would prefer to think of an Akkadian or 'Amorite' proper name whose first part cannot in the meantime be exactly determined; *-pel* could be *-pī-el.* Along the same lines cf. van Uchelen, *op. cit.*, 62. A 'purely linguistic' connection (if one can have such a thing) with the name *amud-pî-el* would be possible if one conjectured *'md'pl* in Gen. 14 (cf. Albright, *op. cit.*, 49f., n.67).

177 *Op. cit.*, 52.

178 I use this description in a somewhat conventional manner without being able to provide a convincing justification for it. One can, however, cite in its favour the fact that many bearers of such names are actually introduced by the description MAR.TU = *amurrûm*; cf. I. J. Gelb, *La lingua degli Amoriti* (Accademia Nazionale dei Lincei, rendiconti, VIII 13, Rome 1958), 145. I believe, however, that it is entirely possible that it will turn out that Th. Bauer, following B. Landsberger, was on the right road with his description 'east Canaanites'; cf. Th. Bauer, *Die Ostkanaanäer: Eine philologisch-historische Untersuchung über die Wanderschicht der sogenannten 'Amoriter' in Babylonien* (Leipzig 1926); 'Eine Überprüfung der "Amoriter"-Frage', *ZA* 38, 1929, 153–60. The description 'Canaanites' in D. O. Edzard, *Die 'zweite Zwischenzeit' Babyloniens* (Wiesbaden 1957), 30 n.127 and *passim,* is too general; W. v. Soden, *WO* 3.3, 1966, 178 n.1, now says 'early Canaanites'. One must always keep in mind the fact that both 'Amorite' and '(east-/early-) Canaanite' as descriptions of languages are artificial creations (analogous to 'Semitic'). The classification proposed by M. Noth, *Die israelitischen Personennamen im Rahmen der gemeinsemitischen Namengebung* (BWANT III 10, 1928), 44–55; 'Zum Problem der "Ostkanaanäer"', *ZA* 39, 1930, 221f.; 'Mari und Israel, eine Personennamenstudie', *Geschichte und Altes Testament* (BHTh 16, 1953), 152; *Die Ursprünge des alten Israel im Lichte neuer Quellen* (Arbeitsgemeinschaft für Forschung des Landes Nordrhein-Westfalen, Geisteswissenschaften, 94, Cologne and Opladen 1961), 29–33, 'proto-Aramaic' is incorrect and should be avoided since it does not correspond to the linguistic character of the names and does not even fit the appellatives cited by Noth from the Mari texts; on this cf. aptly D. O. Edzard, 'Mari und Aramäer?', *ZA* 56, 1964, 142–9.

ʿapiru of the nineteenth century BC, a 'caravaneer' who carried on the trade of donkey caravaneering which flourished at that time.[179] Even apart from doubts as to this interpretation of the term *ʿapiru*, one must, of course, question whether the archaic traits of Gen. 14 which seem to indicate the Middle and Late Bronze Age really rest on authentic historical tradition. They could equally well be attributed to intentional archaizing in a late text[180] which has thus acquired the appearance of great antiquity. Eissfeldt[181] has already pointed out that the narrative betrays a certain affinity with the book of Judith or, to be more precise, with the historical exposition in Judith 1.1–16. There we find, in a literary work of the second century BC,[182] in the attempt to describe a fictitious event in the period of the restoration of the cult of the Jerusalem temple, that is in the late sixth century, that the protagonists are provided with very ancient names but are set in a framework abounding in historical incongruities. Thus 'Nebuchadnezzar',[183] 'who ruled

[179] *Op. cit.*, 40–54. My criticism of Albright's interpretation of the term *ʿapiru* is not directed against his reconstruction of caravaneering in the second millennium (*op. cit.*, 40–43) for which the researches of H. Lewy, 'The Assload, the Sack and Other Measures of Capacity', *RSO* 39, 1964, 181–97, may well prove fruitful.

[180] In this context there should be recalled the so-called 'cruciform monument of Maništušu' (*CT* XXXII 1–4) which purports to be an inscription of king Maništušu, son of Sargon I, but which, according to I. J. Gelb, 'The Date of the Cruciform Monument of Maništušu', *JNES* 8, 1949, 346–8; *Old Akkadian Writing and Grammar* (MAD 2, 1952), 11, is a forgery of the Old Babylonian period in favour of the É.BABBAR temple of Sippar, and, according to E. Sollberger, *JEOL* 7.20, 1967/68, 50–70, even comes from the neo-Babylonian period.

[181] *Einleitung in das Alte Testament* (Tübingen ²1956), 726; (*ibid.* ³1964), 795; ET *The Old Testament: An Introduction* (Oxford 1965), 586.

[182] This is the usual position. J. M. Grintz, *Sēfer yᵉhūdīt: Taḥzoret ha-nosaḥ ha-mᵉqōrī bᵉ-ṣērūf māvō', pērūšīm ū-maftēḥōt* (Jerusalem 1957), 15–17 would rather date the book in the later part of the Achaemenian period (Artaxerxes II, fourth century). The geographical horizon of the book may well be late Achaemenian (see below n. 186), but this does not mean that it was necessarily also written in that period.

[183] After what has been said above, it is pointless to inquire after the identity of this 'Nebuchadnezzar'. Even the revival of the hypothesis that he is the Armenian Araḫa, son of Haldita, who in the confusion at the accession of Darius I after the failure of Nidintu-Bēl ('Nebuchadnezzar III') set himself up as Babylonian king with the name 'Nebuchadnezzar (IV) son of Nabonidus' (G. Brunner, *Der Nabuchodonosor des Buches Judith: Beitrag zur Geschichte Israels nach dem Exil und des ersten Regierungsjahres Darius' I.*, Berlin ²1959) by C. Schedl, 'Nabuchodonosor, Arpakšad und Darius: Untersuchungen zum Buch Judith', *ZDMG* 115, 1965, 242–54, must be regarded as a failure. For this 'Nebuchadnezzar IV' was, in spite of all the efforts of Brunner and Schedl,

over the Assyrians in the great city of Nineveh' (Judith 1.1) fights against 'Arphaxad' (*Αρφαξαδ*) 'who ruled over the Medes in Ecbatana' (*ibid.*). The alleged king of the Medes is also encountered in the biblical tables of nations under the name *'arpakšad* (G. *Αρφαξαδ*)[184] probably as a Mesopotamian people or city (Gen. 10.22, 24; 11.10–13; I Chron. 1.17f., 24). A similar case is that of the field of battle where the two 'kings' fight. The region of Ragau (*Ραγαυ*), where the 'great plain' lies (Judith 1.5) and where 'Arphaxad' is eventually killed by 'Nebuchadnezzar' (1.15), is perhaps a distant reflection of the name of one of the Median capitals, *Ragā* (*Ραγαι* or *Ραγοι*),[185] but is more probably to be connected with the *reʿū* (G *Ραγαυ*) of the Priestly table of nations in Gen. 11.18–21 (I Chron. 1.25). The tables of nations could also be used in order to explain the curious pseudo-geography of the book.[186] In view of all this, it is not very surprising if, in Judith 1.6, there appears

---

an ephemeral figure who did not have the power to make a military attack against the Iranian uplands or Palestine. Since he was able to survive for only four months, only his first year is recorded in the sources: A. Goetze, 'Additions to Parker and Dubberstein's Babylonian Chronology', *JNES* 3, 1944, 45; R. A. Parker and W. H. Dubberstein, *Babylonian Chronology 626 B.C.–A.D. 75* (Brown University Studies 19, Providence ²1956), 16. In the original records there is not a single reference to the practice assumed by Schedl, *op. cit.*, 246–8, that the usurper counted the years of his reign from the end of the rule of Nabonidus his supposed father. In Judith 1.1, 13; 2.1 the reference cannot be to the twelfth, seventeenth and eighteenth years of this 'Nebuchadnezzar IV' who was defeated, captured and killed in the first year of his reign by Darius (*bisūtūn* inscription Pers. III 76–IV 2 [VAB III, 54–57 §§49–51]; cf. IV 28–30 [*ibid.* 60f. §52]). On this cf. also W. Hinz, 'Das erste Jahr des Grosskönigs Darius', *ZDMG* 92, 1938, 161f.; A. Poebel, 'Chronology of Darius' First Year of Reign', *AJSL* 55, 1938, 289–91, 302f.; A. T. Olmstead, 'Darius and his Behistun Inscription', *ibid.*, 402f.; A. Poebel, 'The Duration of the Reign of Smerdis, the Magian, and the Reigns of Nebuchadnezzar III and Nebuchadnezzar IV', *AJSL* 56, 1939, 131–44; also K. Galling, 'Politische Wandlungen zwischen Nabonid und Darius' (1953/54), *Studien zur Geschichte Israels im persischen Zeitalter* (Tübingen 1964), 50f.

184 The name has not yet been identified; I cannot accept what W. Brandenstein, *Sprachgeschichte und Wortbedeutung: Festschrift A. Debrunner* (Berne 1954), 59f., says on this.

185 Old Persian *ragā*, Elamite *rag-ga5-*, Akkadian *ra-ga-aʾ*: *bisūtūn* inscription Pers. II 71f. = Elam. II 54 = Bab. II 59 (VAB III, 38f. §32); Pers. III 2f. = Elam. II 73 (*ibid.*, 42 §36); additional references in Grintz, *op. cit.*, 72, on Judith 1.8; cf. also F. Stummer, *Geographie des Buches Judith* (Bibelwissenschaftliche Reihe 3, Stuttgart 1947), 22.

186 The author of the book of Judith has very nebulous conceptions of the 'wider world', and these presuppose the Achaemenian empire; the impression made by his Palestinian geography is to say the least conflicting.

as 'king of the Elymaeans', that is of the Elamites, a certain 'Arioch' (*Αριωχ*) who probably owes his existence to a confusion between our Chedorlaomer of Elam and Arioch of Ellasar. Here, therefore, we can see how such ancient names were felt to be 'exotic' and found their way into and through later literary works. Another Arioch appears in Dan. 2.14f., 24f. as an official (*rab ṭabbāḥayyā'*) of king 'Nebuchadnezzar' in Babylon. Thus, the name appears to have enjoyed a certain vogue among the pseudepigrapha in the Persian-Hellenistic period. In the case of Gen. 14 this means at least that we cannot deduce from the ancient personal names an equal antiquity for the tradition as a whole. The description of Abraham as *hā'ibrī* could, therefore, equally well be authentic or archaistic fiction. In the same place, however, Gen. 14.13, there is mentioned, alongside Abraham, Mamre, apparently a personification[187] of the traditional dwelling-place of Abraham at Hebron and certainly not a historical personage. He is here, and only here, described as 'the Amorite' (*hā'emōrī*). The parallelism in the introduction of these two personages is certainly not accidental. It would lead us to suppose that when the author of our text wished to associate his fictitious ('Amorite')[188] 'country-dweller' 'Mamre' with the 'father of the Israelites', he went back to the description of the Israelites as 'Hebrews', a description which had for long been and in his own time certainly was ar-

[187] For Abraham's residence near Hebron J uses *'ēlōnē mamrē'* (Gen. 13.18; 18.1), P only *mamrē'* (sometimes as a definition of the site of the 'ancestral grave of the patriarchs': Gen. 23.17, 19; 25.9; 35.27; 49.30; 50.13). The fact that in Gen. 14.13, 24 we probably have personifications of places round Hebron also emerges from the fact that 'Eshcol', the 'brother' of 'Mamre', can scarcely be separated from the 'valley of grapes' (*naḥal 'eškōl* Num. 13.23f.; cf. 32.9; Deut. 1.24) which must be located in the Negeb also in the neighbourhood of Hebron. A similar situation must be envisaged for 'Aner' although no comparable place name can be suggested in the region; the Levitical city of Aner (*'ānēr*) in the tribe of Manasseh (I Chron. 6.55) which proves the use of the name as a toponym, probably owes its existence to a textual corruption (Josh. 21.25 has 'Taanach'). One should also note that in Gen. 14.13 with *be'ēlōnē mamrē'* the linguistic usage of J is adopted while what follows has no parallels in the rest of the tradition. There is general agreement that Mamre is to be located on the site of the *ḥaram* of *rāmet el-ḫalīl* about 3 km. (2 miles) north of the old city of Hebron (*el-ḫalīl*) (cf. *BRL* 275–9 *s.v.* Hebron).

[188] On the designation of the pre-Israelite inhabitants of Palestine as 'Amorites' (*'emōrī*) cf. M. Noth, 'Num. 21 als Glied der "Hexateuch"-Erzählung', *ZAW* 58, 1940/41, 182–9. With regard to the two passages in Gen. 14, Noth, *op. cit.*, 185 assumes that *'emōrī* serves as a general name for 'pre-Israelites' similar to the linguistic usage of the E-source.

chaistic. Here, then, *ʿibrī* is understood in accordance with normal post-biblical linguistic usage as an ethnic term and says nothing either about the nineteenth century BC in general or about Abraham and the relationship of his descendants to the *ʿapiru*. At any rate, such a far-reaching hypothesis as that of Albright's cannot be built on such a precarious foundation.

12. With regard to the question of the identity of the *ʿapiru*-people of the ancient Near Eastern texts of the second millennium with the biblical Hebrews, there emerges from our discussion of the two terms the following:

(*a*) On the presupposition that *ʿapiru* is formed on the basis of the noun form **faʿil-*, the etymological relationship of the word with the Hebrew *ʿibrī* can be established.[189]

(*b*) The situation of the *ʿebed ʿibrī* of the 'Book of the Covenant' (Ex. 21.2–6) can be compared with that of the *ʿapiru*-people of the *wardūtu*-contracts from Nuzu.[190]

(*c*) The description as *ʿibrīm* of the Israelites who were resisting Philistine claims to supremacy can perhaps be explained as analogous to the name *ʿapiru* which was given in the Amarna letters to those elements of the population of Syria-Palestine who were rebelling against Egyptian rule.[191]

(*d*) The passages in the Joseph story and the exodus narratives, as well as the examples from late Old Testament and subsequent writings, seem to understand the word *ʿibrī* as an archaic way of describing the 'Israelite' nation.[192] The connection with the *ʿapiru* is extremely indirect.[193]

The picture which we have to sketch is much more complex than Albright, Mendenhall and others supposed. It now seems out of the question to regard without closer examination the terms 'Hebrews' and 'Israelites' as synonyms and to lump the 'Israelites'/'Hebrews' together with the *ʿapiru*-people. Finally, the fact that the word *ʿibrī* appears only in certain clearly defined groups of texts cautions us against the idea that the terms 'Hebrew' and

[189] See above pp. 74–82.

[190] See above pp. 85–7.

[191] See above pp. 87f.

[192] See above pp. 88–93.

[193] If the suggestion made under (*c*) is right, the description of the 'Israelites' in Egypt as 'Hebrews' could be explained as a retrogressive transposition of the description used by the Philistines into the Egyptian period which was understood as the pre-history of the settlement in Palestine.

'Israelite' are interchangeable at will. At the same time, it is not possible either to regard the *b^enē yiśrā'ēl*[194] of the Old Testament settlement narratives simply as *'ibrīm* and *'apiru*-people. Since, in addition, the *'apiru* of the Amarna letters, as we have shown,[195] do not fill the role which Mendenhall ascribes to them, his hypothesis of the Israelite settlement must be rejected as being without sufficient foundation.[196]

2. NOMADS OF THE SECOND MILLENNIUM

1. The thesis that the Israelite settlement was essentially a social upheaval within Canaanite society at the end of the Bronze Age with no statistically significant immigration from outside overlooks the fact that at all periods Israel was vitally conscious of not being autochthonous in Canaan. The fact that this awareness usually finds expression in the sources at our disposal in kerygmatic formulations[1] is no reason for denying it historical relevance. This is all the less permissible since the Old Testament itself, as we have seen, has retained indications that the 'Israelites' who entered the cultivated land came from the context of life in the steppe and were originally not agriculturalists but breeders of small cattle.[2] In his attempted reconstruction of the settlement Mendenhall has also

[194] On the basis of the theories of Alt and Noth presented above, the names of individual tribes will have stood in the place of 'Israelites' in a stage of the tradition which is preserved now only in fragments.

[195] See above pp. 71–4.

[196] Cf. also the criticism in J. A. Soggin, 'La conquista israelitica della Palestina nei sec. XIII e XII e le scoperte archeologiche', *Protestantesimo* 17, 1962, 208 (*appendice*), which agrees on the whole with the objections raised here.

[1] It is unnecessary to provide detailed references for this assertion since the concept is present everywhere in the older parts of the Old Testament down to Deuteronomy. I refer only to the particularly fine expression of it in Deut. 6.10–12. Cf. also G. v. Rad, 'Es ist noch eine Ruhe vorhanden dem Volke Gottes. Eine biblische Begriffsuntersuchung' (1933), *Gesammelte Studien zum Alten Testament* (ThB 8, 1958), 101–108 (ET 'There remains still a rest for the people of God: An investigation of a biblical conception' in *The Problem of the Hexateuch and Other Essays*, Edinburgh and London 1965, 94–102); 'Verheissenes Land und Jahwehs Land im Hexateuch' (1943), *ibid.*, 87–100 (ET 'The Promised Land and Yahweh's Land in the Hexateuch', *ibid.*, 79–93).

[2] See above pp. 5f. and cf. also Num. 32.16, 24, 36, where it is stated with regard to the tribes of Reuben and Gad that the first measures taken by them after the occupation of their territory was the building of *gidrōt ṣōn* 'sheepfolds' and *'ārīm* 'cities', i.e. permanent settlements (see below pp. 115–20 on *ḥaṣirātum* and *ālānū* in the Mari texts).

not noticed that of the lines of tradition which have been woven together in the present historical picture of Israel it is not the 'exodus-Sinai' traditions but the traditions of the 'fathers' which serve as the ideological basis for the occupation of the agricultural land east and west of the Jordan.[3] According to the general consensus of opinion, however, these traditions reflect conditions in the (Middle and) Late Bronze Age in the steppe region[4] which stretched between the thickly populated areas of southern Mesopotamia ('Sumer and Akkad') and Phoenicia-Palestine, a region whose inhabitants were, for the most part, breeders of sheep and therefore necessarily mobile and whom we have described hitherto in this work in the usual terms of 'semi-nomads' or 'nomads with small cattle'. In this respect one must remember that the 'fathers' to whom the divine promise of land is addressed are described against an Aramaean background.[5] This may be anachronistic, and that would fit the description of them as a 'people', since the Aramaeans are known, at the earliest,[6] from the time of Tiglath-pileser I;[7] but it does prove that the Israelites were completely aware of their ancestors' connections with the territories on the

[3] On the promise of land to the 'fathers' cf. A. Alt, 'Der Gott der Väter' (1929), *Kl.Schr.* I, 65f. (ET 'The God of the Fathers' in *Essays on Old Testament History and Religion*, Oxford 1966, 64f.); G. v. Rad, *Das erste Buch Mose, Genesis* (ATD 2–4, ^{4}1956), 14f. (ET *Genesis*, London ^{2}1963, 20ff.). J. Hoftijzer, *Die Verheissungen an die drei Erzväter* (Leiden 1956), seems to me to confuse the actual circumstances when he assumes that 'a tradition of promise (*scil.* of land) first arose after the connection between the patriarchal period and the exodus period had already occurred both from the religious and from the traditio-historical point of view' (*op. cit.*, 98), that is 'first in the period when the existence of the nation was seriously threatened or perhaps first during the exile' (*ibid.*, 99).

[4] On the definition of this steppe region see R. de Vaux, *RB* 56, 1949, 12–14 with map p. 13.

[5] Cf. Gen. 22.20f.; 28.5 (; 29.4, 14); 31.20, 24, 47 etc. and J. C. L. Gibson, 'Light from Mari on the Patriarchs', *JSS* 7, 1962, 53f. It is not quite clear whether the expression *'^{a}rammī* (*'ōbēd*) in Deut. 26.5 has the ethnic meaning 'Aramaean' or the sociological meaning 'bedouin' (cf. the secondary use in Akkadian of the original tribal names *tid(a)num*, MAR.TU = *amurrû*, *sutû*, ḪA.NA = *ḫanû*, *aḫlamû*).

[6] See Preface.

[7] *aḫ-la-mi/mì-i* ^{KUR}*ar-ma-(a-)ya*^{MEŠ} Prism V 46f. (*AKA* 73); ^{KUR}*aḫ-la-me-e* $^{\text{(KUR)}}$*ar-ma-a-ya*^{MEŠ} *KAH* II 63 III 4f.; 71, 19; *aḫ-la-mì-i* [^{KUR}*a*]*r-ma-a-ya* ^{MEŠ} Weidner I, 29f. (*AfO* 18, 1957/58, 344); $^{\text{(KUR)}}$*aḫ-la-me-e* ^{KUR}*ar-ma-a-ya*^{MEŠ} Weidner II, 34 (*ibid.*, 350); cf. J.-R. Kupper, *Les nomades en Mésopotamie au temps des rois de Mari* (1957), 111 and n. 1. The description 'Aramaean *Aḫlamû*' presumably means Aramaean bedouin and not that the *Aḫlamū* people of the older sources were 'Aramaean'. On the *Aḫlamû* cf. Kupper, *op. cit.*, 104–15,

upper Euphrates and with the nomadic area of *jebel bišrī* and of the fact that they formed part of the population of that area, who were breeders of small cattle.[8] In this connection we must single out the concept of the 'God of the fathers' which Albrecht Alt[9] has convincingly explained on the basis of the circumstances of non-sedentary or semi-sedentary life. Even if modifications of Alt's thesis are necessary in detail,[10] one cannot deny that the concept of 'gods of the way'[11] can be explained only with difficulty from

---

132–8; P. Sacchi, 'Per una storia di Aram. II. Gli Aḫlamu nel sec. XI a.C.', *PP* 14, fasc. 65, 1959, 131–4; S. Moscati, 'The "Aramaean Ahlamu" ', *JSS* 4, 1959, 303–7; S. Yeivin, 'The ʿAmu', *ʿAtiqot* 2, 1959, 163f. The alleged 'Aramaean' passages cited by N. Schneider, 'Aram und Aramäer in der Ur III-Zeit', *Bibl* 30, 1949, 109–11; S. Moscati, 'Sugli origini degli Aramei', *RSO* 26, 1951, 16–22; A. Dupont-Sommer, 'Sur les débuts de l'histoire araméenne', *SVT* 1, 1953, 40–49 must be deleted from the discussion since in every case the connection of the place name or personal name in question with the Aramaeans of the later second and first millennia is very unlikely. On this see Kupper, *op. cit.*, 112–14; I. J. Gelb, *JCS* 15, 1961, 28 n. 5; on the Ugaritic personal name *army* (*WUS* 408) = ^{I}*ar-me-ya* RS 15.37, 13 (*PRU* III, 35) or *a-ri-mu-ya* Alalaḫ 148, 57, also M. Liverani, *Storia di Ugarit nell'età degli archivi politici* (Studi Semitici 6, Rome 1962), 153f.; R. A. Uyechi, *A Study of Ugaritic Alphabetic Personal Names* (Thesis Brandeis University, Waltham, Mass., 1961, typewritten), 64. Moscati's criticism (*JSS* 4, 304 n. 3) does not convince me.

[8] On the meaning of *jebel bišrī* cf. J. Lewy, *ZA* 40, 1929, 270; B. Maisler, *JPOS* 17, 1937, 139; D. O. Edzard, *Die 'zweite Zwischenzeit' Babyloniens*, Wiesbaden 1957, 34–36; H. Klengel, *Benjaminiten und Hanäer zur Zeit der Könige von Mari* (Diss. phil. Berlin 1958), 55; Kupper, *op. cit.*, 136, 149f.; Gelb, *op. cit.*, 30, 31f.

[9] 'Der Gott der Väter' (1929), *Kl.Schr.* I, 1–78 (ET 'The God of the Fathers' in *Essays on Old Testament History and Religion*, Oxford 1966, 3–77).

[10] Cf. J. Hoftijzer, *Die Verheissungen an die drei Erzväter* (Leiden 1957); L. Rost, 'Die Gottesverehrung der Patriarchen im Lichte der Pentateuchquellen', *SVT* 7, 1960, 346–59; F. M. Cross Jr., 'Yahweh and the God of the Patriarchs', *HThR* 55, 1962, 225–59. Complete rejection by S. Mowinckel, *Palestina før Israel* (Oslo 1965), 131. The Old Assyrian material on the 'personal God' ('protector God'; on this cf. also H. Hirsch, *Untersuchungen zur altassyrischen Religion, AfO* Bh. 13/14, 1961, 35–45) cited by J. Lewy, 'Les textes paléo-assyriens et l'Ancien Testament', *RHR* 110, 1934, 50–56, must be taken into account in any new treatment of the problem alongside the much later inscriptional material gathered by Alt (*op. cit.*, 68–77; ET, 67–76) (otherwise Alt, *op. cit.*, 31 addition to n. 1; ET, 32 addition to n. 77). The solution, however, would be quite different from that of Hoftijzer. The most recent contribution by H. Hirsch, 'Gott der Väter', *AfO* 21, 1966, 56–58 does not come to terms sufficiently with the problems raised by the scholarly debate and therefore takes us no further.

[11] The difference between the 'religion of the way' and the 'religion of the place' I owe to J. Hempel, who has expounded it at several points in his lecture 'Das Alte Testament im Rahmen der allgemeinen Religionsgeschichte'

the situation of agricultural populations. In the Old Testament itself there are still traces of a time when the 'Gods of the fathers' had not yet been identified with Yahweh.[12] Yahweh, the God of Israel 'from Egypt onwards' belongs, from the point of view both of the history of tradition and of the history of religion, in another context, and I do not hesitate to regard the 'day of Shechem', the event which lies behind Josh. 24, as the day when this God was accepted by those tribes already in the land and to interpret it as the day when the Israelite Yahweh-amphictyony was founded.[13] The significance of this event is difficult to evaluate correctly. It meant no less than that the Israelite tribes, in their transition to sedentary life, were prevented from becoming assimilated, in the way that their kinsmen in Mesopotamia and Syria had become, to the social conditions of the agricultural land and from becoming absorbed into the resident population and its culture. The religious conflicts of the tenth–eighth centuries in the northern kingdom of Israel show how protracted the conflict concerning assimilation or 'apartheid' was, and we can not conceive how it would have ended if the brutal assault of Assyrian power in the eighth century had not radically altered the situation. Yahweh was not a God of the agricultural land, a God of Canaan, either; he, too, came from the steppe or even from the desert and from a nomadic context, but, as far as we can ascertain, he was, at the end of the second millennium and the beginning of the first, not a 'God of the way' but a 'God of the place' who had his dwelling and also a cultic centre, or cultic centres, in the mountains of Seir, in Edom, in Sinai.[14] The worship offered to him in the circle of the Israelite

---

which I heard in Göttingen in the summer semester of 1959. The idea comes from E. Lehmann, *Stället och vägen: Ett religionshistorisk perspektiv* (Stockholm 1917).

[12] This is clear in Gen. 31.53a where the 'god of Nahor' (*'elōhē nāḥōr*) and the 'god of Abraham' (*'elōhē 'abrāhām*) are set side by side in such a way that it is impossible to think of Yahweh in connection with the latter. A correct recollection from the point of view of the history of religion has also been preserved in Josh. 24.2.

[13] See above p.40 and cf. also R. Smend, *Jahwekrieg und Stämmebund: Erwägungen zur ältesten Geschichte Israels* (FRLANT 84, 1963), 77f.

[14] The so-called 'Kenite hypothesis', which cannot be definitely proved but which is nevertheless probable, is presupposed here. Broadly speaking it states that Yahweh, the God of Israel, was originally a God who dwelt in the Edomite mountains (*har śe'īr*) or in Sinai, the God of the nomads of the Negeb and of Edom, of the Kenites and/or the Midianites, and

tribes is therefore secondary *vis-à-vis* that offered to the 'Gods of the fathers'. The fact that he eventually absorbed the gods of Abraham, Isaac and Jacob is a consequence of the transition to sedentary life and the upheaval in tribal life associated with it.

2. For the description of the nomadism of the second millennium BC we have today a considerably larger number of primary sources at our disposal than had, for example, Alt, who had primarily to work with inferences drawn from the conditions of present-day Arab 'semi-nomads' in Palestine. The rich discoveries

---

reached the Israelites from there. As far as I am aware, the thesis appears for the first time in Richard von der Alm (i.e. F. W. Ghillany), *Theologische Briefe an die Gebildeten der deutschen Nation* I (Leipzig 1862), 320–22, 480–83, then independently in C. P. Tiele, *Vergelijkende Geschiedenis van de Egyptische en Mesopotamische Godsdiensten – Egypte, Babel-Assur, Yemen, 'Harran, Fenicie, Israel* (*Vergelijkende Geschiedenis der oude Godsdiensten* I, Amsterdam 1869/72), 558–60, and became widespread after that: on this cf. the references in H. H. Rowley, *From Joseph to Joshua* (London [4]1958), 149–56; G. v. Rad, *Theologie des Alten Testaments* I (Munich [2]1958), 18–21 (ET *Old Testament Theology* I, Edinburgh and London 1962, 8–11); further now R. Smend, *Jahwekrieg*, 96f.; A. H. J. Gunneweg, 'Mose in Midian', *ZThK* 61, 1964, 1–9; H. Heyde, *Kain, der erste Jahweverehrer: Die ursprüngliche Bedeutung der Sage von Kain und ihre Auswirkungen in Israel* (ATh I 23, 1965), 32–34. It can perhaps be supported by the name of a country or tribe which appears in Egyptian sources and which seems to correspond phonetically to the Hebrew divine name **yahwe* and, in addition, to be localized in the Sinai peninsula. It occurs for the first time – if indeed it is this name – in the form *'a/'ì-h-w-a-u* in the autobiography of the official *ẖtyy* on a limestone stele in tomb 65 in Thebes (*JEA* 4, 1917, plate IX line 10; XIth dynasty) as a supplier of *byꜣ pśḏ* ('shining copper' or 'iron' = ?), then in the lists of foreign nations of Amenophis III in *sōleb* in Nubia in the combination *tꜣ šꜣś.w ya-hu-w*( ) 'the bedouin of Jah(u)wi' (IV N 4α2; II 69; J. Leclant, *Les fouilles de Soleb* [*Nubie soudanaise*]. *Quelques remarques sur les écussons des peuples envoûtés de la salle hypostyle du secteur IV* [NAG 1965: 13], 215 figs. c, e and plate 15 – the reading *ya-h-w*( ) would also be possible). The list of Rameses II in *'amāra* west is dependent on those of Amenophis III and there the same form (with *rwḏ* a scribal error for *wꜣ*) occurs (R. Giveon, *VT* 14, 1964, 244; cf. the indistinct photograph in *JEA* 25, 1939, plate XIV 4). Finally, *yi-ha* occurs in two lists of Rameses III in *medīnet hābū* (J. Simons, *Handbook for the Study of Egyptian Topographical Lists Relating to Western Asia*, Leiden 1937, XXVII 115; XXIX 13; A. Jirku, *Die ägyptischen Listen palästinensischer und syrischer Ortsnamen, Klio* Bh. 38, Leipzig 1937, XXII 115; XXIII 1). The connection of the name with **yahwe*, which is not beyond doubt in view of the various Egyptian forms, was made in R. Giveon, 'Toponymes ouest-assiatiques à Soleb', *VT* 14, 1964, 244f., 255; Leclant, *op. cit.*, 216; S. Herrmann, 'Der alttestamentliche Gottesname', *EvTh* 26, 1966, 281–93; 'Der Name Jhwꜣ in den Inschriften von Soleb', *Fourth World Congress of Jewish Studies, Papers*, I (Jerusalem 1967), 213–16. The 'gnesio-Lutheran' protest against the 'Kenite hypothesis' (*Lutherischer Rundblick* 12, 1964, 41) does not deserve any scholarly attention apart from the insults directed against Eissfeldt.

of cuneiform texts in the old royal city of Mari (*tell ḥarīrī*)[15] on the Euphrates, especially from the period of king Zimri-Lim, the confederate and later ill-fated opponent of the great Ḫammurapi of Babylon, have put us in the position of being able to draw a more exact picture of the process of the settlement of nomads or 'semi-nomads' than the one on which Alt based the historical explanation of the Israelite settlement. But first of all a few basic remarks are necessary about the term 'nomad' in the second millennium. Hitherto the term 'bedouin' (*badawī*) has been avoided if possible in order to obviate any association with modern Arabian tribes of camel breeders. Of course, as Mendenhall[16] rightly states, the picture which the Arabian bedouin tribes offered to the European traveller in the second half of last century has exerted an enormous influence on the discussion of 'Israelite bedouinism'; yet, as far as we know, in the territories of the Near East for which we have a sufficient number of archaeological and epigraphic sources, there were no camel nomads. If the fairly marked tendency, which has recently become strong again, towards an early date for the domestication of the single humped camel (*Camelus dromedarius L.*)[17] (for our purposes we are concerned with it alone) is correct,[18]

[15] I have given a brief bibliography of the excavations in *ZDPV* 80, 1964, 152 n. 7. The textual finds have been published primarily in the series *Archives Royales de Mari* (*ARM* = *TCL* XXIIff.) and discussed in a parallel series with the same title (*ARMT*); texts published elsewhere than *ARM*(*T*) are listed in H. B. Huffmon, *Amorite Personal Names in the Mari Texts: A Structural and Lexical Study* (Baltimore 1965), 274–7.

[16] 'The Hebrew Conquest of Palestine', *BA* 25, 1962, 68f.

[17] E.g. B. Brentjes, 'Das Kamel im Alten Orient', *Klio* 38, 1960, 33–48; *Die Haustierwerdung im Orient. Ein archäologischer Beitrag zur Zoologie* (Die neue Brehm-Bücherei 344, Wittenberg/Stuttgart 1965), 54–57. For the late dating especially R. Walz, 'Zum Problem des Zeitpunkts der Domestikation der altweltlichen Cameliden', *ZDMG* 101, 1951, 29–51; 'Neue Untersuchungen zum Domestikationsproblem der altweltlichen Cameliden', *ZDMG* 104, 1954, 48–50; W. F. Albright, 'Zur Zähmung des Kamels', *ZAW* 62, 1950, 315; *Archaeology and the Religion of Israel* (Baltimore ³1953), 96f., 132f.

[18] The archaeological finds which have been considered to be representations of camels dating from the late third and early second millennia (lists: R. de Vaux, *RB* 56, 1949, 7–9; Walz, *ZDMG* 101, 33–37; Brentjes, *Klio* 38, 33f.) contribute nothing, even in so far as they are clear, which does not seem to me to be the case in every instance, to the problem of the emergence of full bedouin culture in the Arabian peninsula. The patriarchs, who were certainly nomads with small cattle, may well have possessed the odd camel in Palestine, so that the mention of camels in Genesis (list in de Vaux, *op. cit.*, 7 and n. 1) need not necessarily be considered anachronistic. A similar explanation may be given for the appearance of the dromedary (anše-a-ab-ba: *i-bi-lu*) already in the original Old Babylonian form of the series ur$_5$(ḪAR)-ra: *ḫubullu* (RS

then it is clear that the development of camel nomadism as an economic system in the territories bordering on the 'fertile crescent' most probably first occurred, as Albright, Walz and Dostal[19] suggest, within a relatively short period before the thirteenth/twelfth century, so that in fact the Midianite and Amalekite camel troops who oppressed the Israelite tribes in the time of Gideon are the first real bedouin attested in the historical sources.[20] In addition, the inability of the Israelites, who had only recently become sedentary, to defend themselves against this attack shows fairly clearly that the use of the camel in a *g̱azū* represented something new for them and that they, therefore, had certainly not been camel nomads before the settlement. Basically, that was in any case not to be expected. In what follows, then, we have to reckon only with groups of breeders of small cattle, i.e. primarily sheep.

3. From the point of view of farmers and merchants settled in

---

17.40 III 22, *MSL* VIII 1, 102) and in the series itself (Ḫḫ XIII 366, *MSL* VIII 1. 51) in a list of domestic animals, even if the reference, as W. G. Lambert, *BASOR* 160, 1960, 45 correctly remarks, cannot be pressed, since alongside it another wild animal, the 'donkey of the steppe' (anše-edin-na: *sír-ri-mu*, RS 17.40 III 17, *op. cit.*; Ḫḫ XIII 374, *op. cit.*, 52), probably the onager (A. Salonen, *Hippologica Accadica*, Acta Academiae Scientiarum Fennicae 100, Helsinki 1955, 45f.; *sirrimu* is the word which was earlier read as '*purīmu*' and erroneously connected with the Hebr. *pere*') is mentioned in the same context. Further, according to D. J. Wiseman's revised reading (*JCS* 13, 1959, 29), fodder for a camel would be mentioned in the text Alalaḫ 269.59 (fifteenth century) which would therefore need to be either domesticated or else kept wild or half-tame in a zoo; however, instead of Wiseman's ^{ANŠE}GAM!.MAL! (pseudologogram for *gammalu*) Lambert, *op. cit.*, 42f., reads DÁRA.BAR! = *ayyalu* 'deer'. On the keeping of fallow deer in the ancient East cf. Brentjes, *Haustierwerdung*, 63–65, and the representation of a fallow deer, led by a cord and a collar and therefore tame, on a Syrian ivory from Ugarit in Brentjes, *ibid.*, 64 fig. 61. According to M. Dietrich and O. Loretz, *Theologische Revue* 65, 1969, 365, ANSE.GUR!.NUN! = *kūdanu*(*m*) 'mule' should be read; see already *AHw* 499[a]. Untenable is J. Aistleitner's explanation of the Ugaritic word *udr* (*CTA* 4 IV/V 79.102) as 'camel' (*WUS* 97), by which he appears to mean a camel caravan bringing precious stones (*ilqṣm*) for the building of Baal's palace (cf. M. Weippert, *GGA* 216, 1964, 186). The meaning 'camel' does not fit the context, and the Akk. *udru* which has been compared with *udr* is a late Iranian, perhaps Median, loanword in Akkadian which corresponds to the Avestian *uštra-* (cf. Sanskrit *úṣṭra-* 'camel, buffalo'; on the other hand Achaemenian Old Persian *uša-* in *ušabari-* 'mounted on a camel' < **uša-* < **uštra-*). Akk. *-dr-* is a simplified substitution for *-štr-*.

[19] Cf. now especially W. Dostal, 'Zur Frage der Entwicklung des Beduinentums', *Archiv für Völkerkunde* 13, 1958, 1–14.

[20] Judg. 6.5; 7.12; 8.21, 26.

cities and villages, the 'man of the steppe',[21] 'who lives in the hills,[22] is a barbarian devoid of any culture, one 'who knows no house,[23] and no cities,[24] who, since he does not cultivate the soil, 'knows no crops',[25] who, at the best, now and again digs up wild truffles[26] and, in highly uncivilized fashion, 'eats raw flesh'.[27] He ignores the refined forms of social intercourse of the urbane world[28] and, after his death, is not ritually interred.[29] Since he does not accommodate himself to the usual forms of social intercourse and often troubles the country by his marauding raids,[30] the central authority and the population must protect themselves against the threat from the 'hills'. It is said of Šū-Suen, king of Ur, that he erected a wall against the nomadic MAR.TU-people[31] and also the '(high) wall against the hills'[32] which is attested in the formula from the nineteenth year of Ḫammurapi of Babylon, will have to be explained in similar terms. If these defensive measures proved of no avail, then one would eventually have to have recourse to weapons and attack the 'people of the steppe' with force; we have abundant information concerning such encounters

[21] lú-líl-lá *TCL* XV 9, VI 23 *par.* (according to D. O. Edzard, *Die 'zweite Zwischenzeit' Babyloniens*, 1957, 32 no. 1f); cf. *ARM* VIII 10, 1 (1 SAGÌR *é-a-tu-kúl-ti šum-šu* LÚ.LÍL 'a slave called Ea-tukulti, a "man of the steppe"'.

[22] ḫur-sag-gá tuš-a *TCL* XV 9 VI 23 *par.* (Edzard, *ibid.*).

[23] é-nu-zu *ibid.* 22 *par.* (Edzard, *ibid.*); u4-ti-la-na é nu-tuku-a 'who knows no house as long as he lives' *SEM* 58 IV 28 (Edzard, *op. cit.*, 32 no. 1g).

[24] uru^{ki}-nu-zu *SEM* 58 IV 28 (Edzard, *ibid.*); ul-ta uru^{ki}-nu-zu 'who have never known any cities' *UET* I 206 (Edzard, *op. cit.*, 33 no. 2e).

[25] lú-še-nu-zu *TCL* XVI 66 v°. 12′ (Edzard, *op. cit.*, 31 no. 1d); *SEM* 1 V 11′ (Edzard, *op. cit.*, 32 no. 1e).

[26] uzu-diri kur-da mu-un-ba-al-la 'who digs up truffles in the hills' *SEM* 58 IV 26 (Edzard, *op. cit.*, 32 no. 1g). On the 'truffles' (uzu-diri) cf. B. Landsberger, *Die Fauna des alten Mesopotamien nach der 14. Tafel des Serie ḪAR.RA = ḫubullu* (Leipzig 1934), 111; Edzard, *op. cit.*, 31f. n. 131.

[27] uzu-nu-šeg6-gá al-kú-e *SEM* 58 IV 27 (Edzard, *op. cit.*, 32 no. 1g).

[28] du10-gúr nu-zu-àm 'who does not know how to bend the knee' *ibid.* 26 (Edzard, *ibid.*).

[29] u4-ba!-ug6-ga-na ki nu-túm-mu-dam *ibid.* 29 (Edzard, *ibid.*). The expression 'who is not buried after his death' is surely to be understood as paraphrased in the text above (cf. Edzard).

[30] ke-en-ge ki-uri nigín-na-a-ba MAR.TU lú-še-nu-zu ḫu-mu-zi 'in the whole of Sumer and Akkad may the MAR.TU "who know no crops" rise up' *SEM* 1 V 10′f. (Lugalbanda and Enmerkar, Edzard, *op. cit.*, 32 no. 1e).

[31] u4 bàd-MAR.TU-*mu-ri-iq-ti-id-ni-im* mu-dù-a ù nè-MAR.TU ma-da-né-e bí-in-gi4-a 'when he (*scil.* Šū-Suen) had built the "MAR.TU wall which keeps back the bedouin" and had driven out the forces of the MAR.TU from his land' *ZA* 29, 180f.: 20–26 (Edzard, *op. cit.*, 33 no. 2c).

[32] bàd-(maḫ)-igi-ḫur-sag-gá Edzard, *op. cit.*, 181 and n. 998.

between the sedentary population and nomads in the second millennium BC.[33] From the opposite, nomadic side, of course, a quite different impression is received. We even have direct testimony to this in the Old Testament itself, in the birth oracle of Ishmael (Gen. 16.12) which comes perhaps from Ishmaelite circles or at any rate from circles familiar with bedouin romanticism. Here the proud self-awareness of the free-roving man finds this expression:[34]

hū' yihyeh pere' 'ādām
yādō bakkōl w^e^yad kōl bō
w^eʿ^al p^e^nē kol-'eḥāw yiškōn

He will be a man like a wild ass –
His hand against everyone, everyone's hand against him!
He lives in the face of all his brothers.[35]

4. But let us now turn to the texts from Mari which, of course, are separated from the period of 'Joshua' and the settlement of the Israelite tribes by a good five hundred years[36] but which, however, stand nearer in time to that period than do the modern parallels. For our purposes, we shall have to make a selection from the wealth of material which has been exhaustively discussed by J.-R. Kupper[37] and shall deal primarily with the 'Benjamin-

[33] See, e.g., n.31 above and the year formulae of Jaḫdun-Lim and Zimri-Lim of Mari discussed below pp.123f. and n.94.

[34] Cf. the estimate of the passage in H. Gunkel, *Die Urgeschichte und die Patriarchen (das erste Buch Mosis)* (SAT I 1, ²1921), 147, and in G. v. Rad, *Das erste Buch Mose – Genesis* (ATD 2–4, ⁴1956), 164 (ET *Genesis*, London ²1963, 189). For a picture of the *pere'* cf. Job 39.5–8.

[35] The translation of the third line of the saying is known to be disputed; various possibilities have been suggested, such as 'east of all his brothers will he dwell' (e.g. E. Reuss, *Die heilige Geschichte und das Gesetz: Der Pentateuch und Josua, Das Alte Testament übersetzt, eingeleitet und erklärt*, III, Braunschweig 1893, 243) or 'he lives in defiance of all his brothers' (cf., e.g., GesB[17], 649[b] *s.v.* **pāne* I 1e; Gunkel, *op. cit.*, 145; v. Rad, *op. cit.*, 164 [ET, 189]). The attempt is made above, in loose dependence on the Hebrew text, to express what seems to me to be meant (cf. Gunkel and v. Rad) without regard for ultimate philological precision.

[36] This approximate reckoning corresponds both to the so-called 'medium chronology' and to the so-called 'short chronology'.

[37] *Les nomades en Mésopotamie au temps des rois de Mari* (Bibliothèque de la Faculté de Philosophie et Lettres de l' Université de Liège 142, Paris 1957); cf. G. Dossin, 'Les bédouins dans les textes de Mari', *L'antica società beduina. Studi . . . raccolti da F. Gabrieli* (Studi Semitici 2, Rome 1959), 35–51; J.-R. Kupper, 'Le rôle des nomades dans l'histoire de la Mésopotamie ancienne', *JESHO* 2, 1959, 113–27; H. Klengel, 'Zu einigen Problemen des altvorderasiatischen Nomadentums', *ArOr* 30, 1962, 585–96; 'Sesshafte und Noma-

ites'[38] of Mari who have been much discussed since Dossin's basic article of 1939, with these not least on account of the interest which Old Testament studies have had in them.

5. It must, of course, be clearly stated at the outset that the name 'Benjaminites' can, at the most, now be used only as a conventional designation. The hebraizing explanation, suggested by Dossin in 1939, of the usual written forms of the name DUMU.MEŠ *ya-mi-in/na/ni*[39] as **binī*^{MES}*-yamīna* is certainly incorrect. Since, in the first place, there can be doubt as to the reading of the Sumeriogram DUMU.MEŠ 'sons', at least two possibilities could be discussed:

(*a*) Since, in the case of the element *yamīn-*, we are not dealing with an Akkadian word but with one which may fairly certainly be attributed to the language of the 'Benjaminites' and since this language, on the evidence of the personal names, must have been an 'Amorite' dialect,[40] DUMU.MEŠ could be read, as Dossin himself intended, as 'Amorite'. This would most probably give **banū yamīn(a/i)*.

(*b*) The regular Akkadian reading of DUMU is *marū*, plural (DUMU.MEŠ) *mārū*. Since the name occurs in an Akkadian context, it could also be read as **mārū yamīn(a/i)*.

Meanwhile, we know that in fact **mārū yamīn(a/i)* is to be read,[41] a reading which does not, of course, exclude the possibility

den in der alten Geschichte Mesopotamiens', *Saeculum* 17, 1966, 205–22. Reference should also be made to the researches of Dossin, Edzard and Kupper mentioned above n. 8 and below n. 38. I was unable to consult the work of J. T. Luke, *Pastoralism and Politics in the Mari Period: A Re-Examination of the Character and Political Significance of the Major West Semitic Tribal Groups on the Middle Euphrates* (Thesis, University of Michigan, Ann Arbor 1965).

[38] G. Dossin, 'Benjaminites dans les textes de Mari' *Mélanges syriens offerts à Monsieur René Dussaud . . . par ses amis et ses élèves* (BAH 30, 1939), 981–96; Kupper, *op. cit.*, 47–81.

[39] One example of each: DUMU.MEŠ *ya-mi-in ARM* I 6.6f.; DUMU.MEŠ *ya-mi-na ARM* II 36.12; DUMU.MEŠ *ya-mi-ni ARMT* XI 27.10. Other forms, partly from still unpublished texts, in G. Dossin, *RA* 52, 1958, 60.

[40] On 'Amorite' see above ch. III 1 n. 178.

[41] This solution of DUMU.MEŠ *yamīn(a/i)* is supposed in H. Tadmor, *JNES* 17, 1958, 130 n. 12; cf. I. J. Gelb, *JCS* 15, 1961, 37f., on the basis of the assertion that 'Amorite' words in Mari are not written logographically. The supposition becomes a certainty by the interchange of *ma-ar mi-i* and DUMU.MEŠ *mi-i* in year-formulae of Zimri-Lim; cf. MU *zi-im-ri-li-im da*ʾ*-aw-da-am ša ma-ar mi-i i-du-ku ARMT* XI 43.18–21 with MU *zi-im-ri-li-im da-aw-da-am ša* DUMU.MEŠ *mi-i i-du-ku ARMT* XI 18.16–19; 19.15–18; 20.14–17; 21.8–11; 24.7–10; 44.10–14. *Mi-i* is apparently a contraction for *yamīn-*, as is clear from

that the people may, in their own language, have called themselves **banū yamīn(a/i)*. **Mārū yamīn(a/i)* perhaps means 'people of the south', i.e. 'who live in the south'.[42] Since, however, the word *mārū*, like the word *b^enē* in the older forms of the name of the Israelite tribe of Benjamin, does not properly belong to the name,[43] it is better if, in future, we speak of *Jaminites*. This term has the additional advantage of avoiding confusion or over-hasty identification of these people with the biblical Benjaminites.

6. The Jaminites mentioned in our texts live, as a rule, in the region of the kingdom of Mari. It is, however, obvious that they are not originally indigenous there but are treated by the royal administration as immigrants and viewed with suspicion. When it is stated on one occasion that they 'do not return to their land' (*a-na ma-ti-šu-nu ú-ul i-tu-úr-ru-nim*),[44] that surely means that in the region of Mari they are regarded as foreigners. 'Their land' is also more often simply referred to as 'above', that is as 'mountains' or 'hills' in contrast to the Euphrates valley. According to Dossin,[45]

---

the fact that the formula also occurs in the form MU *zi-im-ri-li-im da-aw-da-am ša* DUMU.MEŠ *ya-mi-na i-du-ku* and the like (G. Dossin, *Les noms d'années et d'éponymes dans les 'Archives de Mari'*, Studia Mariana, Leiden 1950, 55 n.6 variant c). Cf. M.(L.) Burke, 'Un nouveau nom d'année du règne de Zimri-Lim?', *RA* 52, 1958, 57–59 (publication of *ARMT* XI 43); G. Dossin, 'À propos du nom des Benjaminites dans les "Archives de Mari",' *RA* 52, 1958, 60–62; M. L. Burke, *ARMT* XI (1963), 124 and n.2. On the reading *dawdâm* instead of **dawidâm* see H. Tadmor, 'Historical Implications of the Correct Rendering of Akkadian *dâku*', *JNES* 17, 1958, 129–31; on the phonetic values presupposed there for PI, viz. *aw/(ew)/iw/uw*, see J.-R. Kupper, *op. cit.*, 50 n.1; B. Landsberger in Tadmor, *op. cit.*, 130; I. J. Gelb, 'WA = *aw*, *iw*, *uw* in Cuneiform Writing', *JNES* 20, 1961, 194–8; E. Reiner, 'The Phonological Interpretation of a Subsystem in the Akkadian Syllabary', *From the Workshop of the Chicago Assyrian Dictionary: Studies Presented to A. L. Oppenheim, June 7, 1964* (Chicago 1964), 170f.; K. Deller, *Or* NS 34, 1965, 76 and n.1. G. Dossin, in M. L. Burke, *ARMT* XI (1963), 124 n.2, proposes the reading am_x; similarly J. Aro, *OLZ* 54, 1961, 604. On the etymology of the word *dabdû(m)/dawdû(m)/damdû* '(crushing) defeat' cf. Landsberger in Tadmor, *op. cit.*, 129, and on the contrary (surely correctly) Gelb, *op. cit.*, 196; on the other hand W. v. Soden, *AfO* 18, 1957, 122 and on the contrary Tadmor, *op. cit.*, 130 n.7. (On am_x cf. now G. Dossin, *RA* 61, 1967, 19–22.)

[42] Doubted by Gelb, *op. cit.*, 38.

[43] On this cf. K.-D. Schunck, *Benjamin: Untersuchungen zur Entstehung und Geschichte eines israelitischen Stammes* (BZAW 86, 1963), 4–6.

[44] *ARM* I 6.12.

[45] *Mélanges Dussaud* (see above n.38; abbreviated in the following as *Mél. Duss.*), 986. The texts cited from Dossin's article are designated according to W. v. Soden's procedure (*AHw*) by the page and from top to bottom with the letters a, b, c, d . . .

it is true, this is taken to refer to upper Mesopotamia, but one text, which speaks of an illegal crossing of the Euphrates by the Jaminites in the direction of the Bisir mountains (*a-na* KUR *bi-*[*s*]*i-ir*),[46] seems to indicate that the 'hills' of the Jaminites and of the nomads in general who were threatening Mari are to be found in the region of *jebel bišrī*.[47] Kinsmen (*aḫḫū*) of the Jaminites are also to be found 'on the other side' (of the frontier? of the Euphrates?) (*i-na e-bé-er-tim*) in the kingdom of Jamḫad,[48] the Rabbû or Rabbāyu who also appear frequently elsewhere in the Mari texts.[49] The hereditary economic system of the Jaminites was, of course, as was only to be expected from the fact that they originated in the steppe, the breeding and pasturing of small cattle, and this even in the region of Mari itself in spite of all the attempts on the part of the administration to make them sedentary and restrict them to regular farming. There is one mention, in a context which is, unfortunately, preserved in only a very fragmentary state, of the Jaminites pasturing sheep in the 'Euphrates meadow' (*aḫ purattim*) which lay within the territory of Mari (UDU.ḪÁ *na-wu-um* [*ša* DUMU.M]EŠ [*y*]*a-mi-na a-na aḫ* ÍDUD.KIB.NUN.NA[. . .).[50] The rights of pasturage, in this instance, are laid down by the state,[51] presumably by treaty.[52] Restricted possibilities of pasturage have, as

[46] *ARM* V 27.25f.

[47] On the mountains ba11-sal-la/*ba-sa-ar*/*bi-si-ir* see the references to literature on *jebel bišrī* above n. 8.

[48] *ARM* I 6.9f. Jamḫad is the name of the kingdom of Ḫalab (Aleppo).

[49] *ARM* I 24.2′ (cf. *ARMT* XV, 132 n.1); IV 6.5; VII 133.5; 211.17; VIII 11.30; *Mél.Duss.* 985: a.

[50] *ARM* II 90.7f.; cf. D. O. Edzard, *ZA* 53, 1959, 169. On *nawûm* see below pp. 116f. and n. 61.

[51] *ARM* I 43.10′–12′.

[52] Negative assertion in a letter from Jakīm-Addu to Zimri-Lim *Mél.Duss.* 984:a: (21) . . . *ki-ma ša i-na pa-ni-tim* (22) *i-nu-ma* DUM[U.MEŠ *ya-mi*]*-na ur-du-nim-ma* (23) *i-na sa-ga-ra-tim*KI *úš-bu* (24) *ù a-*[*n*]*a* LUGAL [*a*]*q-bu-ú um-ma a-na-ku-ma* (25) ANŠE*ḫa-a-ri ša* DUM[U.MEŠ] *ya-m*[*i*]*-na la ta-qa-tal* '. . . at that time when the Jaminites came down and settled in Sagarātum I said to the king: "Do not make a treaty with the Jaminites."' On the expression used here for 'make a treaty', viz. 'slay an ass' cf. G. Dossin, *Syria* 19, 1938, 108; M. Noth, 'Das alttestamentliche Bundschliessen im Lichte eines Mari-Textes' (1955), *Gesammelte Studien zum Alten Testament* (ThB 6, ²1960), 142–54 (ET 'Old Testament Covenant-making in the Light of a Text from Mari', *The Laws in the Pentateuch and Other Studies,* Edinburgh and London 1966, 108–17); *Die Ursprünge des alten Israel im Lichte neuer Quellen* (Arbeitsgemeinschaft für Forschung des Landes Nordrhein-Westfalen, Geisteswissenschaften, 94, Cologne and Opladen 1961), 21. So far, besides the passage mentioned, the following occurrences of the expression in the texts from Mari are known: (ii) *ARM* II 37.6–14 (Noth's principal text): (6) *a-na ḫa-a-ri-im qa-ta-li-im*

their consequence, transhumance, and this, since the movements of the nomads could not be strictly supervised, would surely be looked upon by the authorities with mistrust and would be prevented wherever possible.[53] As such a movement in connection with transhumance we must surely understand the crossing, anticipated by Zimri-Lim and his officials, of the Ubrabû, a sub-division of the Jaminites,[54] to the Rabbû, their 'brothers' (*aḫḫū*) living – as

---

(7) *bi-ri-it* ḪA.NA.MEŠ *ù i-da-ma-ra-aṣ* (8) *mì-ra-na-am ù ḫa-az-za-am iš-šu-ni-im-ma* (9) *be-lí ap-la-aḫ-ma-a mì-ra-na-am* (10) *ù ḫa-az-za-am ú-ul ad-di-in* (11) [*ḫa*]*-a-ra-am* DUMU *a-ta-ni-im* (12) *a-na-ku ú-š*[*a*]*-aq-ti-il* (13) [*s*]*a-li-ma-am bi-ri-it* ḪA.NA.MEŠ (14) *ù i-da-ma-ra-aṣ aš-ku-*[*u*]*n* 'to make a treaty between Hanaeans and Idamaraṣ a young dog and a she-goat were produced. However, I was afraid of my lord and did not permit the dog and the goat. I had an ass of good stock killed; I brought about an alliance between the Hanaeans and the Idamaraṣ.' (iii) *Mél.Duss.* 986: a, 10–14: (10) I*ás-di-ta-ki-im ù* LUGAL.MEŠ *ša za-al-ma-qi-im*KI[!?] (11) LÚ*su-ga-gu*MEŠ *ù* LÚŠU.GI.MEŠ [*š*]*a* DUMU.MEŠ *ya-mi-na* (12) *i-na* É.SUEN *ša ḫa-ar-ra-nim*KI ANŠE*ḫa-a-ri iq-tu-*[*ú-l*]*u* 'Asditakim, the kings of Zalmaqum (and) the *sugāgū* and elders of the Jaminites made a treaty in the Sîn-temple of Harran.' (iv) *Mél.Duss.* 991:b: *a-na mi-nim ta-aḫ-mu-uṭ-ma it-ti zi-im-ri-li-im* [*ù* DUMU *si-i*]*m-a-al* ANŠE*ḫa-a-ri ta-aq-tu-ul ù i-ša-ri-iš it-ti-šu-nu ta-da-ab-bu-ub* 'why have you hastily made a treaty with Zimri-Lim and the Sim'alites and come to an agreement with them?' (v) *Syria* 19, 109: 21–23: (21) *ù a-na a*[*b*]*-bé-e i-da-ma-ra-aṣ*KI *ù* [*a-du-na*]-DIŠKUR *šu-pu-ur-ma* (22) *a-na ṣe-ri-ka li-*[*i*]*l-li-ku-nim-ma* (23) *ḫa-a-ra-am ša sa-li-mi-im qú-tu-ul-ma it-ti-šu-nu i-ša-ri-iš du-b*[*u-u*]*b* 'and write to the "fathers" (*šuyūḫ*) of Idamaraṣ and to Adūna-Adad to come to you and make a treaty (and) come to an agreement with them.' (vi) *Syria* 19, 108: (16) *na-aš-pa-ar-tam an-ni-tam a-na bi-na-ištar* (17) *aš-pu-ur* I*bi-na-ištar ke-em i-pu-ul* (18) *um-ma-a-mi it-ti qar-ni-li-im* (19) ANŠE*ḫa-a-ra-am aq-tu-ul ù i-na ni-iš* DINGIR.MEŠ (20) *a-na-ku a-na qar-ni-li-im ke-em aq-bi* (21) *um-ma a-na-ku-ma šum-ma a-na zi-im-ri-li-im* (22) *ù um-ma-na-ti-šu tu-qá-al-la-al* (23) *a-na-ku a-na be-el a-wa-ti-ka a-ta-ar* 'This message have I sent to Bina-Ištar. Bina-Ištar has answered thus: "I have made a treaty with Qarni-Lim and said on oath to Qarni-Lim: If you offend against Zimri-Lim and his troops, I shall become your enemy".' (vii) Recently the expression has also appeared in a letter from Zimri-Lim of Mari to Ḫadnurapi found in *tell er-rimāḥ*: ANŠE*ḫa-a-ri i ni-iq-tu-ul* 'let us make a treaty'; with the same meaning in the same text there also occurs: *ni-iš* DINGIR.MEŠ *bi-ri-ni li-iš-ša-ak-nu-ma* 'an oath is sworn between us' (TR 4012; see S. Page, *Iraq* 30, 1968, 89).

For 'make a treaty' one can also say in Mari *epēšu* + *salīmam*, e.g. *Mél. Duss.* 991:c, 23f.

[53] Cf. *ARM* II 92.5–29 and, by way of contrast, *Mél.Duss.* 989:d.

[54] This is inferred in the following way: In the foundation document of the Šamaš temple e-girzal-an-ki (written phonetically É.GI.IR.ZA.LA.AN.KI = *bīt tašīlat šamê u erṣetim*) of Jaḫdun-Lim the three enemy kings I*la-ú-um* LUGAL *sa-ma-nim*KI *ù ma-at ub-ra-bi-im* I*ba-aḫ-lu-ku-li-im* LUGAL *tu-tu-ul*KI *ù ma-at am-na-ni-im* I*a-ya-lum* LUGAL *a-ba-at-tim*KI *ù ma-at ra-ab-bi-im* (III 4–9; *Syria* 32, 1955, 14) are described in the course of the narrative as 3 LUGAL.MEŠ *an-nu-ti-im ša* DUMU *mi-im* 'these three kings of the Jaminites' (III 20f.) (on the

we have seen – in Jamḫad, a crossing of which we hear in a letter to the king.[55] At any rate, a change of pasture – forced on them by circumstances – on the part of the already settled Jaminites is viewed with similar mistrust. A significant text in this respect is ARM II 102.9–16:

9 LÚ.MEŠ *ša ki-ma i-na sa-ga-ra-tim*^{KI}
10 *wa-aš-bu e-li-iš-ma pa-nu-šu-nu*
11 *ù* UDU.ḪA-*šu-nu ša i-na la-as-q*[*í*]-*im*
12 *i-ka-la e-li-iš-ma ú-še-še-ru*
13 *ša ki-ma i-ša-al-lu*
14 *um-ma-a-mi ri-tum*
15 *ú-ul i-ba-aš-ši-ma*
16 *ù* <*e*>-*li-iš nu-še-še-*[*er*]

'all the people who dwell in Sagarātum[56] (turn) their faces to the hills (*eliš*), and their sheep which graze on the *lasqum*[57] do they drive to the hills. Everyone who was called to account (said) as follows: "There is no (more) pasturage; therefore we drive to the hills." '[58] For pasturing, the Jaminites also have *ḫaṣirātum* and *tarbaṣātum* (TÙR.ḪÁ),[59] i.e. stockyards and cattle pens, in which

interpretation of *šarrānu* and *mār mīm* see above n. 41 and bellow nn. 81 and 94). It is clear from this that at least the three tribes mentioned belong to the Jaminites; of the cities, in any case, Samānum is known from other passages to be Jaminite (see below n. 64). In *ARM* III 50.10–13, 1 ^{LÚ}*ub-ra-bu-u*[*m*] 1 ^{LÚ}*ya-ḫu-ur-r*[*u-u*]*m ù* <1 ^{LÚ}> *aw*(PI)-*na-nu-*[*um*] are also summed up as 3 LÚ.MEŠ *an-nu-tum ša* DUMU.MEŠ [*y*]*a-mi-na*. On this cf. also H. Klengel, *Benjaminiten und Hanäer zur Zeit der Könige von Mari* (Thesis, Berlin 1958, typewritten), 16–19.

[55] *ARM* I 6.9f.; see above n. 48.

[56] Elsewhere too Sagarātum figures as a Jaminite centre; cf. above n. 52 and *ARMT* XV, 132 *s.v.* Sagarātum; Kupper, *op. cit.*, *passim* (see Index p. 279ᵃ *s.v.*).

[57] *Lasqum/lašqum*, in spite of the isolated determination with KI (*la-ás-qí-im*^{KI}) in *Mél.Duss.*, 986f. n. 1, is surely not a place name (see also below n. 64) but the designation of a particular type of pasture land; cf. D. O. Edzard, *ZA* 53, 1959, 170 n. 8; W. v. Soden, *AHw* 539ᵇ.

[58] In the German edition of this book the passage was interpreted differently; I have however been convinced by the criticism of W. L. Moran, *CBQ* 30, 1968, 644f.

[59] *Mél.Duss.* 989:d: (4) *aš-šum ḫa-ṣí-ra-tim ù* TÙR.ḪÁ (5) *ša* ḪA.NA.A DUMU.MEŠ *ya-mi-im* (6) *ma-ḫa-ṣí-im ù ba-li-iḫ šu-bu-ri-im be-lí ú-we-er-an-ni* 'with reference to the fact that my lord has ordered me to destroy the yards and pens of the Jaminite "Hanaeans" and make (them) cross the Baliḫ . . .' The form *ya-mi-im* is not an error for **ya-mi-na* (so G. Dossin, *Mél. Duss.*, 989 n. 3) but, as the other reference in *ARMT* XII 33 (see below n. 94) shows, is the middle step between *yamīn*(*a*/*i*) and *mīm* (see above n. 41).

connection one should also note that *ḫasirātum* is an 'Amorite' word corresponding to Hebrew *ḥaṣērōt*.[60] The Jaminites' small cattle, like that of the Hanaeans (who were also still partly nomadic) and of the city dwellers themselves, is found in the 'pasture land' (*nawûm*),[61] either in the 'Euphrates meadow' (*aḫ purattim*)[62] or perhaps in the territory of Idamaraṣ;[63] *nawûm* is then also used

---

Klengel, *op. cit.,* 28; *WZ* Berlin 8, 1958/59, 212, takes ḪA.NA.A DUMU.MEŠ *ya-mi-im* to mean 'Benjaminites settled or living in Hana'; but I think it more probable that the name of the Hanaeans is used here as a secondary appellative for 'nomads' (see above n. 5). On the Hanaeans cf. generally Kupper, *op. cit.*, 1–46; Klengel, *op. cit.* (Thesis), 20–28; on the *ḫaṣirātum,* Klengel, *ibid.*, 84f.; Noth, *Ursprünge,* 37; D. O. Edzard, *ZA* 56, 1964, 145.

60 *Ḥaṣērīm* of the Ishmaelites alongside *ṭīrōt* Gen. 25.16, of the Kedarites alongside *'ārīm* Isa. 42.11: *yiśśeʾū midbār weʿārāw ḥaṣērīm tēšēb qēdār* 'let the desert and its "cities" lift up (their voice), the villages that Kedar inhabits' (NŚ' absolutely for NŚ' + *qōl*: Num. 14.1; Isa. 3.7; 42.2; Job 21.12; the conjectures proposed for these passages in BHK³ are unnecessary).

61 D. O. Edzard's definition of the term *nawûm* (later *namû*) as 'the herds of a nomadic tribe together with the members of the tribe who are with them and accompany them' ('Altbabylonisch *nawûm*', *ZA* 53, 1959, 168–73; cf. A. Falkenstein in Edzard, *Die 'zweite Zwischenzeit' Babyloniens* (1957), 106 n. 522) seems to me to be too one-sided and does not always do justice to the passages cited. One has to arrange his material thus:

(1) (primary meaning) 'pasture land' *ARM* II 45.9′–11′; V 23.10–13; BE VI: 1, 72; *Era* IV 66; *Mél.-Duss.* 988:a; 992:b; *RA* 36, 49:4f.; VAB VI 22.9–12; 71.11; 77.5; 225.12; YOS X 56 II 37–39.

(2) (derived from [1]: contents of the pasture land) 'herd(s together with shepherds)' *ARM* II 35.7–11, 19f.; 59.4–6; 90.7–10; III 15.10–20; VI 42.18f.; *Mél.-Duss.* 986f. n.1; 989:c; *Syria* 19, 109 (Bannum to Zimri-Lim); YOS X 13.11; 36 I 35.

(3) Decision not possible (in most cases probably 1) *ARM* I 6.26–28, 41–43 (ḪA.NA *ša nawîm*); 42.5–7 (ḪA.NA.MEŠ *ša nawîm*); II 48.8f.; 98.4′–10′; *Mél.-Duss.* 991: c.

Hebr. *nāwe* means 'pasture land' at least in the following passages: II Sam. 7.8; Isa. 65.10; Jer. 23.3; 33.12; 50.19; Ezek. 25.5; 34.14; Amos 1.2; Zeph. 2.6; Ps. 23.1f.; I Chron. 17.7. Literature on *nawûm/namû* in Edzard, *op. cit.*, 168 nn.1 and 2; cf. further Klengel, Thesis, 80–82; *WZ* Berlin 8, 1958/59, 213f.; Noth, *Ursprünge,* 16, 30 and n.61; Edzard, *ZA* 56, 1964, 146. The denominative verb from *nawûm* in Akkadian, *nawûm* Dt (*MAOG* 11: 33, 1; *RA* 38, 83:11) means 'to be made into pasture land'; on this concept cf. *KUB* VII 60 III 23–30; Jer. 33.12; Ezek. 25.5; Zeph. 2.6.

On the exact meaning of the expression *ḫibrum ša nawîm* (*ARM* VIII 11.21; cf. *ḫibrum* in a defective context I 119. 10 and in the unpublished texts A 1296, 2605, 2796, 2801) one can so far say hardly anything that is not merely supposition; cf. J. Bottéro, *Le problème des Ḫabiru à la 4e Rencontre Assyriologique Internationale* (Cahiers de la Société Asiatique 12, Paris 1954), 204; Kupper, *op. cit.*, 20 n.1; P. Fronzaroli, *AGI* 45, 1960, 45–47; M. Noth, *op. cit.*, 35f.; D. O. Edzard, *ZA* 56, 1964, 145.

62 *ARM* II 90.7–10; *Mél.-Duss.* 988:a; 989:c.

63 *Syria* 19, 109 (Bannum to Zimri-Lim).

for the herds together with the shepherds. In the region of Mari, both Jaminites and Hanaeans have, besides the shelters already mentioned as being used for cattle rearing, *ālānû*[64] and *kaprātum*,[65] i.e., according to normal Akkadian usage, 'cities' and 'villages'. They possess arable land which presumably belongs to the royal estate[66] and for which they are subjected to the *šibšum*,[67] and they grow barley (*še'um*).[68] All of this indicates that the Jaminites are at the point of transition from the nomadic life to the sedentary life. It is true that we do not know exactly what special sense the words *ālum* and *kaprum* have. Kupper[69] says, certainly correctly, that they cannot be cities built by the nomads themselves; in his opinion they are 'flimsy shelters which the non-sedentary population use from time to time when they return from a change of pasture, or which are used by their womenfolk and children when they set off for the *rezzou*'. Similar judgments are passed by Fronzaroli:[70] 'not real cities, but "villages" used by the Semites of the

[64] *ālānû* of the Hanaeans: *ARM* II 48.9, 10; of the Jaminites: *ARM* II 92.5,12; III 12.19, 25; 16.5; 21.5; 38.15, 17, 25; *Mél.Duss.* 984:b (= *RA* 35, 178f.: 14f.), c; 993:c. The following are mentioned by name as *ālānû* of the Jaminites: Dumtēn (*ARM* III 38.17; on the reading of the name cf. *ARMT* XIII, 169 on no. 124; J.-R. Kupper, *Syria* 41, 1964, 105 and n. 2), Ilum-Muluk (*Mél.Duss.* 994:e, f; *RA* 35, 178f.: 111f.; cf. also below n. 76), Samānum (*Mél.Duss.* 994:e; *RA* 35, 178f.: 10; cf. also above n. 54), Raqqum (*Mél. Duss.* 994:e), Rasāyum (*Mél. Duss.* 994:f.), Dabiriš (*ibid.*) and perhaps Mišlān (*RA* 35, 178f.: 13). On the settlement of the Jaminites in Sagarātum see above n. 52. Cf. also Klengel, Thesis, 49–53 where, however, *lasqum* is wrongly understood as a place name (p. 53) and Zurubbān is incorrectly listed among the Jaminite settlements (pp. 49f.).

[65] *Mél.Duss.* 984:d, e.

[66] Cf. Kupper, *Nomades*, 58; 'Correspondance de Kibri-Dagan', *Syria* 41, 1964, 109.

[67] *Mél.Duss.* 985:b. The exact definition of the *šibšu*(*m*), which is attested from the Old to the Neo-Babylonian period, has not yet been achieved. All that is certain is that it is a tax or tribute paid in kind. On this cf. amongst the most recent literature E. Ebeling, *Bruchstücke einer mittelassyrischen Vorschriftensammlung für die Akklimatisierung und Trainierung von Wagenpferden* (VIO 7, 1951), 15; J. J. Finkelstein, *JCS* 7, 1953, 140; 15, 1961, 95f.; A. Goetze, *Sumer* 14, 1958, 39; F. R. Kraus, *Ein Edikt des Königs Ammi-Ṣaduqa von Babylon* (Studia et Documenta ad Iura Orientis antiqui pertinentia 5, Leiden 1958), 126–32; H. Klengel, *WZ* Berlin 8, 1958/59, 216[b]; M. L. Burke, *ARMT* XI (1963), 130f.; J.-R. Kupper, *Syria* 41, 1964, 109.

[68] *Še'um* of the Jaminites is mentioned in *Mél.Duss.* 985: a, 15′; 989: c, 26.

[69] *Nomades*, 13f. Similarly P. Sacchi, *PP* 14, fasc. 65, 1959, 132f.

[70] 'L'ordinamento gentilizio semitico e i testi di Mari', *AGI* 45, 1960, 41. Fronzaroli adopts this position even against the theory, represented, e.g., by L. Matouš, 'Einige Bemerkungen zum Beduinenproblem im alten Mesopotamien', *ArOr* 26, 1958, 633, that *ālum* here is to be understood in the sense

steppes', and by Klengel:[71] 'settlements' to be distinguished from cities and villages. In my opinion these definitions are somewhat too one-sided. It is true that, on the basis of the conventional phraseology in *Mél.Duss.* 993: c, 8′–10′:

> *[i]-na qi-bi-it* ᴰ*da-gan ù* ᴰ*i-[t]úr-me-er be-lí da-aw-da-am ša na-ak-ri-šu i-du-uk-ma a-la-ni-šu-nu a-na ti-li-im ù ka-ar-mi-im ú-te-er*
>
> 'on the instructions of Dagan and Iturmer my lord has dealt his enemies (*scil.* the Jaminites) a (crushing) defeat and has transformed their cities into heaps of ruins and wasteland'

with its mention of the *telāl* of Jaminite cities, one must guard against drawing any too far-reaching conclusions about the nature of these *ālānu*;[72] but a few passages in the Mari texts suggest that it was not simply a question of 'tent villages' but also of permanent settlements outside the walled cities such as Mari, Terqa etc.[73] We can, therefore, accept the definition of Edzard,[74] which leaves room for all possibilities that might arise: 'any place in which a tribe or part of a tribe settles permanently or temporarily, either a collection of tents and mud huts or a larger, village-like settlement'. When, in the list in *Mél.Duss.* 994:f, six Jaminites are mentioned, by name and by their place of residence, as having been released from being prisoners of war (*waššurūtum*), the way in which they are described presupposes that we are dealing here with members of a tribe who are settled in permanent quarters and who are also subject to the jurisdiction[75] of the king of Mari. This is clear also in *Mél.Duss.* 994:e where the official Ilišu-naṣir sends the following inquiry to the king, probably after Zimri-Lim's great victory over the Jaminites (cf. *Mél.Duss.* 994:f) which we shall discuss shortly:

---

of the etymologically related Hebr. *'ōhel* as 'tent'. There is no proof that this meaning was even known in Akkadian.

[71] Thesis, 94–98.

[72] Stereotyped expression for the destruction of 'cities'; cf. the foundation document of the Šamaš temple of Jaḫdun-Lim (see above n. 54) III 26f.; IV 1 (*Syria* 32, 1955, 15).

[73] Cf. Kupper, *op. cit.*, 14, 57, 76 and n. 1, 77 and n. 1; J. C. L. Gibson, 'Light from Mari on the Patriarchs', *JSS* 7, 1962, 57f.

[74] *ZA* 53, 1959, 171; cf. 56, 1964, 145.

[75] *ARM* II 92.5f., 11–20, 21f., 24–27. Alongside this they probably had a tribal jurisdiction of their own represented particularly in the institution of the *šāpiṭum*; on this cf. Fronzaroli, *op. cit.*, 51–54; M. Noth, *Ursprünge*, 17; D. O. Edzard, *ZA* 56, 1964, 147; W. Richter, *ZAW* 77, 1965, 64–68.

i-na ṣa-bi-im^{MEŠ} DUMU.MEŠ *ya-mi-na ša be-lí i-na qa-at-tu-na-an*^{KI} *i-zi-bu* 12 LÚ.TUR.MEŠ [. . . . . .]ḪÁ TUR.MEŠ [. . . . . .]*ša i-na i-lu-um-mu-lu-uk*^{KI} [*s*]*a-ma-nim ù* [*r*]*a-aq-*[*q*]*í-im*^{KI} *wa-aš-bu be-lí ṭe*$_4$*-em* LÚ.MEŠ [*š*]*u-nu-ti ša wa-aš-šu-ri-šu-nu ù la wa-aš-šu-ri-šu-nu li-iš-pu-ra-am*

'amongst the Jaminites whom my lord has left in (the city of) Qattunān are twelve young men . . . who belong to (the cities of) Ilum-Muluk,[76] Samānum and Raqqum. Let my lord send me instructions whether those men are to be set free or not'.

Here we are clearly dealing with Jaminites who, although they are settled in the cities mentioned (that is clearly indicated by the stative *wašbū*), went out to battle against Zimri-Lim with their kinsmen in the steppe and on that occasion were taken prisoner by the king. Even the Jaminite 'city' of Dumtēn appears, according to the text of *Mél.Duss.* 989:a = *ARM* III 38.15–26 which we shall discuss later, to have been a permanent settlement. How, on the other hand, the nomads came to have *kaprātum*[77] is shown in two excerpts from letters of Ḫaliḫadum to Zimri-Lim *Mél.Duss.* 984:d, e, of which I reproduce e here:

[76] In passing I draw attention to the fact that this place name can figure in the discussion about the existence or non-existence of the god 'Moloch' (*mōlek*) (along these lines cf. already G. Dossin, *RA* 35, 1938, 178 and n.1; A. Bea, *Bibl* 20, 1939, 415). The name also occurs in the forms DINGIR-*mu-lu-uk*^{KI} (*ARM* III 73.20), DINGIR-*mu-lu-ka-yi*^{KI} (*ARM* III 59.8; *nisba*) and *i-lu-ma*^{sic}*-li-ka-yi*^{KI} (*RA* 35, 178 n.1; *nisba*). Besides it, there occurs in the texts from Ugarit a place-name ^{URU}*mu-lu-uk*^{KI}(?) or ^{URU}*mu-lu-uk-ki*(?) (RS 12.34 + 43, 32 [*PRU* III, 193]; 16.170, v°. 6′, 7′ [*ibid.*, 91]) and an 'Amorite' personal name *i-tar-mu-lu-uk* (Th. Bauer, *Die Ostkanaanäer*, Leipzig 1926, 23). In the case of *mul*(*u*)*k*- it is not simply another form for *malik*-, but probably the abstract noun **mulk*- 'kingdom' (cf. Arab. *mulkun*) and the same is probably the case with the Hebr. *mōlek*. On the phenomenon of *abstractum pro concreto* it is enough to refer here to Phoen. *mmlkt* which often stands for *mlk* 'king'.

[77] It is impossible to determine from the texts the difference between *ālānû* and *kaprātum* in relationship to the nomadic population in the territory round Mari. According to D. O. Edzard, *ZA* 53, 1959, 171 n.11; 56, 1964, 145, *kaprum* is 'village', an 'expression for small settlements of the sedentary population on the flat land', according to M. Noth, *op. cit.*, 16f. and n.22, 'apparently really a complex of storehouses . . . such as itinerant shepherds are in the habit of having even today to store and secure the produce of their work in the fields'. The connections between *kaprātum* and the storing of grain which are mentioned by Noth, *op. cit.*, n.22, can be explained from the sense 'villages' just as easily as from the sense 'storehouses'.

6 *ki-im be-lí iš-pu-ram*
7 *um-ma-mi* ḪA.NA.MEŠ *an-ni-iš*
8 *li-ir-dam-ma i-na ka-ap-ra-at*
9 DUMU.MEŠ *ya-mi-na* 1 *ka-ap-ra-am*
10 *li-il-qú-ma li-ku-lu*
11 *an-ni-tam be-lí iš-pu-ra-am-ma*

'Thus has my lord written to me: "The Hanaeans may settle here; amongst the villages of the Jaminites they may take (possession of) and make use of[78] a village." This has my lord written.'

This means that the *kaprātum* at least were assigned to the (nomadic) owners on the authority of the state. That this was the case also with respect to the *ālānû* there is no evidence, but it is nevertheless probable. This would mean that it is a question of existing establishments which the state had at its disposal for nomadic tribes of sheep breeders in order to facilitate their transition to a sedentary life and their incorporation into the state confederacy. In the case of the Jaminites,[79] this appears to have been a difficult undertaking which ended in violent conflicts and in catastrophe for the Jaminites. For the nomads were unable to accustom themselves quickly enough to the obligations which the state system laid upon its subjects. The much discussed 'nomadic ideal'[80] emerges from the words of the *sugāgum*[81] of the Jaminite 'city'

[78] On *akālum* 'eat' in the sense 'make use of' see *AHw* 27[a] *s.v. akālu(m)* 7b.

[79] The relationship of the Hanaeans to the central government of Mari was apparently of a friendly nature even if not always free of tensions; cf. Kupper, *op. cit.*, 21–40; Matouš, *ArOr* 26, 1958, 633.

[80] On this cf. the classic study by K. Budde, 'Das nomadische Ideal im Alten Testament', *Preussische Jahrbücher* 85, 1896, 57ff.; further J. W. Flight, 'The Nomadic Idea and Ideal in the Old Testament', *JBL* 42, 1923, 158–226; G. Nyström, *Beduinentum und Jahwismus: Eine soziologisch-religionsgeschichtliche Untersuchung zum Alten Testament* (Lund 1946); also M. Y. Ben-Gavriel, 'Das nomadische Ideal in der Bibel', *Stimmen der Zeit* 88, 1962/3, 253–63.

[81] On the meaning of the word *sugāgum* (probably to be read thus, not *suqāqum*) cf. G. Dossin, *RHA* fasc. 15, 1939, 72 n. 2; J.-R. Kupper, *RA* 41, 1947, 164; *Nomades*, 16–19; H. Klengel, Thesis, 103–19; *WZ* Berlin 8, 1958/9, 217–19; P. Fronzaroli, *AGI* 45, 1960, 54–56, on the etymology P. Fronzaroli, '*Su-ga-gu-um* "sceicco"', *PP* 14 fasc. 66, 1959, 189–93; E. E. Knudsen, 'Cases of Free Variants in the Akkadian *q* Phoneme', *JCS* 15, 1961, 87[a] and n. 24.

Kupper's distinction between three categories of *sugāgū* (1. 'Chiefs of clans or villages who generally form a kind of college'; 2. '*muḫtār*'; 3. 'agent in the service of the king') is not convincing (against it also Fronzaroli, *AGI*

(*ālum*) of Dumtēn who replies to the royal official concerning the demand to submit to forced labour: LÚ*na-ak-rum l*[*e*]*-el-li-kam-ma i-na a-li-ni-ma li-it-ba-la-an-ni-ti* 'let the enemy come and drag us away out of our "city"!'[82] The 'enemy' is the power of the state represented by the royal official and his men. It is, therefore, not surprising that we frequently encounter the Jaminites (and also the Hanaeans) on *ghazawāt* (described in Akkadian as *šaḫāṭum*,[83] *qalālum*,[84] *riḫṣum*,[85] *ṭēm nukurtim*)[86] which are usually directed

---

45, 54f.). It is possible to work solely with Kupper's second sense in every case and to see in the *sugāgum* an official who is actually chosen by the notables of a place but installed by the king (*ARM* I 119; V 24) and who has to carry out administrative duties (it should be noted that in *ARM* V 24.11, 20 the terms *šāpirūtum* and *sugāgūtum* are used interchangeably for the same office). In the passage cited here we are dealing with an act of defiance of the consequences of which for the *sugāgum* we have no knowledge. In contrast to the *sugāgū* ('*maḫātīr*') of the Jaminites who are completely or partly sedentary, the *šuyūḫ* of the 'free' Jaminites are called *šarrānu* (LUGAL.MEŠ *ša* DUMU.MEŠ *ya-mi-na* *ARM* II 36.11f.; III 70.4'; *Mél.Duss.* 988:b, 36; cf. the two year-formulae of Zimri-Lim MU *zi-im-ri-li-im da-aw-da-am ša* DUMU.MEŠ *ya-mi-na i-na sa-ga-ra-tim*KI *i-du-ku ù* LUGAL.MEŠ-*šu-nu ik-šu-du* 'year in which Zimri-Lim inflicted a (crushing) defeat on the Jaminites at (*ina*) Sagarātum and took their "kings" prisoner' and MU *zi-im-ri-li-im da-aw-da-am ša* DUMU.MEŠ *ya-mi-na ù* LUGAL.MEŠ-*šu-nu i-du-ku* 'year in which Zimri-Lim inflicted a (crushing) defeat on the Jaminites and their "kings"' *Mél.Duss.* 981; *Studia Mariana,* 1950, 55 no. 6 with variant b; cf. above n. 41 and below n. 94). Klengel, Thesis, *loc. cit.* would not regard the difference noted here as valid and identifies *šarrānu* and *sugāgū* (both = *šuyūḫ*); slightly differently *WZ* Berlin 8, 217f. The situation is different if city kings together with the title 'king of the city of X' also have the title 'king of the land of Y' where Y is a tribal name; see the foundation document of the Šamaš temple of Jaḫdun-Lim III 4–9 (*Syria* 32, 1955, 14; cf. above n. 54) and the title 'king of Mari, (Tuttul) and of the land of ḪA.NA' (Kupper, *op. cit.* 30). Here there is expressed the claim to control of the nomads living in the territory of the city in question, a claim formulated entirely in accordance with the political structure of the Mesopotamian states. Cf. generally Kupper, *op. cit.*, 30f.

82 *Mél.Duss.* 989:a = *ARM* III 38.19–22. According to W. L. Moran, *CBQ* 30, 1968, 645, the reaction of the *sugāgum* betrays a general human and natural 'distaste for forced labour' which is not necessarily characteristic of nomads. It must of course be borne in mind that in the nomadic-bedouin milieu animosity against any kind of forced labour finds particularly vehement and fundamental expression (an experience which in our own century the Turks had with the Arabs) and that the inhabitants of Dumtēn are people whose distance from the nomadic life of the steppe is still quite small. Whether the reference to Codex Ḫammurapi (§30 and) §31 is relevant in this context I am not sure.

83 *Mél.Duss.* 987:e+988:a; 988:c; 991:d.

84 *Mél.Duss.* 987:c.

85 *Mél.Duss.* 988:b. *Riḫṣum* is best rendered by '(hostile) attack'.

86 *Mél.Duss.* 989:b.

against the herds of the *nawûm*,[87] but which also occasionally lead to greater acts of violence.[88] Here too it is worthwhile to cite a significant example from a letter of Zimri-Lim to a certain Jašši-Dagan:

4 *iš-tu* u$_4$*-mi-im ša a-na a-aḫ* ^{ÍD}UD.KIB.NUN.NA *ú-ra-am-me-e-em*
5 DUMU.MEŠ *ya-mi-na ši-ta-ḫu-ṭì-im qa-tam iš-ta-ka-nu*
6 1-*šu iš-ḫi-ṭú-ma* UDU.ḪÁ *ma-da-tim il-qú-ú*
7 *ṣa-ba-am né-eḫ-ra-ra-am wa-ar-ki-šu-nu aṭ-ru-ud-ma*
8 *da-aw-da-šu-nu i-du-ku iš-te-*[*en*] *i-na li-ib-su-nu*
9 *ú-ul ú-ṣí ù* UDU.ḪÁ *ma-li il-qú-ú ú-te-ru-nim*
10 *iš-nu-ú ap-pu-na iš-ḫi-ṭú* UDU.ḪÁ *il-qú-ú-ma*
11 *né-eḫ-ra-ra-am aṭ-ru-ud ik-šu-ud-su-nu-ti-ma*
12 *d*[*a*]*-a*[*w-da-š*]*u-nu i-du-ku ù* UDU.ḪÁ *ša il-qú-ú ú-te-ru-nim*
13 [*iš*]*-li-šu*[89] *ap-pu-na qa-tam-ma i-pu-šu*
14 [. . . . . . M]EŠ *ma-li i-ša-ḫi-ṭú ú-ul i-ša-al-li-mu*

'From the day when I had gone to the Euphrates meadow,[90] the Jaminites carried out raids without ceasing:[91] On one occasion they stole and took away many sheep. I sent police troops[92] after them (and) they defeated them, so that not a single one escaped, and they brought back all the sheep which they had taken. – Again they made a second raid and took sheep; but I

[87] References in D. O. Edzard, 'Altbabylonisch *nawûm*', *ZA* 53, 1959, 169. See also above pp. 116f. and n. 61.

[88] *Ki-ma* 3 *me-tim ṣa-ab* LÚ [. . .] [*y*]*a-* [*m*]*i-nu-um i-du-ku ta-aš-pu-ra-am* 'you have written (to me) that the *yamīnûm* (Jaminite) has killed about three hundred of the "man" (see above ch. II 1 n. 11) of . . . (?)' *ARM* I 67.6f. The interpretation of the section is not quite certain.

[89] Reading proposed by D. O. Edzard, *ZA* 53, 1959, 169 n. 7; G. Dossin restores [*ú-ša-a*]*l-li-šu*. But Edzard points to the fact that according to *GAG* §88g *šalāšum* D means 'to treble'; for 'to do for the third time' *šalāšum* G is used. Analogously in line 10 *šanûm* G (not D) 'to do for the second time' (*šanûm* D = 'to double/to repeat' > 'to narrate').

[90] 1st sing. pret. vent. D *ramû: urammêm* < **urammi-am*; cf. A. Finet, *L'Accadien des lettres de Mari* (Académie Royale de Belgique, classe des Lettres et des Sciences morales et politiques, Mémoires, II 51, Brussels 1956), 153 §59d. On *ramû* 'throw' in the sense of 'betake oneself' cf. G *ma-ḫa-ri-iš ab-bé-e-šu a-na ma-li-ku-ti ir-me* 'before his fathers he (*scil.* Marduk) received princely dignity (literally: he betook himself to princely dignity)' *Enūma eliš* IV 2; D (cf. *ARMT* XV, 249: 'se déplacer') *ARM* I 19 v°. 9; 36.24; inf. D *rummû* ('emigration') *ARM* I 19 v°. 5, 7.

[91] Pret. Gt.; see *GAG* §92f.

[92] Probably actually 'auxiliary troops'; *ne'rārum* 'help' (W. v. Soden, *Or* NS 20, 1951, 258 and n. 4), on the verb *na'arrurum* 'hasten to help' (v. Soden, *ibid.*, 258ff.).

sent the police and they caught them and defeated them and brought back the sheep which they had taken. – Again, they did the same a third time; but no one . . . who had taken part in the raid derived any benefit from it."[93]

The text of the report speaks for itself, and it is therefore completely understandable that Zimri-Lim should have decided to 'solve' the Jaminite problem by force. We do not know when the king inflicted the crushing defeat on the trouble-makers at Sagarātum; it must, however, have appeared so significant to him that he designated two different years with reference to this event.[94] The

[93] *Mél.Duss.* 988:c.

[94] As far as I am aware it has not yet been established which years of Zimri-Lim's reign are involved here; cf. now however the attempted classification in M. Birot, *ARMT* XII (1964), 16–18. The following variants of the formula are known to me:
Year 1
(a) MU *zi-im-ri-li-im da-aw-da-am ša* DUMU.MEŠ *ya-mi-na i-na sa-ga-ra-tim*KI *i-du-ku ù* LUGAL.MEŠ-*šu-nu ik-su-du*: *Mél.Duss.* 981; *Studia Mariana*, 55 no. 6. Cf. above n. 81.
(b) MU *zi-im-ri-li-im da-aw-da-am ša* DUMU.MEŠ *ya-mi-na i-na sa-ga-ra-tim*Ki *i-du-ku: Mél.Duss., ibid.*; *Studia Mariana*, 55 no. 6 var. a.
(c) MU *zi-im-ri-li-im da-aw-da-am ša* DUMU.MEŠ *ya-mi-na ù* LUGAL.MEŠ-*šu-nu i-du-ku*: *Mél.Duss., ibid.; Studia Mariana*, 55 no. 6 var. b. Cf. above n. 81.
(d) MU *zi-im-ri-li-im da-aw-da-am ša* DUMU.MEŠ *ya-mi-na i-du-ku*: *Mél.Duss., ibid.; Studia Mariana*, 55 no. 6 var. c; *ARM(T)* VII 87.13–16; 88.23–26; XI 25.13–15 (,*16); 26.12–15; XII 27; 28; 31 (DUMU.ME *ya-mi-na*); 34; 38; 43; 44; 46; 56; 106 (cf. *ARMT* XII, 34 n. 1).
(e) MU *zi-im-ri-li-im da-aw-da-am ša* DUMU.MEŠ *ya-mi-ni i-du-ku*: *ARMT* XI 27.8–11; 28.11–14; 29.13–15; 30.8–11; 31.6–9; 32.8–11; 33.11–14; 34.18–21; 35.8–11; 36.7–10; 37.11–14; 38.13–16; 39.8–11; 40.7–10; 41.6′–9′; 42.8–11; 46.17–20; 47.14′–17′; XII 42 (DUMU.MEŠ [*mi*] *ya-mi-ni*); 47; 49–52; 54; 55; 57–81; 83; 86; 90–102; 104; 108 (cf. on d).
(f) MU *zi-im-ri-li-im da-aw-da-am ša* DUMU.MEŠ *ya-mi-nim i-du-ku*: *ARMT* XII 82; 85; 87; 89 (cf. on d).
(g) MU *zi-im-ri-li-im da-aw-da-am ša* DUMU.MEŠ *ya-mi-im i-du-ku*: *ARMT* XII 33 (cf. on d); see also above n. 59.
(h) [MU *zi*]-*im-ri-li-im* [*da-aw*]-*da*-[*a*]*m* [*ša* DUMU.MEŠ *ya-m*]*i-i* [*i-du*]-*ku*: *ARMT* XI 23.7–10; XII 35; 52 (DUMU.MEŠ *ya-mi*) (see on d); cf. also G. Dossin, *RA* 52, 1958, 60.
(i) MU *zi-im-ri-li-im da-aw-da-am ša* DUMU.MEŠ *mi-i i-du-ku*: *ARMT* XI 18.16–19; 19.15–18; 20.14–17; 21.8–11; 24.7–10; 44.10–14; XII 20–26; 29; 30; 37; 40; 41; 45; 107 (DUMU.MEŠ *mi-e*) (cf. on d). On this see above n. 41.
(k) MU *zi-im-ri-li-im da-aw-da-am ša ma-ar mi-i i-du-ku*) *ARMT* XI 43.18–21. On this see above n. 41.
Year 2
(a) *ša-ni-tum* MU *ša zi-im-ri-li-im da-aw-da-am ša* DUMU.MEŠ *ya-mi-ni i-du-ku*: *Mél.Duss.* 982; *ARMT* XI 48.7–11.
(b) *ša-ni-tum ša-tu ša zi-im-ri-li-im da-aw-da-am ša* DUMU.MEŠ *ya-mi-ni i-du-ku*:

effect was felt also elsewhere;[95] for the following excerpt from the report of a governor to the king also appears to refer to the great battle against the Jaminites:

8′ *ša-ni-tam aš-šum* DUMU.MEŠ *ya-aw-ma-ḫa-ma-yi*^{KI}
9′ *ša be-lí iš-pu-ra-am iš-tu u*$_4$*-mi-im*
10′ *ša be-lí i-na na-we-e* DUMU.MEŠ *ya-mi-in*
11′ *im-ḫa-ṣu it-ta-[al-k]u-nim*
12′ *ma-am-ma i-na ḫa-al-ṣ[i]-ya*
13′ *ú-ul i-ba-aš-ši*
14′ *ḫa-al-ṣu-um ša-lim*

'Further: Concerning the Jawmahamaeans,[96] concerning whom my lord has written (to me): Since the day when my lord

---

ARMT XII 108; 109 (?, only *ya-*[is preserved) (cf. *ARMT* XII, 61 n. 1).
(c) MU.2 *zi-im-ri-li-im da-aw-da-am ša* DUMU.MEŠ *ya-mi-na i-du-ku*: Dossin, *Mél.Duss.* 982 n. 1.
Two year-formulae of Jaḫdun-Lim, father of Zimri-Lim, which refer to the Jaminites are known:
(a) MU.I.KÁM *ya-aḫ-du-li-im a-na* ḪE.EN *i-li-ku-ma ù na-wa-am ša* DUMU.MEŠ *ya-mi-na a-na qa-ti-šu i-dì-in*: *Studia Mariana*, 52 no. 6.
(b) MU.I.KÁM *ya-aḫ-du-li-im da-aw-da-am ša* DUMU *ya-mi-na i-du-ku*: *ARM* VIII 75.21–23.
The form MU.I.KÁM (really 'first year') means – according to the parallels – probably simply *šattum* 'year'. Whether both formulae refer to the same event or to two different events cannot be determined with certainty. Obscure, too, is the relationship between the names of the two years and the victory, referred to in the foundation document of the Šamaš temple of Jaḫdun-Lim (see above n. 54), of the king over Lā'um of Samānum and Ubrabûm, Ba'lu-Kullim of Tuttul and Awnānum and Ayalum of Abattum and Rabbûm (III 3–27; *Syria* 32, 1955, 14f.) who are referred to in simplified and pejorative fashion as 'kings of the Jaminites' (DUMU *mi-im*) (III 20f.; cf. above n. 54). A connection between the three texts does not seem to me to be impossible, but the material on the reign of Jaḫdun-Lim (in contrast to that on his son's reign) is still too scanty for any certain decision to be reached. On formula (a) we should also note that ḪE.EN is probably the land of ḪA.NA (*ma-at* ḪA.NA, *passim*); cf. the form (KUR.) ḪÉ.A.NA.KI in Kupper, *op. cit.*, 41–43 (read **ḫên*, allomorph of **ḫān-*?). On the forms of the name Jaḫdun-Lim cf. *ARMT* XV, 145; what is meant here is probably the assimilated form **yaḫdullim* or else *-n* at the end of a syllable is not written.

[95] The mention of Jaminite prisoners of war in *Mél.Duss.* 993:d; 994:b–f could refer to the battle at Sagarātum. In what temporal relationship this stands to the defeat of the Jaminites of the 'hills' too (*Mél.Duss.* 993:a, b) cannot be determined.

[96] On the tribal name cf. Kupper, *op. cit.*, 73 n. 1; Klengel, Thesis, 25 and n. 2; *WZ* Berlin 8, 1958/59, 211f.; I. J. Gelb, *JNES* 20, 1961, 195.

defeated the Jaminites in the pasture lands,[97] they have departed; none of them remain in my province. The province is quiet.'[98]

7. The even more extensive material available about the Hanaeans (*ḫanû*) would provide, basically, the same picture, so that we do not have to expound it here in the same way. It is clear that both Jaminites and Hanaeans, in the period of the kings of Mari, were in the process of transition from the nomadic way of life to a semi-sedentary and completely sedentary way of life. Thus, there emerges from the sources a somewhat ambiguous picture of their way of life and of the way in which they earned their living, a picture which has provoked Mendenhall to a not quite exact judgment of Kupper's treatment of the nomad problem: 'Kupper . . . has greatly overestimated the amount of true nomadism in the Mari period. Much of the material refers simply to the seasonal transhumance of sheep-herding villagers.'[99] Certainly in the texts from Mari we see alongside the herds of nomads such as the Jaminites also the herds of the king, of the city-dwellers and villagers and – amongst the latter – those of the Hanaean clans and groups of clans who have meanwhile become semi- or wholly sedentary. But it is clear that the Jaminites as well as the Hanaeans and Sutaeans were regarded by the really sedentary population, both the native Babylonians and the babylonianized 'Amorite' upper classes,[100] as roving barbarian intruders from the world of the steppe, in short, as nomads who were, as far as possible – eventually with assistance from the state – to be settled or restricted to specific areas or driven off.[101] It is almost unnecessary to underline the fact that here, in what is, from the point of view of time and place, relatively close proximity, we can follow *mutatis mutandis* a process which provides a suitable analogy with the picture which Alt and his followers suggest for the course of the Israelite settlement. Like the Israelites, the Jaminites and their kinsmen settle between the towns which they are unable or unwilling to conquer but with which there develops a differentiated system of

[97] This is probably the oblique case of the absolute plural of *nawûm* (on this cf. above n. 61), so that it is to be translated as above.

[98] *Mél.Duss.* 992:b.

[99] 'The Hebrew Conquest of Palestine', *BA* 25, 1962, 69 n. 7.

[100] These upper classes also come originally from a nomadic context but have become completely urbanized and babylonianized.

[101] Klengel, Thesis, 101.

relationships. We see in Mari, as in Palestine, the attempts made, with varying degrees of success, by the established powers to make the intruders their subjects, we see the Jaminites of Dumtēn proudly refusing the submit to forced labour and the tribe of Issachar, on the contrary, on account of the pleasantness of the land, bending its neck to the yoke. That the Jaminites and the Hanaeans, unlike the Israelites, were unable in the end to withstand the established population and became absorbed into it, is to be explained as the result of the different types of political structure in Mesopotamia and Palestine and of certain characteristics on Israel's part. All in all, we may conclude that the pattern of the settlement which was developed by Alt originally on the basis of modern Arabian examples, corresponds exactly to the data of the second millennium and, by means of its more convincing arguments, is preferable to that of Mendenhall which, as we have tried to show, suffers from untenable premisses.

IV

ARCHAEOLOGY AND BIBLICAL TRADITIONS

1. THE SITUATION

1. The debate, presented in this study, between the 'schools' of Alt and Albright is less a quarrel about individual historical details – however much this factor plays a part – than a debate about the principles of historiography which has as its starting point the question about the evaluation of the material available for the reconstruction of the Israelite settlement. We have seen that Alt and his followers and fellow-travellers,[1] on the basis of their literary-critical, form-historical and traditio-historical analysis of the biblical settlement narratives, came to the conclusion that these narratives were of a predominantly legendary type, were dominated by an aetiological interest and, therefore, were not to be regarded as authentic historical sources. Hence they almost entirely excluded these texts from the investigation of 'what actually happened' and turned to original records from the ancient Near East. The special character of this material occasioned the conclusion that the problem of the Israelite settlement would have to be studied by means of investigations into the history of territorial divisions. From this there arose the theory of the settlement in two stages, the gradual transition of nomadic breeders of small cattle to a sedentary way of life in the power-political and economic vacuum between the Canaanite city-states, with the following period of consolidation and rounding off of the territories won in this way.

2. Albright and his followers,[2] on the other hand, doubted whether such far-reaching historical conclusions could be reached on the basis of literary analysis and asserted that the fixed form of all ancient tradition was unable to provide later scholars with the

[1] See above ch. II 1, pp. 5–46.
[2] See above ch. II 2, pp. 46–55.

means of judging its 'historicity' or 'non-historicity' on the basis of criteria concerning form or type. Rather, on every occasion, evidence from outside this tradition ('external evidence') needed to be adduced, evidence which is at our disposal, thanks to archaeological activity in Palestine and elsewhere, in the form of 'archaeological facts' and thanks to the philology of the ancient Near East with its numerous original texts.

2. THE VALUE OF ARCHAEOLOGICAL DISCOVERIES

1. Martin Noth[1] in particular has always rejected the accusation that the line of investigation laid down by Alt did not pay sufficient attention to the 'external evidence'; rather, it is that the relevance of this material is evaluated differently by the two sides. This is especially clear when the 'archaeological facts' are utilized by Albright and his followers in support of the biblical accounts of the settlement. This expression needs closer examination.

2. First of all, the destructions, indicated by archaeology, of certain Palestinian cities in the thirteenth and twelfth centuries, i.e. in the period established for the Israelite settlement, are regarded as 'evidence' for the historical correctness of the corresponding Old Testament conquest narratives.[2] The parallelism or identification is obvious, but the historian must, nevertheless, ask for evidence. Such proof would be simple if the conquerors had left their victory steles behind on the ruins of the Late Bronze Age Canaanite cities. So far, however, no documents of this nature have come to light in Palestine from the period in question, and, in view of the intensive archaeological activity since the twenties, it may well be doubted whether discoveries of this nature will be made in the future.[3] This means, however, that archaeological

[1] His systematic articles on the problems discussed here are to be understood along these lines; cf. M. Noth, 'Grundsätzliches zur geschichtlichen Deutung archäologischer Befunde auf dem Boden Palästinas', *PJ* 34, 1938, 7–22; 'Hat die Bibel doch recht?', *Festschrift für Günther Dehn zum 75. Geburtstag* (Neukirchen 1957), 7–22; 'Der Beitrag der Archäologie zur Geschichte Israels', *SVT* 7, 1960, 262–82.

[2] See above pp. 47–55.

[3] The situation for the period of Assyrian expansion is different from that for the 'dark age'. At the present time we know of stele fragments, probably

finds are essentially silent evidence. Anyone who is familiar with Palestinian archaeology knows that excavations, on the other hand, usually bring to light such fragile objects as fragments of walls or burial places containing objects of daily public or private use covered with deposits of earth and rubble. Seldom enough is anything written found alongside, a cuneiform tablet or an ostrakon, and if there is, it mostly has to do with circumstances of administration or trade and therefore is of significance only for linguistics and cultural history. Obviously these finds can be used as evidence only by means of methodical interpretation.[4] The established stratifications then have to be fitted into a chronology which is, at first relative and is then, where possible, made absolute, a chronology which emerges from the comparison of this particular archaeological sequence with other sites which have already been classified. If the result is not from the start to be influenced or perhaps prejudiced by non-archaeological factors, one must first of all avoid identifying the excavated site with one which is known from tradition and projecting the latter's history, which has been handed down in a literary form, on to the archaeological findings; this is, rather, a second, later step which nevertheless seems to me also to presuppose a critical evaluation of the tradition. The first step can only be the interpretation of the archaeological findings on the basis of internal criteria and by analogy with other findings. This means, however, that archaeological results should not be presented in a positivist[5] fashion as

---

of Sargon II, from two places in Palestine, Samaria (*sebaṣṭiye*) and Ashdod (*esdūd*, modern *'ašdōd*); cf. M. Weippert, *ZDPV* 80, 1964, 154f. and n.14. The fragments from Ashdod have now been published by H. Tadmor, *EI* 8, 1967, 241–5 and plate 41; cf. *BA* 29, 1966, 95 fig. 11.

[4] The discussion of archaeological methodology must of necessity be brief here and greatly simplify the difficult problems. Good recent introductions can be found in W. F. Albright, *The Archaeology of Palestine* (Pelican Book A 199, Harmondsworth [5]1960), 7–22; H. J. Franken and C. A. Franken-Battershill, *A Primer of Old Testament Archaeology* (Leiden 1963); cf. generally also Sir Mortimer Wheeler, *Archaeology from the Earth* (Pelican Book A 356, Harmondsworth 1956), etc.

[5] In the face of current misunderstanding, it must be particularly stressed here that the basic position of the 'American Archaeological School' (the description in W. F. Albright, *Samuel and the Beginnings of the Prophetic Movement*, The Goldenson Lecture for 1961, Cincinnati n.d., 4) is *positivist*, not fundamentalist; cf. e.g., a methodological demand such as that of Bright: '*Objective*, external evidence is always required', J. Bright, *Early Israel in Recent History Writing: A Study in Method* (SBT, First Series 19, 1956), 91

'facts' which speak for themselves, unalterable and sacrosanct; as results of methodical interpretation, 'archaeological facts', whose existence cannot be denied, are already theoretical.[6]

3. If one accepts this suggestion, then the conflagration levels of the thirteenth to twelfth century which are under discussion here must first of all be examined without reference to the Israelite settlement and the biblical traditions concerning it. In this respect, there immediately emerges the fact that, taken by themselves, they are not very eloquent. Usually they tell us only that the catastrophe was caused or accompanied by fire; they are, for the most part, silent as to the cause of the catastrophe or as to who brought it about. If we accept provisionally that, in actual fact, as is maintained, it was a conqueror attacking from without, then, on the basis of our methodical principles, it is not immediately obvious from the archaeological findings who this was. We are aware, from the Amarna letters of the fourteenth century, of the constant and universal conflict that raged in Syria–Palestine when the *pax aegyptiaca*, originally established by Tuthmosis III and preserved or re-established, with varying degrees of success, by his successors,[7] collapsed because of weakness or lack of interest[8] on the part of the Egyptian government. Since the rule of the Pharaohs in most parts of Palestine in the thirteenth to twelfth century was scarcely even nominal,[9] we must in any case reckon with the fact

(italics mine). Only in order to avoid the possible impression that this claim has a polemical purpose, I remark explicitly that the science of history, in so far as it is not sheer speculation, always and necessarily contains an inherent tendency to positivism in so far as it derives its knowledge from observation of material which has to be examined methodically. The problem treated here involves only the criticism of the actuality of this material.

[6] One may be permitted to quote Goethe at this point: 'The ideal would be to grasp *that everything which is actual is already theoretical*. The blue of the sky reveals to us the basic law of chromatics. Do not look for anything behind the phenomena; they themselves are the instruction' (italics mine); *Betrachtungen im Sinne der Wanderer – Kunst, Ethisches, Natur* (Goethe's Werke, Vollständige Ausgabe letzter Hand, XXII, Stuttgart and Tübingen [Cotta] 1829), 251.

[7] See above pp. 9ff.

[8] Thus apparently under Amenophis IV (Akhnaton) who ignored the appeals of his Asian vassals (Amarna letters); cf., e.g., H. Brunner, 'Echnaton und sein Versuch einer religiösen Reform', *Universitas* 17, 1962, 153f.

[9] One can accept that the Egyptians during the later period were mainly interested in the defence of the most important overland routes such as the *via maris*. In Megiddo (*tell el-mutesellim*) the base of a statue of as late a ruler as Rameses VI has been found: *Megiddo II, Seasons of 1935–39* (OIP 62, 1948),

that the general state of war between the city-states and the territorial states could have continued even without organized attacks from without. Wright himself admits this with regard to the twelfth century and would like to think what must not be excluded as a possibility, namely that the 'Israelites' participated in these wars;[10] nor is there any reason for not admitting a similar situation with regard to the thirteenth century. The conflagration levels, therefore, could have been caused by very different people who cannot be immediately identified from the written sources and among whom, of course, there may well have been 'Israelites'.[11] One must, of course, also note that large-scale destructions are a common phenomenon in the eastern Mediterranean in that period. And this still leaves completely aside the consideration that such great fire-disasters must not be attributed solely to events of war. Destructive fires can have many causes, and anyone who knows the closely-packed houses of Late Bronze Age cities in Palestine will not be surprised that, as in the similarly closely-built European cities of the Middle Ages, what started as a relatively small fire could reduce larger sections of a city and even whole cities to ashes. In addition, Palestine is one of the main earthquake regions in the world. It is obvious that when houses collapse during an earthquake fires can start and quickly spread. It is not always possible, however, for archaeology to establish the occurrence of an earthquake on the basis of shifts in the terrain and of the remains of walls. Thus, for example, the destruction of the Late

---

135–8; photographs pp. 137f., figs. 374 and 375. After their settlement, the Philistines emerged, as nominal Egyptian vassals, in legal succession to the Pharaohs; cf. A. Alt, 'Ägyptische Tempel in Palästina und die Landnahme der Philister' (1944), *Kl.Schr.* I, 229f.; B. Mazar, 'The Philistines and the Rise of Israel and Tyre', *Proceedings of the Israel Academy of Sciences and Humanities*, I 7 (Jerusalem 1964), 1f.; G. E. Wright, 'Fresh Evidence For the Philistine Story', *BA* 29, 1966, 72. Even David and Solomon seem to have taken this into consideration (Wright, *op. cit.*, 84).

[10] See above pp. 52f.

[11] By way of analogy cf. R. v. Uslar, *Studien zu den frühgeschichtlichen Befestigungen zwischen Nordsee und Alpen* (BJ Bh.11, 1964), 220: In Germany 'archaeological findings are not exactly productive of destruction levels which can be linked with specific events. Such events were chiefly the invasions of the Norsemen and the Hungarians. However, in view of admittedly sparse written assertions (which to my knowledge have not yet been systematically gathered together) from a period in the tenth century which is, in any case, lacking in sources, one must reckon with destructions caused by feuds and other internal altercations.'

Bronze Age sanctuary at *tell dēr ʿallā* in the twelfth century could have been connected with events of the period of the Israelite settlement such as the 'conquest' of 'Gilead' or the 'territorial expansion' in Wright's sense – or indeed also with the activity of the Philistines[12] or of raiding bands from the east – if H. J. Franken had not localized the source of the fire and realized that its probable cause had been an earthquake.[13]

4. In addition, the 'sharp break in culture' between the last settlements of the Late Bronze Age and the first of the Early Iron age, established in the excavations at, for example, Bethel (*bētīn*), has been regarded by Albright and his followers as an archaeological indication of the Israelite settlement.[14] In this case, too, reservations must be made since the transition from the culture of the Late Bronze Age to that of the Early Iron Age took place under similar catastrophic circumstances throughout the whole area of the eastern Mediterranean (§3). The cause of the cultural decline here is not to be sought primarily in population upheavals so that the anti-civilization nomadism of the 'Israelite' immigrants into Palestine is regarded as responsible for the primitive wall and pottery techniques of Iron I. One cannot simply conclude from such a change in material culture that a change in population has taken place, since experience teaches how quickly people of a lower level of culture accommodate themselves, as they settle, to the higher level of their new home, especially in those cases where, as at the Israelite settlement, the established population is not

[12] In the course of the Dutch excavations 'Philistine pottery' is said to have been found on *tell dēr ʿallā*, which G. E. Wright, *op. cit.*, 73f. takes as evidence for Philistine expansion also east of the Jordan. From the outset this is questionable from a methodological point of view; it is much more likely that the vessels (?) arrived by way of trade or as votive offerings in the not unimportant sanctuary of *tell dēr ʿallā* from the coastal plain (cf. *ZDPV* 82, 1966, 291f.). On the evaluation of the clay tablet inscriptions from *tell dēr ʿallā* which are also claimed for the Philistines (Wright, *op. cit.*, 73 with reference to R. de Vaux, W. F. Albright and F. M. Cross Jr.) cf. already M. Weippert, *ZDPV* 82, 1966, 299–310, especially 302 n. 153. The process of elimination does not necessarily lead to the Philistines since we cannot be sure that we already know all the local Semitic or non-Semitic scripts in the area of Syria-Palestine.

[13] H. J. Franken, 'The Excavations at Deir ʿAllā in Jordan, 2nd Season', *VT* 11, 1961, 363–7; 'Excavations at Deir ʿAllā, Season 1964, Preliminary Report', *VT* 14, 1964, 418; *Opgravingen in Bijbelse grond: past het of past het niet* (Tentoonstellingscatalogus 8, Rijksmuseum van Oudheden, Leiden 1965), 8f.; cf. also M. Weippert, *ZDPV* 80, 1964, 189.

[14] See above pp. 46–8.

stamped out but, at least in large numbers, continues to live alongside and among the new arrivals. In any case, the deterioration in the material culture of Palestine, which led eventually to the state of affairs in the First Iron Age, had already begun in the Late Bronze Age[15] and was most probably caused by the rapid and simultaneous decline in political and economic stability, so that the break which actually becomes obvious in the thirteenth and twelfth centuries can be explained by the collapse of the previous government of the country and its economic system. The self-dissolution of the city-state system then made possible, of course, the infiltration of nomads who later, when they had become sedentary, formed the confederacy of the twelve tribes of Israel;[16] but by themselves, however, they were not the cause either of the collapse of the political system or of the decline of Late Bronze Age culture but, at most, expedited and exploited them. Only with the period of the early monarchy, when a relatively stable political system had once again become established in the country, does the material culture begin to rise above the poverty of that of the First Iron Age.[17]

5. In this connection one must also ask to what extent, in any case, one can come to conclusions about changes in population on the basis of differences in pottery styles. It seems to me that many

[15] Cf. K. M. Kenyon, *Archaeology in the Holy Land* (London ²1965), 209.

[16] An analogous situation is clear for the irruption of nomads into Syria and Mesopotamia as early as the third and second millennia; cf. J.-R. Kupper, *Les nomades en Mésopotamie au temps des rois de Mari* (Paris 1957), *passim*; D. O. Edzard, *Die 'zweite Zwischenzeit' Babyloniens* (Wiesbaden 1957), 44–48.

[17] That the process, as far as we can tell, began earlier in Edom supports our theory. In the process of their settlement, which occurred at the same period of time as that of the Israelites, the Edomites found an area scarcely occupied by a sedentary population and could therefore consolidate themselves considerably earlier than the Israelites (cf. Gen. 36.31), who had to contend over centuries with the Canaanites and later also with the Philistine-Canaanite cities. It was this that was the main factor, it seems to me, in delaying the formation of the Israelite state, and not a resistance to kingship, a resistance reputedly determined by 'nomadic' or religious considerations but which can almost only be deduced from deuteronomistic texts. On the beautifully painted Edomite pottery from the twelfth/eleventh century, on which above all our estimate of the consolidation of Edom is based, cf. N. Glueck, *The Other Side of the Jordan* (New Haven 1940), *passim* (cf. Index p. 206ᵃ *s.v.* Pottery, Edomite, and p. 23 fig. 6 and p. 25 fig. 7); Y. Aharoni, *PEQ* 94, 1962, 66f. (with a dating which has since come in need of revision, cf. Rothenberg); B. Rothenberg, *Das Heilige Land* 97, 1965, 19 n. 2; *Museum Haaretz Tel-Aviv Bulletin* 7, 1965, 26–28; *ZDPV* 82, 1966, 133f. and n. 7; M. Weippert, *ibid.*, 280 n. 35.

of the ideas about population movements and invasions developed from the study of pottery are based on an over-interpretation of the material; even in the case of the so-called *ḵẖirbet kerak* ware, in which characteristics typical of Asia Minor are obvious,[18] it does not seem to me to be obvious that they were introduced into the country as the result of mass migration. One should, rather, think of the migration of individual families of potters – as is surely the case also with the so-called 'Philistine pottery'[19] – or else of imports or of local imitations of imported articles which enjoyed a fairly wide popularity for a certain time and then disappeared again. No one will want to deduce from the extremely numerous imitations of Mycenaean ring ware in Palestine that there had been a 'Mycenaean invasion'. Conquerors quickly become assimilated to their new environment; the Philistines are an obvious example.[20] Thus it also appears to me to be very dubious whether the so-called 'Collared Rim Ware' which Albright and Aharoni, since it is usually found in new settlements of the Iron I Age, interpret as a type of genuine Israelite pottery,[21] can really be so closely associated with the 'Israelites'; the same type is also found in Megiddo (*tell el-mutesellim*),[22] which remained Canaanite till as late as the tenth century,[23] and we are surely dealing here with a particular fashion of the Early Iron Age. The fact that this particular type of pottery appears particularly frequently in the new

[18] Cf. S. Hood, *AnSt* 1, 1951, 116–19; W. F. Albright, *The Archaeology of Palestine*^{5}, 76f. K. M. Kenyon actually calls the *ḵẖirbet kerak* ware imported pottery, and this deserves closer consideration: *op. cit.*, 113, 127. Strong arguments for a movement of population are, however, to be found in R. Amiran, *AnSt* 15, 1965, 165–9; *AJA* 72, 1968, 317f.; cf. also W. F. Albright, *Yahweh and the Gods of Canaan* (London 1968), 98.

[19] K. Galling orally; cf. *SVT* 15, 1966, 155 n. 2. For the opposite position cf. now T. Dothan, *Ha-p^{e}lištīm w^e-tarbūtām hā-ḥ^{o}mrīt* (Jerusalem 1967), 71–208 *passim*.

[20] Cf. the lexicon article by H. Donner and M. Weippert mentioned above ch. III 1 n. 35.

[21] Cf. W. F. Albright, *AASOR* 4, 1923, 10; *The Archaeology of Palestine*^{5}, 118; Y. Aharoni, *Sēqer ba-gālīl: yišūvīm yiśrā'ēlīyīm w^e-ḥarsēhēm*, *EI* 4, 1956, 63f.; *Hitnaḥ^{a}lūt šivṭē yiśrā'ēl ba-gālīl hā-ʿelyōn* (Jerusalem 1957), 21–23; 'Problems of the Israelite Conquest in the Light of Archaeological Discoveries', *AS* 2.2/3, 1957, 146, 149; R. Amiran, *Ha-qērāmīqā ha-q^{e}dūmā šel 'ereṣ-yiśrā'ēl mē-rēšīt ha-t^{e}qūfā ha-nē'ōlītīt w^e-ʿad ḥurban bayit rīšōn* (Jerusalem 1963), 282f.

[22] *Megiddo I, Seasons of 1925–34, Strata I–V*, by R. S. Lamon and G. M. Shipton (OIP 42, 1939), 150; *Megiddo II, Seasons of 1935–39* (OIP 62, 1948), plate 83:1, 2, 4, levels VII and VI.

[23] Cf. A. Alt, 'Megiddo im Übergang vom kanaanäischen zum israelitischen Zeitalter' (1944), *Kl.Schr.* I 256–73.

settlements of the period (§6) is not therefore unduly surprising.

6. The only archaeological fact which can, with a great degree of probability, be connected with the settlement of the 'Israelite' tribes is the colonization of the Palestinian hill country which is clearly seen in numerous small country settlements of the early Iron Age I.[24] And that is precisely what one expects on the basis of the settlement theories of the 'school' of Albrecht Alt. Obviously, here too, one cannot decide definitely in individual cases whether we are dealing with an 'Israelite' village or a Canaanite one; but there is, nevertheless, a stronger probability in favour of 'Israelites'.

7. The discussion of the archaeological contribution to the reconstruction of the process of the settlement of the Israelite tribes can be brought to a close at this point. The result is largely negative or, at the very best, uncertain; where definite statements are possible, these support the settlement theories of Alt and Noth rather than those of Albright and his followers. In the question of conflagration levels it must be conceded that 'Israelites', too, could have taken part in the destructions even if they need not necessarily have been the main protagonists. If historical judgments are in the main probability judgments[25] which are achieved by balancing various related or divergent possibilities ('balance of probability'),[26] it seems obvious to me that the archaeological side of the balance, both in general and in individual cases, can

[24] Examples for the tribal territory of Benjamin in K.-D. Schunck, *Benjamin: Untersuchungen zur Enstehung und Geschichte eines israelitischen Stammes* (BZAW 86, 1963), 21; for the Shephelah in A. Saarisalo, 'Topographical Researches in the Shephela', *JPOS* 11, 1931, 19; for Galilee in Saarisalo, 'Topographical Researches in Galilee', *JPOS* 9, 1929, 38–40; Aharoni, *EI* 4, 1956, 59f. The extensive settlement of the Palestinian hill country is suggested also by the discovery of plastered cisterns dating from towards the end of the Late Bronze Age; cf. W. F. Albright, 'The Rôle of the Canaanites in the History of Civilization' (1942), *The Bible and the Ancient Near East: Essays in Honor of William Foxwell Albright* (Garden City 1961), 341, 358 n. 72.

[25] The methodological demand of historical criticism 'states that in the domain of history there are only probability judgments, some greater than others, and that against every tradition there must be first of all measured off the degree of probability appropriate to it'; E. Troeltsch, 'Über historische und dogmatische Methode in der Theologie' (1898), *Gesammelte Schriften* II (Tübingen 1913), 731.

[26] On this term cf. Bright, *Early Israel*, 88f.; J. A. Soggin, 'Ancient Biblical Traditions and Modern Archaeological Discoveries', *BA* 23, 1960, 99; 'Alttestamentliche Glaubenszeugnisse und geschichtliche Wirklichkeit', *ThZ* 17, 1961, 397; 'La conquista israelitica della Palestina nei sec. XIII e XII e le scoperte archeologiche', *Protestantesimo* 17, 1962, 206.

have only little weight. The weight of proof falls almost entirely on the literary traditions which, in Albright's view too,[27] cannot do justice to this task without additional support. Thus, the search for 'archaeological facts' as 'external evidence' for the Israelite settlement actually leads back in a circle to the point of departure. *There must always be literary, formal, and traditio-historical criticism.*

3. THE LITERARY PROBLEM

1. The remaining literary problem of the Israelite settlement can, for our purposes, be reduced to the double question whether the Old Testament accounts, especially those in Josh. 2–11, are correctly designated as aetiological narratives, and what historical consequences can be deduced from this classification should it prove to be correct. Bright in particular – following Albright – has sharply criticized the methodological premiss of the 'school' of Alt and Noth, according to which aetiology is to be regarded as one of the essential factors in the formation of the tradition, and has designated the aetiological factor within the historical tradition as secondary.[1] His argument has been accepted by Wright,[2] and it is, in fact, necessary to correct in many places the picture sketched by Alt and Noth; but it may be questioned whether Bright's argument and evidence are really convincing in their present form. In order to decide on the question of priority between the aetiological factor and the historical tradition, Bright demands the examination of those historical traditions which appear in an aetiological form but whose origin can be established. He cites and examines with this end in view American traditions, gives a parodied traditio-historical analysis of them after the manner of Noth and comes to the conclusion that the aetiological factor, where it exists and is bound to the tradition, says nothing about the historicity of that tradition: 'external evidence is required'.[3] As far as I can judge, Bright's examples are based, partly

[27] W. F. Albright, 'The Israelite Conquest of Palestine in the Light of Archaeology', *BASOR* 74, 1939, 12.

[1] Bright, *Early Israel*, 91ff. For Albright see above pp. 46ff., for Alt and Noth pp. 20ff. I follow up Bright's argument here only in so far as it is of relevance to the settlement debate.

[2] G. E. Wright, *JBR* 28, 1960, 188.

[3] Bright, *op. cit.*; the quotation p. 97. On 'external evidence' see above p. 47.

at any rate, on weak foundations. Neither the story of the landing of the Pilgrim Fathers at Plymouth[4] nor that of the first Thanksgiving Day[5] nor even the 'Weemsian legend' of George Washington's throwing abilities at the Rappahannock[6] are aetiologies but can exist by themselves even without the object or custom that has become attached to them. They even existed by themselves for a longer or shorter period within American mythology in written or oral form: Plymouth Rock was created in the context of the canonization of the 'settlement traditions' of New England at the time of the War of Independence when the need arose to give to the new national consciousness which was emerging or which had to be created its commemorative or cultic sites, the annual 'Thanksgiving Day' festival spread from about 1864 onwards in the crisis of the War of Independence and the 'Reconstruction' probably from a similar motive, and the throwing custom at the Rappahannock at Fredericksburg, Va., was first begun in 1936 for reasons of 'publicity' or for commercial reasons.[7] From the testimony of these traditions it emerges that the first two are authentic reports of historical occurrences while the last one belongs to the type of biographical legend in which a hero's decisive characteristics are presented as having already been in evidence in his childhood.[8] In Parson Weems' book on Washington[9] there

[4] *Ibid.*, 94.

[5] *Ibid.*, 95.

[6] *Ibid.*, 95–97. The original is on p. 21 of Cunliffe's edition of Weems' biography of Washington mentioned below in n. 9. The traditionist, according to Weems, is Col. Lewis Willis, 'his (*scil.* Washington's) play-mate and kinsman'; the story is, however, sheer invention.

[7] *Ibid.*, 96 and n. 1.

[8] On this cf. M. Dibelius, *Die Formgeschichte des Evangeliums* (Tübingen [3]1959), 119ff. (ET *From Tradition to Gospel*, London 1934, 106ff.); R. Bultmann, *Die Geschichte der synoptischen Tradition* (FRLANT 29, [4]1958), 327f., 330, 331, 334f. (ET *History of the Synoptic Tradition*, Oxford 1963, 300f., 302, 304, 306f.).

The point can also be well illustrated from American mythology. None of the 'Weemsian legends' has permeated the American consciousness like that of 'George Washington and the Cherry Tree' (p. 12 of the edition of Weems' book mentioned below n. 9). The Washington of the anecdote is presented as a six-year-old boy. Strange to say, however, in the painting by Grant Wood 'Parson Weems' Fable' he has the features of the adult as he appears in the 'canonical' representations. The interest of the legend is caught exactly.

[9] The book appeared for the first time in 1800 (Baltimore) with the title *The Life and Memorable Actions of George Washington* and underwent innumerable editions. The definitive text is that of the ninth edition: M. L. Weems, *The Life of George Washington with Curious Anecdotes Equally Honourable to Himself*

is a whole cycle of such anecdotes;[10] similar anecdotes are related, for example, also about Jesus in the infancy narratives of the apocryphal gospels and even in the New Testament (Luke 2.41–52) or about Abraham Lincoln.[11] These remarks alone are surely sufficient to show that in the case of the three examples mentioned by Bright quite different literary, social and historical circumstances are present from those operative in the settlement narratives of Josh. 2–11. Yet his indication that the aetiological factor there is secondary has a certain significance.

2. B. S. Childs[12] in particular has shown convincingly that the formula 'to this day' or the like, which Alt and Noth had regarded as an almost infallible sign of aetiological form,[13] has, in the majority of instances in the Old Testament, in fact been introduced secondarily as an editorial comment on existing traditions, like similar formulae in Greek aetiological narratives. On the other hand, Herodotus (II 154, 182 *et al.*) and Pausanias (I 10.5; II 3.7; 22.3) use related expressions in order to state that for aspects of the traditions that are being reported visible evidence is still to hand. According to Childs, the formulae are found mostly with non-aetiological material, which does not, of course, conversely, exclude their use in aetiological narratives. Childs' asser-

---

and Exemplary to his Young Countrymen (Philadelphia 1809). The last edition, to which reference is made here: *The Life of Washington, By Mason L. Weems*, Edited by Marcus Cunliffe (The John Harvard Library, Cambridge, Mass., 1962). On this cf. D. Wecter, *The Hero in America: A Chronicle of Hero-Worship* (New York 1941), 132–6; W. A. Bryan, 'The Genesis of Weems' "Life of Washington" ', *Americana* 36, 1942, 147–65; M. Cunliffe, 'Parson Weems and George Washington's Cherry Tree', *BJRL* 45, 1962/63, 58–96 (reprinted in his edition of the book pp. IX–LXII); further also W. A. Bryan, *George Washington in American Literature, 1775–1865* (New York 1952), 94–96, 237f.

[10] *Op. cit.* (ed. Cunliffe), 9ff. On the further traditio-history of these childhood legends see Cunliffe, *ibid.*, XXI–XXIII.

[11] Cf. R. B. Basler, *The Lincoln Legend: A Study in Changing Conceptions* (Boston and New York 1935), 120–23: 'The Model Boy'; Wecter, *op. cit.*, 226–9.

[12] B. S. Childs, 'A Study of the Formula "Until this Day" ', *JBL* 82, 1963, 279–92. The study by J. L. Seeligmann which comes to similar conclusions, 'Aetiological Elements in Biblical Historiography', *Zion* 26, 1961, 141–69 (Hebr.) is known to me only from the reference in *ZAW* 74, 1962, 348. Similarly also Bright, *op. cit.*, 94.

[13] See above pp. 21f. More sceptically now M. Noth, 'Der Beitrag der Archäologie zur Geschichte Israels', *SVT* 7, 1960, 279.

tions can also be applied, following his example, to the settlement accounts in Josh. 2–11 which are under discussion here, in such a manner that the house of Rahab and the ruptured walls of the *tell* of Jericho,[14] the *tell*, the heap of stones and the tree (?) of Ai, the stones and trees (?)[15] in front of the cave of Makkedah and the Gibeonite cult-servants, were all regarded and were intended to be regarded as visible evidence of the reported occurrences. Thus, the occurrence of the formula 'to this day' or the like could be no certain indication for or against the aetiological character of the tradition; the latter must, rather, be established by other, internal indications. The 'eyewitness formula' is, therefore, generally a *donum superadditum*, since in many cases it simply may not be there.

3. Now, the problem of historical aetiology can also surely be regarded from another point of view than hitherto. General experience leaves us in no doubt as to the ability of striking phenomena to form traditions.[16] If once one analyses against their historical background, the *Schwedenschanzen* or *Tillyschanzen*[17] which are found all over Germany, it soon emerges that quite different types of fortifications of both prehistoric and historical periods have been described by these names. Popular tradition has correctly established the fortificatory nature of the sites, and they have been embedded in a context the 'historicity' of which can on no account be doubted: the Thirty Years' War. I do not know to what extent elaborate narratives are connected with these *Schwedenschanzen* or *Tillyschanzen*; the aetiological character of the description is, however, clear. It is obvious, and not to be disputed, that the names are relatively recent and may belong, at the

[14] H. J. Franken, 'Tell es-Sultan and Old Testament Jericho', *OTS* 14, 1965, 196–8, 200, who refutes for sound reasons the Albright-Kenyon erosion hypothesis (see above p. 50 and ch. II 2 n. 25), assumes that the (Canaanite?) family of Rahab probably lived in the oasis of Jericho and at the most occupied insignificant quarters on the *tell* itself. The aetiology would have been occasioned by the Rahab settlement of the oasis and by the ruins of the Middle Bronze city. I can only concur with Franken's discussion in its entirety (*op. cit.*, 189–200).

[15] On the problem of the exact determination of the meaning of *'ēṣ(īm)* see above ch. II 1 n. 69.

[16] Along the same lines cf. also M. A. Beek, *JSS* 4, 1959, 72.

[17] Cf., e.g., W. D. Asmus, *Germania* 36, 1958, 233f.; R. v. Uslar, *Studien zu den frühgeschichtlichen Befestigungen zwischen Nordsee und Alpen* (BJ Bh. 11, 1964), 180 and fig. 79. I am unaware of any comprehensive study of the constructions designated by these names. It may well be that some of them are actually connected with the Thirty Years' War.

earliest, to the middle or second half of the seventeenth century. Since, on the other hand, archaeologists can determine precisely that most of these ruined fortifications have nothing to do with the Thirty Years' War, the names must be attributed to an attempt on the part of the local population to connect these remarkable sites with a particularly impressive event of the recent past, as far back as popular historical recollection can reach.[18] This observation can be applied to the local tradition of Chattanooga cited by Bright[19] as well as to the Israelite settlement traditions.

4. The narrative about Sergeant Roper's heroic deed in the 'Battle above the Clouds' is without doubt attached to Lookout Mountain which towers above the Chattanooga in the south, or, to be more precise, to a single topographical feature of this mountain ridge, namely Roper's Rock, whose name the narrative explains. Bright[20] himself declares that the story is 'pure fancy' and that the name 'Roper's Rock', like other comparable place-names in the United States, may go back to a forgotten pioneer family called Roper which once settled there. However, it can easily be understood how the inexplicable name became associated in the popular mind with an event in the Civil War; Bragg's retreat and the occupation of Chattanooga by Union forces under Rosencrans in September 1863 and the subsequent battles around the heights surrounding the town, Missionary Ridge and Lookout Mountain, which led, by November, to the complete expulsion of the Confederates, marked a decisive turning-point for the inhabitants of Chattanooga – and of the whole of Tennessee, the conquest of which by the Union troops was more or less completed by these events – exactly comparable to the effect of the First World War in Germany. The Civil War was, therefore, an obvious background for the aetiology of Roper's Rock,[21] quite apart from

[18] Other constructions are called *Heidenschanzen*, although they clearly originate, partly, in the Christian era. Here the aetiology has remote antiquity in view.

[19] *Op. cit.*, 97–100.

[20] *Ibid.*, 99f.

[21] Bright, *op. cit.*, 99, describes the formation of the tradition in graphic terms: 'There is Roper's Rock, and it is a striking cliff; and people asked the natives why it was so called. And the natives, loath to be caught short by Yankee tourists, came up with the tale. Nor was it sheer, wilful fabrication. Traditions of the Civil War hover like ghosts on the ridges about Chattanooga. It was natural for people honestly to suppose that the height of Lookout Mt, most commanding of all, had a part in the events.'

the question of whether Grant and Hooker had ever had a Sergeant Roper under them or not in the 'Battle above the Clouds' and from the fact that the famous 'Battle' was, in actual fact, nothing more than a limited engagement between sentries and shock troops.[22]

5. A similar supposition can be made in the case of the so-called Benjaminite settlement tradition in Josh. 2ff., especially with regard to the narratives of the conquest of Jericho and Ai. It has already been stressed several times in this study that the excavations undertaken on the sites of these places, *tell es-sulṭān* near *erīḥā* and *et-tell* near *dēr dubwān*, have shown that in the period in which the Israelite settlement is usually, and correctly, placed, both *telāl* were not occupied but lay deserted.[23] According to the theory of Alt and Noth, the existence of these deserted sites within Benjaminite tribal territory occasioned the aetiological narratives of the destruction of the cities by the Benjaminites – later, in the all-Israelite expansion, by the 'Israelites'.[24] This is now easily understandable. If the final phase of the settlement, the 'territorial expansion', was, with Alt, one of warlike encroachments on the part of the consolidated Israelite tribes into the territory of the city-states, then naturally, from then on, the experience that now – as opposed to earlier – they were able to hold their own against the professional Canaanite troops and their chariot corps and themselves pass to the attack on fortified cities, impressed on the historical memory the picture of a conquest and drove from the consciousness the much less dramatic and, in parts, the less glorious events of the period of peaceful settlement; nothing was easier, then, than that the great mounds of ruins within the tribal territory should be attributed to similar events of the past. In spite of Bright, then, these narratives are deeply imbued with an aetiological interest, even if individual details have been provided only later and secondarily with aetiological indications of the type *ʿad hayyōm hazze*. What we have, fundamentally, then, is that a definite historical picture of the settlement has produced the traditions. This does not, of course, exclude the possibility of

[22] On the events cf. J. G. Randall, *The Civil War and Reconstruction* (Boston and New York ²1953), 533–8; C. Eaton, *A History of the Southern Confederacy* (New York 1954), 280–4.

[23] See above pp. 49f., 53f.

[24] See above pp. 21f., 25ff.

being able to regard the accounts of the conquest of Hazor (Josh. 11.1–9, 10–15), Bethel (Judg. 1.22–26) and Laish/Dan (Judg. 18) as genuine historical traditions from the period of territorial expansion.[25]

6. Finally, we still have to discuss the problem of the localization of such traditions in particular places, a problem which Bright has treated with particular reference to the patriarchal narratives.[26] There can be no doubt that there are local traditions with a definite point of localization and that, on the other hand, traditions can also move.[27] The story of the 'Battle above the Clouds' and Roper's Rock is a localized story of this type which could be told only in Chattanooga, Tenn. and which, from there, was transferred to the nation's history books. Bright himself alludes to this when he remarks of Roper's Rock: 'Thereby hangs a story' or, more generally, when he localizes traditions about the Civil War on the heights around Chattanooga.[28] Is this not an example of localized traditions? One cannot say that the 'theatre of operation' is all that gives the impression of localization in a particular place:[29] these stories belong to Chattanooga and are handed down there, as Bright affirms from his own experience in the case of the 'Battle above the Clouds'.[30] They presuppose nothing but definite localities and the very general background of the Civil War with the predominantly bitter experiences of the inhabitants of these places in that event. The situation is quite different in the case of Bright's other examples. Of course the surrender of the British at Yorktown is no more a Virginian tradition than is the Civil War, whose main theatre was Virginia. Nor is the Declaration of Independence of 1776 a Pennsylvanian one because it was drawn up, for specific reasons, in Philadelphia, Pa.[31] These traditions are, rather, already fundamentally all-American because they presuppose the emergence and existence of the union, and they cannot, therefore, be used as arguments

[25] On Noth's evaluation of Josh. 11.10–15 see above pp. 36f. and ch. II 1 n. 104.

[26] *Op. cit.*, 100–104.

[27] On this cf. A. Alt, 'Die Wallfahrt von Sichem nach Bethel' (1938), *Kl.Schr.* I, 79–88; W. F. Albright, 'The Israelite Conquest of Palestine in the Light of Archaeology', *BASOR* 74, 1939, 14.

[28] *Op. cit.*, 98, 99. Cf. also above n. 21.

[29] So Bright, *op. cit.*, 101f.

[30] *Ibid.*, 98, 99.

[31] *Ibid.*, 102.

here.[32] The case is different again with the transference of the 'Weemsian legend', which we have already discussed, of George Washington's legendary abilities at throwing,[33] a legend which is told not only – as in Weems – about the Rappahannock at Fredericksburg but also about Natural Bridge in Virginia, the Hudson at the New Jersey palisades and the Potomac at Mount Vernon where Washington lived in his old age near Washington, D.C.[34] Here the 'tradition' – which, in the cases mentioned, certainly goes back to Weems[35] – as Bright[36] correctly remarks, has followed the man when the latter had become an all-American figure in whom the places with which he had been more closely associated wished to have a share.[37] In contrast to the United States, this wider unity was attained only relatively late in Israel. I should like, therefore, very tentatively, to propose the following classification of the narratives about the prehistory and early history of Israel:

1. *Old Tribal Traditions* having an aetiological or a historical character. These are originally localized in a particular place or among a particular tribe, and they have become all-Israelite only with the emergence of an all-Israelite organization. This latter is also the reason for the introduction of Joshua into the settlement narratives. Examples: The conquest of Jericho and Ai, the battle at Gibeon, the conquest of Hazor and Bethel.[38]

2. *Traditions Reflecting the Amphictyony*. These have a historical

[32] Unless one accepts that the all-Israelite element existed from the outset; thus explicitly Bright, *op. cit.*, 111ff. This is of course possible only if one differentiates the texts not methodically but on the basis of subjective 'probability'.

[33] Above pp. 137f.

[34] Natural Bridge and Hudson: Cunliffe, *op. cit.*, XLI and n. 52; Potomac: Bright, *op. cit.*, 102f. and n. 2.

[35] Cf. again Cunliffe, *op. cit.*, XXI, XLI, XLIIf. and nn. 56f.

[36] *Op. cit.*, 103.

[37] In this sense Bright's concept 'tied to people', which he proposes in opposition to 'tied to places' (*op. cit.*, 102f.; on the definition of Israel as 'people', *ibid.*, 112–14), can be accepted. It is clear, however, that this is a second stage in the formation of the tradition.

[38] On the interpretation of local traditions in the light of an inclusive whole cf. W. Zimmerli, 'Die historisch-kritische Bibelwissenschaft und die Verkündigungsaufgabe der Kirche', *EvTh* 23, 1963, 27. I can also cite an example from my own 'background': In every Franconian school the history of the state of Bavaria from the sixth century onwards is taught as the common history, although the forebears of the schoolchildren cannot have participated in it before 1803, 1806, 1812, 1815 or even 1921.

character and are originally all-Israelite. Examples: The assembly at Shechem (Josh. 24.1–27), the infamy perpetrated at Gibeah and the vengeance wrought on Benjamin by the confederated tribes (Judg. 19f.).

3. *Late Traditions*, often in a deuteronomistic form. These are originally all-Israelite since they presuppose not only the formation of the state but also a post-amphictyonic picture of the premonarchical period. Examples: The framework narrative in the books of Joshua and Judges.[39]

[39] It is of no importance here whether one thinks of the framework as having emerged complete or by stages.

V

CONCLUSION

IT WOULD GO beyond the scope of this work if, at this point, we were to undertake a detailed analysis of the Old Testament settlement texts on the basis of the results of our discussion. Rather, let me simply stress by way of conclusion that it seems to me that the picture, suggested by Alt and his followers, of the occupation of Palestine by those who later formed the Israelite tribes has, in its main features, stood the test of the far-reaching criticism both of its general features and of specific details by the 'American Archaeological School'. This result has not been forced; it has emerged in the course of our investigations after thorough and, as far as possible, objective examination of the opposing theories. The 'subjective'[1] methods of the 'school' of Alt seem to me to provide a 'more objective' picture and one which corresponds better with the sources than do those of his critics, whom we are more justified in calling 'subjective' in so far as it can be shown that Albright and his followers all too often attribute to their material more than it can bear and are, at times, even compelled, explicitly or implicitly, to accommodate either the biblical traditions to the archaeological 'facts'[2] or else the results of investigations to the statements of the texts.[3] This does not, however, mean that all the

[1] Described thus by G. E. Wright, *JNES* 5, 1946, 112; Bright, *op. cit.*, 92, cf. 109.

[2] Example of Ai: Albright, above pp. 50f.; L. H. Vincent, 'Les fouilles d'et-Tell', *RB* 46, 1937, 262–6; disagreement with the localization on the basis of biblicist treatment of the text and of archaeological finds in J. M. Grintz, '"'Ai which is beside Beth-Aven": A Re-examination of the Identity of 'Ai', *Bibl* 42, 1961, 201–16; B.-Z. Luria, *Meqōmāh šel hā-'ay ('Iyūnīm be-sēfer yehōšūa': Diyūnē hā-ḥūg la-miqrā' be-vēt Dāwīd ben-Guriyōn dīn we-ḥešbōn mālē' – Pirsūmē hā-ḥevrā le-ḥēqer ha-miqrā' be-yiśrā'ēl* 9, Jerusalem 1960, 12–41; J. Simons, 'Een opmerking over het 'Aj-probleem', *JEOL* 9, 1944, 157–62. See also ch. II 1 n. 52.

[3] Example of Jericho: Albright, above p. 50.

results achieved by Alt and Noth and their fellow-travellers and continuers are to be adopted without modification. For example, on the basis of Alt's sketch of the territorial relationships within Palestine before the arrival of the Israelites and their kinsfolk[4] one cannot conclude that the normal form of political organization in the hill country as opposed to the valleys and plains was the 'larger territorial system'.[5] The examples cited – the kingdom of Lab'ayu and his sons in Shechem and the rule of Tagu – are particular powers which arose because of the fact that particularly energetic and unscrupulous dynasties extended their area of control from the basis of one city-state at the expense of other city-states.[6] The city lists of the Egyptian kings as well as the place names in the Amarna texts show only that the mountain regions of Palestine were scarcely colonized. Only in this way did they furnish sufficient room for the peaceful settlement of nomads with small cattle in search of land. Although the basis of proof is relatively slight, I, too, should like to connect this first phase of the settlement of those who later became the Israelites with the Leah tribes and the annexed Bilhah and Zilpah tribes.[7] If the Rachel tribes are thought of as having immigrated later and, according to Smend,[8] having brought with them both the worship of Yahweh and the 'Yahweh War', then they may well have provided the impetus for the second phase of the process, the territorial expansion, which then became determinative for the historical picture of the conquest of Palestine which we have in the Old Testament traditions.

[4] See above pp. 15f.

[5] For this reason I also have reservations about the picture of Bezek as a great power drawn by P. Welten, 'Bezeq', *ZDPV* 81, 1965, 144f. on the basis of Judg. 1.4–7 and with specific reference to Alt.

[6] As the Amarna letters show, this was an every-day occurrence in the city-state territories of the plains and valleys.

[7] The annexation of the Bilhah-group to Rachel must be due to later systematization and intended symmetry; cf. M. Noth, *Das System der zwölf Stämme Israels* (BWANT IV 1, 1930), 27f., 83–85; less decisively O. Eissfeldt, 'Jakob-Lea und Jakob-Rahel', *Gottes Wort und Gottes Land: Festschrift für Hans-Wilhelm Hertzberg zum 70. Geburtstag* (Göttingen 1965), 51f.

[8] R. Smend, *Jahwekrieg und Stämmebund: Erwägungen zur ältesten Geschichte Israels* (FRLANT 84, 1963).

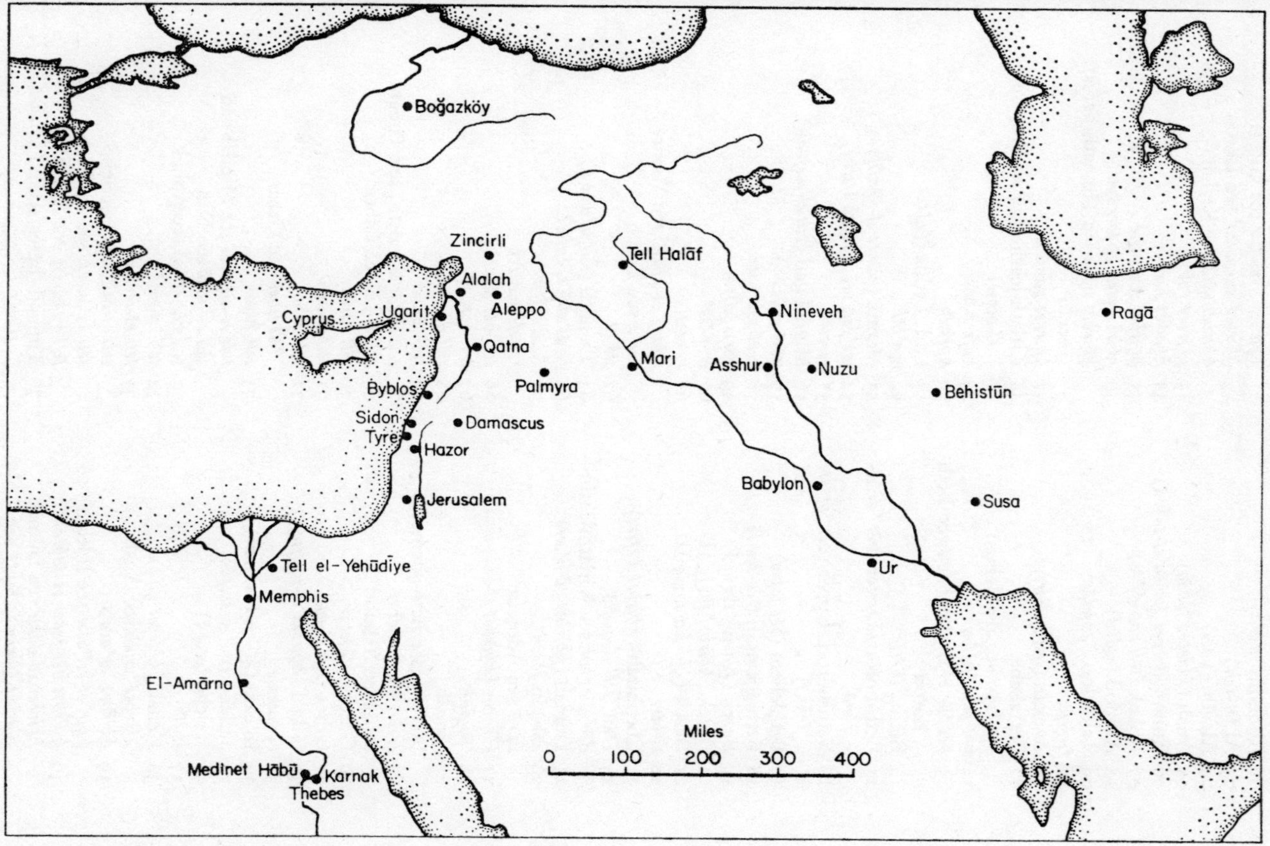

Boğazköy
Zincirli
Tell Halāf
Alalah
Aleppo
Ugarit
Cyprus
Nineveh
Raga
Qatna
Mari
Asshur
Nuzu
Palmyra
Byblos
Behistūn
Sidon
Damascus
Tyre
Hazor
Babylon
Jerusalem
Susa
Tell el-Yehūdiye
Ur
Memphis
El-Amārna
Miles
0 100 200 300 400
Medinet Hābū
Karnak
Thebes

01 *ābil*
02 Adoraim (*dūrā*)
03 Ai (*et-tell*)
04 Aijalon (*yālō*)
05 Anab (*k̲h̲irbet ʿanāb*)
06 Anim (*k̲h̲irbet ġuwēn et-taḥtā*)
07 Aphek (*tell rās el-ʿēn*)
08 Ashdod (*esdūd*)
09 Ashkelon (*ʿasqelān*)
10 *ʿayyūn*
11 Azekah (*tell z̲akarīye*)
12 Beersheba
bēt laḥm see Bethlehem
13 *bēt mak/qdūm*
bēt ʿūr el-fōqā/et-taḥtā see Beth-horon
14 Bethel (*bētīn*)
15 Beth-horon, Lower (*bēt ʿūr el-fōqā*)
16 Beth-horon, Upper (*bēt ʿūr et-taḥtā*)
17 Bethlehem (*bēt laḥm*)
18 Beth-shemesh (*ʿēn-šems*)
19 Bezek (*k̲h̲irbet ibz̲īq* I)
20 Bezek (*k̲h̲irbet ibz̲īq* II)
21 Bezek (*k̲h̲irbet ibz̲īq* III)
22 *el-bīre*
23 Chephirah (*k̲h̲irbet kefīre*)
24 Dan (*tell el-qāḍī*)
dēr el-az̲har see Kiriath-jearim
25 Dumah (*k̲h̲irbet ed-dōme*)
26 *dūrā* in *jōlān*
dūrā see Adoraim
27 Ekron (*k̲h̲irbet el-muqannaʿ*)
28 *ʿēn dōk*
29 *ʿēn nāb*
ʿēn šems (see Beth-shemesh)
erīḥā see Jericho
esdūd see Ashdod
30 Gezer (*tell jez̲er*)
31 Gibea (*tell el-fūl*)
32 Gilgal (*k̲h̲irbet el-mefjir*)
33 *el-ḥamme*
34 Ibleam (*k̲h̲irbet belʿame*)
35 Jericho (*tell es-sulṭān*)
36 Jericho (*erīḥā*)
37 *el-jīb*
38 Keilah (*k̲h̲irbet qīlā*)
k̲h̲irbet ʿanāb see Anab
39 *k̲h̲irbet ʿarʿara*
k̲h̲irbet belʿame see Ibleam
40 *k̲h̲irbet bēt jaber et-taḥtānī*
k̲h̲irbet ed-dōme see Dumah
k̲h̲irbet ġuwēn et-taḥtā see Anim
41 *k̲h̲irbet ḥayyān*
k̲h̲irbet ibz̲īq see Bezek
42 *k̲h̲irbet iksāf*
k̲h̲irbet kefīre see Chephirah
k̲h̲irbet el-mefjir see Gilgal
k̲h̲irbet muqannaʿ see Ekron
k̲h̲irbet qīlā see Keilah
43 *k̲h̲irbet rabūḍ*
44 *k̲h̲irbet šamʿ*
45 *k̲h̲irbet simūnīye*
46 *k̲h̲irbet/tell eṭ-ṭarrāme*
k̲h̲irbet tibne see Timnath-heres/serah
47 *k̲h̲irbet z̲anūtā*
48 Kiriath-jearim (*dēr el-az̲har* near *el-qerye*)
49 *kufr ḥāris*
50 *kurnub*
51 Lod, Lydda (*ludd*)
52 *maʿlūl*
53 Mamre (*rāmet el-k̲h̲alīl*)
54 *maʿyan mē neptōaḥ* (*liftā*)
55 *mērōn*
56 Migdal-gad (*tell el-mejādil*)
57 *nebī mūsā*
58 *nebī samwīl*
59 *qarn ḥaṭṭīn*
60 *er-rām*
61 *rāmallāh*
rāmet el-k̲h̲alīl see Mamre
ṣarʿā see Zorah
62 *selbīṭ*
63 Taanach (*tell taʿannek*)
64 *telāl abū el-ʿalāʾiq*
65 *telāl miṭlib*
et-tell see Ai
66 *tell bēt mirsim*
67 *tell bornāṭ*
68 *tell dēr ʿallā*
69 *tell ʿēṭūn*
tell el-fārʿa (north) see Tirzah
tell el-fūl see Gibea
70 *tell harbaj*
71 *tell el-ḥesī*
72 *tell ibšar*
tell jez̲er see Gezer
73 *tell kīsān*
tell el-mejādil see Migdal-gad
tell el-qādī see Dan
tell rās el-ʿēn see Aphek
74 *tell eṣ-ṣāfī*
75 *tell eš-šerīʿa*
tell es-sulṭān see Jericho
tell taʿannek see Taanach
tell z̲akarīye see Azekah
76 Timnath-heres/serah (*k̲h̲irbet tibne*)
77 Tirzah (north *tell el-fārʿa*)
yālō see Aijalon
78 Zorah (*ṣarʿā*)

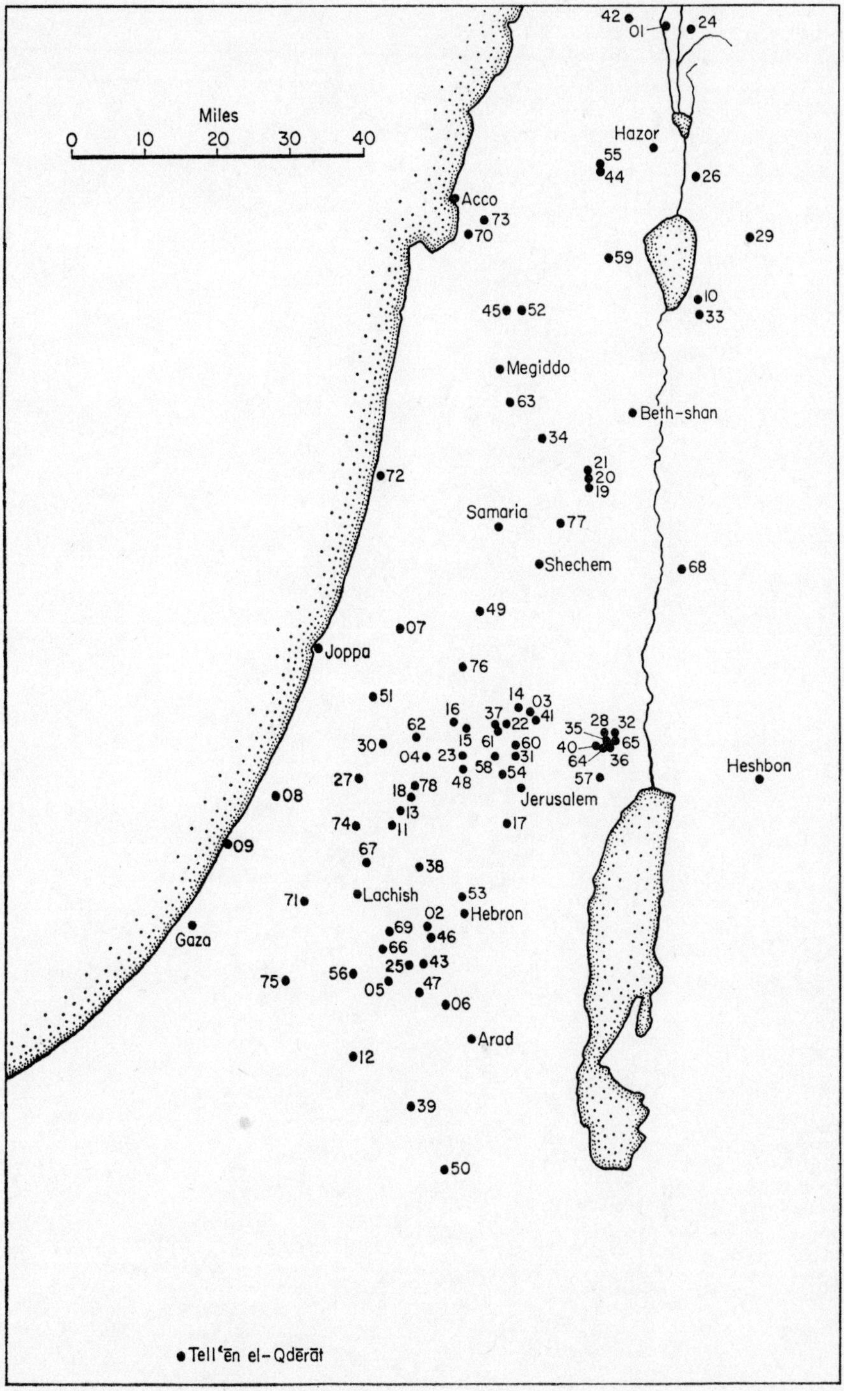
Miles
0 10 20 30 40
Acco
Hazor
Megiddo
Beth-shan
Samaria
Shechem
Joppa
Jerusalem
Heshbon
Lachish
Hebron
Gaza
Arad
Tell ʿēn el-Qdērāt
01 02 03 04 05 06 07 08 09 10 11 12 13 14 15 16 17 18 19 20 21 22 23 24 25 26 27 28 29 30 31 32 33 34 35 36 37 38 39 40 41 42 43 44 45 46 47 48 49 50 51 52 53 54 55 56 57 58 59 60 61 62 63 64 65 66 67 68 69 70 71 72 73 74 75 76 77 78

INDEXES

1. AUTHORS

2. GODS AND MEN

3. PEOPLES AND PLACES

4. SUBJECTS

5. WORDS

Akkadian

abāku, 77
aḫlamû, in the sense of 'bedouin', 103f.
akālum, 120
ālum, pl. *ālānû*, 117, 20
amurrû, in the sense of 'bedouin', 103
awīlu, 8
bašmu, 76
dabdûm, *dawdûm*, *damdû*, 112
dišpu, 76
emantuḫlu, 68
epēšu G+ *salīmam*, 114
epēšu H+ *ana ḫapirī*, 72
erēpu, 78
erpetu, 79
ezēbu Š, 73
gelzuḫlūtu, see *kelzuḫlūtu*
ḫabbātu, 72, 73
ḫabirāya, 75
ḫalāqu, 71
ḫanû, in the sense of 'bedouin', 103
ḫaṣirātum, 115f.
ḫibrum, 116
ḫupšu, 72, 82
ibilu, 107
ilāni (*ša*) *ḫapirī*, 70
kabāsu, 77
kabāšu, 77
kaprum, pl. *kaprātum*, 117–20
kelzuḫlūtu, 72
labāšu, 77
las/*šqum*, 115, 117
malku, 82
mātum: *ša mātim*, 70
napištu(*m*), 78
**našāpu* G D N, 78
nawûm, 116, 122, 125
**nawûm* Dt, 116
ne'rārum, *neḫrārum*, 122
nuššupu, see **našāpu*
parzillu, 75
pirḫāšum PN, 79
piršaʾu, 79
pí-ṭá-te in ERÍN.MEŠ *p.*, 68
puršaʾu, 79
pur'usu, 79
qalālum, 121
rab ešri, 68
ramû G D, 122
riḫsum, 121
sirrimu, 108
sugāgum, 120f.
sugāgūtum, 121
sutû, in the sense of 'bedouin', 103
ṣābu, 67
šaḫāṭum, 121
šalāšum, 122
šanûm, 122
šāpirūtum, 121
šāpiṭum, 118
šarru(*m*), pl. *šarrānu*, 8, 121
šibšum, 117
tarbaṣātum, 115
ṭēm nukurtim, 121
udru, 108
ummānu, 95

Arabic

'fk, 77
baṭanun, 76
badawī, 107
bḏr, 76
burghūṯun, 79
dibsun, 76
firzilun, 75
f'l, 79
kbs, 77
lbs, 77
malikun, 82
mulkun, 119
nbj, 78
nsf, 78
nafsun, 78

Aramaic

'pk, 77

6. REFERENCES

Egyptian Texts

Akkadian and Sumerian Texts

Biblical References